A Concordance to the
Critique of Pure Reason

American University Studies

Series V
Philosophy
Vol. 148

PETER LANG
New York • Washington, D.C./Baltimore
Bern • Frankfurt am Main • Berlin • Vienna • Paris

Jay Reuscher

A Concordance to the
Critique of Pure Reason

PETER LANG
New York • Washington, D.C./Baltimore
Bern • Frankfurt am Main • Berlin • Vienna • Paris

Library of Congress Cataloging-in-Publication Data

Reuscher, John A.
    A concordance to the Critique of pure reason / Jay Reuscher.
      p.   cm. — (American university studies. Series V, Philosophy;
  vol. 148)
    Includes bibliographical references.
    1. Kant, Immanuel, 1724–1804. Kritik der reinen Vernunft—
Concordances. 2. Philosophy, German—18th century—Concordances.
I. Title. II. Series.
B2779.R46   121—dc20   92-36438
ISBN 0-8204-2108-1
ISSN 0739-6392

Die Deutsche Bibliothek-CIP-Einheitsaufnahme

Reuscher, Jay:
The concordance to the Critique of pure reason / Jay Reuscher. - New York;
Berlin; Bern; Franfurt/M.; Paris; Wien: Lang.
  (American university studies: Ser. 5, Philosophy; Vol. 148)
  ISBN 0-8204-2108-1
NE: Kant, Immanuel: Critique of pure reason; HST; American university
studies / 05

The paper in this book meets the guidelines for permanence and durability of
the Committee on Production Guidelines for Book Longevity of the
Council on Library Resources.

© 1996 Peter Lang Publishing, Inc., New York

Printed in the United States of America.

Table of Contents

Preface

There are two parts to this *Concordance*. The first part, *The Linear Index*, contains the list of virtually all the texts of substantive importance in the order of their occurrence in the *Critique Of Pure Reason*. The second part, *The Topical Index*, contains the themes and paradigms to which these texts belong. Together the two parts enable the user both to track particular texts to the various families of texts of which they are members and to study these families themselves as wholes.

The numbers following the texts in *Part One, The Linear Index*, indicate the topics in *Part Two, The Topical Index*, to which they belong. In *Part Two*, the major divisions fall into two classes: 1) The doctrines on the sources, nature, and limits of the competence of the human mind; 2) The doctrines on the object, representations, and subject of mental activity. All other classifications are subsets of these two. The symbols used in abbreviations were selected for the visual convenience of the reader. There is no significance to the order of their occurrence.

Note on the Method of Text Citation

1. I have used Norman Kemp Smith's translation of the *Critique of Pure Reason*. (London: Macmillan and Co., Ltd., 1933).
2. Lines of the text are counted from the line opposite the A and B marginal labels and their numbers placed after the dot. For example, A116.12-16 means lines 12 through 16 counted from the line opposite A116 in the margin.
3. Headings are *not* counted.
4. A numbers have been used as basic and their lines have been counted consecutively *around* the new material Kant wrote for the 1787 edition (as indicated in Kemp Smith's own footnotes).
5. A materials excluded by Kant from the 1787 edition and placed by Kemp Smith below the line are designated by their own marginals.
6. A texts are counted *through* texts omitted in the 1787 edition and located below the line.
7. Materials written for the 1787 edition are the only texts cited by using the B label.
8. Kant's footnotes are designated by the line in the main body of the text to which they were attached by the lowercase letter and are counted in sequence from their own first line regardless of any intervening marginals. For example, B422.14 ftnt a 14-15 means lines 14 and 15 counted from the first line of the footnote although marginal B423 intervenes.
9. There is no significance to the order of the coding symbols used after the text in the *Topical Index*.

PART ONE

LINEAR INDEX

Contents

4   *Contents*

Contents

Linear Index

Preface to First Edition

Avii.1-5	1, 7, 11
6-8	7
Avii.10-	
Aviii.1	7
10-13	1
Ax.12-14	10
Axi.4-	
Axii.3	11
Axii.5-8	11
8-10	8, 11
Axiii.5-6	7
13-19	7, 11
Axiv.9-12	11
12-14	7
14-17	11
20-23	7
Axv.9-14	7
Axvi.16-20	12, 14.2, 14.27
Axvi.20-	
Axvii.2	8, 9
4-7	1
Axvii.7-10	36
Axx.1-7	7, 14.9
7-9	7, 14.9
9-12	11, 14.9
13-18	1, 7
Axxi.1-2	7, 14.9
2-5	11
14-16	7

Preface to Second Edition

Bviii.1-3	7
7-10	7
Bix.1-6	7
7-12	12
Bix.12-14	12, 14, 16
Bix.21-	
Bx.1	12

Bix.21- (Continued)	
2-6	12, 14, 16
11-15	12, 14.7
Bx.18-	
Bxi.1	11
Bxii.1-3	29
3-6	29
6-9	29
Bxiii.3-8	11
8-11	1
11-15	5
Bxiii.19-	
Bxiv.5	5
9-11	7, 14.9
11-13	7, 14.9
Bxvi.12-14	12, 14.7, 14.9
14-17	12, 14.7, 14.9
Bxvii.3-7	31.1
7-15	13, 14.13, 22
17-21	7, 12, 14.13, 14.27
Bxvii.21-	
Bxviii.2	12, 14.2
2-9	1, 12, 14.16
9	
ftnt a	
3-6	1, 12, 14.16
6-12	1, 10, 12, 14.28, 21
Bxiv.1-6	12
Bxix.10-	
Bxx.1	1
1-6	1, 14.27, 17, 18
7-11	7, 17
11-24	10, 12, 14.1, 14.17, 17, 18, 21, 22
Bxxi.1	
ftnt a	
3-10	7, 10, 14.9, 18
Bxxi.19	1, 8, 11, 14.9, 37
Bxxii.4-8	14.9
8-9	1
9-11	7, 14.9
Bxxiii.1-7	7, 9, 11, 12, 14.9, 14.16
7-9	12, 14.7, 14.20
9-16	7, 11, 14.9
Bxxiii.16-	
Bxxiv.1	7, 12, 14.9
1-5	1, 14.9
5-7	7, 14.9
16-20	1

20-21	37
Bxxv.2	37
2-3	37
3-7	37
7-10	37
10-14	37
Bxxv.19-	
Bxxvi.5	1, 12, 14.6, 14.18,, 14.28, 17, 18
7-12	12, 14.22, 14.27, 14.28, 17, 18
Bxxvi.11 ftnt a	
1-3	12, 14.7, 14.14
3-7	8
Bxxvii.2-12	12, 14.4, 14.22, 14.28, 17, 21, 36
Bxxxvii.14-	
Bxxviii.4	1, 12, 14.1, 14.22, 14.28, 17, 18, 21, 36
4-6	1
7-9	1, 36
Bxxxvii.14-	
9-12	1, 36
12-16	1, 17, 21, 22, 36
16-18	1, 36
Bxxix.11-15	21, 37
16-21	37
Bxxix.26-	
Bxxx.9	1, 37
9-11	37
Bxxxi.13-15	1, 14.9
Bxxxi.19-	
Bxxxii.5	1, 10
6-20	37
20-23	37
Bxxxii.23-	
Bxxxiii.3	36, 37
3-5	10, 37
5-14	10, 37
Bxxxvii.20-	
Bxxxviii.3	7, 10
Bxl.1 ftnt a	
14-19	12, 20, 22, 34, 35.3A
24-33	12, 20, 22, 31.1, 34, 35.2, 35.3A, 35.6
33-38	12, 20, 34, 35.3D
38-42	12, 19, 20, 22, 34, 35.2, 35.3A, 35.3D, 35.4E
42-44	
45-50	12, 20, 34, 35.3A, 35.3D
50-53	12, 20, 31.1, 34, 35.2, 35.3A, 35.3D
60-67	12, 20, 22, 23, 34, 35.3A, 35.3D

Introduction

I. The Distinction Between Pure and Empirical Knowledge

B1.1-8	11, 12, 14.12, 14.17, 14.18, 22, 36
8-10	1
12-16	20
B2.3-6	1
B2.24-	
B3.1	1
5-8	1, 36
A1.1-3	20, 29, 36
8-10	1
10-11	1
A1.11-	
A2.2	1
2-4	1, 7
4	7
7-10	7
11-20	1, 7, 12, 14.13

II. We Are in Possession of Certain Modes of *A Priori* Knowledge, and even the Common Understanding is Never Without Them.

B3.9-10	1
10-12	1, 36
12-14	7, 11
14-16	7, 11
B3.16-	
B4.2	1
2-5	1, 7
5-7	1
8-10	1, 7
10-12	1
12-18	1
19-22	1, 7
B4.23-	
B5.2	36
2-10	1
10-13	7
13-16	1
21-22	7
B6.1-7	1
7-10	7

III. Philosophy Stands in Need of a Science Which Shall Determine the Possibility, the Principles, and the Extent of all *A Priori* Knowledge.

A2.21	
A3-4	1, 12, 14.4
5-7	1, 10, 15
B7.6-7	7, 10, 14.9, 37
7-9	11, 14.9
9-12	11
A3.15-20	11
A4.15-22	1, 7
A5.18-23	11
A6.6-11	1, 3, 11

IV. The Distinction Between Analytic and Synthetic Judgments.

B11.19	1
B12.3-7	1
12-15	7
15-20	5
20-22	1
22-25	1
A9.6-9	36
9-12	1, 36
12-15	1, 36
16-20	1, 36
21-25	1, 36
A9.25-	
A10.2	1

V. In all Theoretical Sciences of Reason Synthetic *A Priori* Judgments Are Contained as Principles.

B14.5-6	1
B14.10-15	1
15-19	1
20-22	1
B14.22-	
B15.1	1, 7
1-4	1, 7
5-11	1
12-13	1
13-15	1
15-19	1

B15.19-
    B16.3   1
    3-5   1
B16.5-6   1
    6-10   1
    11-12   1
    12-13   1
    13-17   1
B16.7-
    B17.1   ("B17.1" for the first time) 1
    1-5   1
    5-7   1
    7-9   1
    9-13   1
B16.3-   ("B16.1" for the second time) 1
B16.3-
    B17.3   ("B17.1" foor the second time) 1
    3-6   1
    7-8   7
    8-11   7
B17.11-
    B18.1   7
    3-7   1
    8-11   7
    11-14   7, 10
    14-19   1, 10
    19-21   7

VI. The General Problem of Pure Reason

B19.6-7   7
    8-12   1
B20.14-20   8
    21-22   8
B20.22-
    B21.1   8
    1-5   7, 10
    6-9   7, 10
    9-13   7, 9, 10
    13-16   7
B21.16-
    B22.5   7, 10, 14.9
    6-12   1, 7, 10, 11, 14.9
    12-19   7, 10, 11, 14.9
    19-21   7, 11, 14.9
    22-23   7, 14.9
B22.23-
    B23.3   1

4-9	7, 9, 11
9-14	1, 7, 9, 11
15-17	1
17-21	1, 7, 10
21-23	1, 10
B23.23-	
B24.2	1
2-6	1
7-13	7

VIII. The Idea and the Division of a Special Science, Under the Title "Critique of Pure Reason."

A10.19-	
A11.1	11
1-2	7, 11
2-4	7, 11
4-6	7, 11
7-8	7, 11
10-13	9, 11
A11.17-	
A12.2	1, 9, 11, 12
2-3	7, 11
8-11	11
11-13	1, 11
13-16	1
16-22	7
A12.22-	
A13.3	8, 11
4-6	7, 11
6-9	7, 11
B27.2-3	
3-4	11
A13.10-12	7, 11
12-14	7, 11
14-15	7, 11
15-19	7, 11
19-21	7, 11
A14.8-13	7
14-15	7, 11
15-19	7, 11
A14.23-	
A15.9	1, 7, 37
9-10	1, 11
11-13	1, 37
19-22	1, 4, 9
22-23	1, 9, 12, 14.13, 14.18
23-24	1, 9, 12

I
TRANSCENDENTAL DOCTRINE OF ELEMENTS

FIRST PART. Transcendental Aesthetic

Introduction 1

Section I
Space 2—Metaphysical Exposition of this Concept

13-14	1
15-17	1
17-19	1
19-21	1
A24.20-	
A25.1	1
1-2	1, 7, 22
2-4	1, 7
4-7	1, 7
7	7
8-9	1, 7
9-11	1, 7
11-16	1, 7
17	7, 22
18-20	1
21-23	7
B39.22	7, 22
B40.1-4	7, 11, 22
4-5	1, 11, 22
5-6	7, 11, 22
7-8	1, 7, 22

3—The Transcendental Exposition of the Concept of Space

10-11	7
12-15	7
16-17	7
B40.17-	
B41.3	7, 22
3-5	1, 7, 20
5-8	7, 9
8-11	1
12-14	20
15-20	12, 20, 22
21-23	7

Conclusions from the above Concepts

A26.1-3	1
3-6	1
6-9	1
10-11	20
11-12	7, 20
12-15	12, 14.12, 14.18, 36
15-17	7, 20
17-20	7
21-22	1
22-25	1, 12, 14.12, 14.18, 20, 36

A27.1-2	1
2-6	12, 14.6, 14.18, 14.19
7-9	1
9-12	1
12-15	1
15-23	12, 14.6, 14.18, 14.22, 14.28, 21, 38.1, 38.5
A27.23-	
A28.5	12, 14.9, 20
5-7	20
7-12	20
13-15	1
18-25	20, 22
21-24	1
24-25	7
A28.25-	
A29.2	1
2-4	1
4-7	1
7-8	1
8-13	7
13-14	7
B44.16-18	1, 7
19-26	1
A29.15-220	1, 20
A29.20-	
A30.2	1
2-9	1, 12, 14.17, 14.19, 17, 18, 20 22
9-12	1, 17, 22

Section II
Time 4—Metaphysical Exposition of the Concept of Time

13-14	1
14-17	7
17-19	7
A31.1-2	7
2-4	1, 7
4	7
4-5	7
5-7	1, 7
8-10	7
10-11	1, 7
11-12	1, 7
13-15	1
15-16	1
16-19	7
20-21	1, 7
A31.21-	
A32.1	7, 20

1-2	1
3-4	1
5-6	1
6-7	7
8-10	1
10-11	7
12-17	7

5—The Transcendental Exposition of the Concept of Time

B48.12-15	7
15-20	7
B48.20-	
B49.2	7
2-5	7

6—Conclusions from these Concepts

A32.21-	
A33.1	20
1-4	20
4-6	1, 20
6-8	7, 20
9-10	1, 7, 20, 34, 35.3A
10-11	1, 34
11-13	1
13-14	1
15-17	7
17-20	7
20-22	7
A34.1-2	7
2-4	7
4-6	20
6-9	7
9-11	7, 35.3A
11-16	7
A34.17-	
A35.3	12, 14.1, 14.22, 14.28, 17, 18, 20, 22, 34, 35.3A, 35.4A
3-6	20, 36
7-16	21, 22, 38.1
17-19	12, 14.23
19-22	1, 7
A35.22-	
A36.2	1, 20
3-4	1, 17
4-9	20, 21
9-13	20
13-16	14.1, 20

7—Elucidation

A37.6-7	20
7-9	20
9-11	20, 34, 35.3A
11-16	20
17-18	1
18-22	12, 14.20, 14.23, 20, 21
A38.14-21	12, 14.1, 14.6, 14.22, 14.28, 18, 20, 21, 22
A38.25-	
A39.2	7
5-9	1, 12, 14.22, 14.28, 20, 21
9-11	1
11-15	7, 20
A40.8	1
A41.10-15	1

8—General Observation on Transcendental Aesthetic

A42.2-3	21.22
3-9	17, 18, 21
10-11	17, 18, 21
11-13	1, 13.6, 17
13-14	1, 17
17-20	1, 7, 17
22-24	7, 17, 20
A43.1-4	2, 17, 18
4-5	1, 17
8-11	1, 12, 13.6, 14.7
20-24	7
A44.1-4	2, 17, 18
4-8	12, 14.17, 14.22, 14.28, 17, 18, 20, 22, 36
18-25	1, 12, 14.12, 14.17, 14.18, 17, 20, 21, 22
A45.13-16	1, 12, 14.1, 17, 18, 20, 21
A45.22-	
A46.6	1, 18
6-10	1, 18, 20, 21
10-11	1, 13.2, 18, 20, 21
13-16	17
6-11	1, 17
A46.26-	
A47.4	7, 9
4-6	1, 9
6-13	1
13-17	1, 7
23-25	1, 9
A47.25-	
A48.1	9
1-5	1, 7
5-6	7, 12, 14.13, 14.21

SECOND PART. Transcendental Logic

Introduction. Idea of a Transcendental Logic

I—Logic in General

A50.16- (Continued)
21-22	1, 7
22	1
22-23	1
23-24	1

A51.24-
A52.2	1
2-5	1, 31.1
8-10	1, 7
12-15	7
22-25	5

A53.9-13	1, 7

A53.22-
A54.2	1, 7, 11
5-10	1, 7
11-14	1
14-16	7

A54.25-
A55.5	37
5-7	1, 37

II—Transcendental Logic

8-10	1
10-12	7
12-19	7
19-21	7, 9, 11, 12, 14.25, 21

A55.21-
A56.1	7, 9, 11
2-6	1
6-9	1, 22
12-17	9, 11, 12, 22
19-22	9, 11, 12, 14.17, 14.25, 22

A57.1-3	9, 11, 12, 14.25
4-8	9
8-16	9, 11, 12, 14.16, 14.25, 14.27

III—The Division of General Logic into Analytic and Dialectic

A58.15-19	12
A59.1-4	1
10-14	1
14-16	7
16-18	1, 7
18-19	1
19-22	1

A59.22-
A60.1	7
1-3	1

IV—The Division of Transcendental Logic into Transcendental Analytic and Dialectic

FIRST DIVISION. Transcendental Analytic

Book I
Analytic of Concepts

Chapter I
The Clue to the Discovery of All Pure Concepts of the Understanding

Section 1
The Logical Employment of the Understanding

Section 2
The Logical Function of the Understanding in Judgment

Section 3
The Pure Concepts of the Understanding, or Categories

Chapter II
The Deduction of the Pure Concepts of Understanding

Section I
The Principles of any Transcendental Deduction

A85.4-8	7, 25, 26.9
8-11	1, 12, 14.2, 25
11-13	7, 11, 12, 14.2, 25, 26.5
13-16	5, 25, 26.6
16-17	5, 25, 26.6
18-22	7, 12, 14.2, 25, 26.1, 26.9, 31.1
A85.22-	
A86.3	1, 7, 12, 14.2, 25, 26.6, 26.9
3-4	11
5-8	36
8-11	26.13, 36
11-16	7, 14.4, 25, 26.14, 29, 31.1, 36
16-19	5, 25, 26.8
20-22	1, 7, 25, 26.6, 26.9
A86.23-	
A87.1	1, 25, 26.6
4-6	1, 25, 26.7
6-10	1, 7, 25, 26.6, 26.9
11-14	1, 7, 25, 26.6, 26.9
14-17	2, 7
17-20	7, 25, 26.9
21-24	7, 25, 26.1, 26.9
A87.25-	
A88.1	12, 14.6, 14.7, 14.13, 14.18, 20, 25, 26.1, 31.1
2-5	25, 26.4, 31.1
5-8	7, 12, 14.2, 25, 26.1, 31.1
8-11	1, 7, 12, 14.2, 25, 26.1
11-17	1, 3, 25, 26.7, 26.17
A89.1-5	1, 25, 26.7, 26.17
10-11	12, 14.1, 14.19, 14.23, 20
16-18	1, 12, 14.2, 14.13, 25, 26.1
18-20	1, 12, 14.1, 14.2, 25, 26.1, 31.1
20-21	1, 12, 14.2, 25, 26.1, 31.1
A89.21-	
A90.1	1, 7, 12, 14.2, 25, 26.1
A90.1-3	1, 12, 14.1, 25, 26.1, 31.1
3-6	25, 36
6-9	14.1, 25, 26.1, 31.1, 36
9-12	12, 14.1, 25, 26.1, 31.1
12-15	7, 12, 14.2, 14.6, 14.19, 14.22, 20, 25, 26.1
15-18	7, 12, 14.2, 14.21, 25, 26.1, 26.9, 26.14, 31.1
18-20	12, 25, 26.1, 25.14, 31.1
21-24	25, 26.1, 36
24-25	25, 26.1, 36
A90.25-	
A91.2	12, 14.2, 14.6, 14.18, 25, 26.1, 31.1
2-9	1, 14.4, 25, 26.1, 36
9-11	7, 25, 26.9, 36
A91.11-12	7, 25, 26.9, 36
12-15	1, 5, 14.1, 25., 26.9, 36

15-18	1, 25, 26.9, 36
19-20	1, 7, 25, 26.9, 36
A91.20-	
A92.1	11, 5, 25, 26.9
1-4	25, 26.9

Transition To The Transcendental Deduction Of The Categories

5-8	12, 14.17, 22, 25, 26.1
8-10	2, 12, 14.17, 20, 22, 25, 26.11, 26.20, 29, 36
10-11	1, 12, 14.12, 14.14, 14.17. 14.18, 22, 25, 26.13, 36
11-13	12, 14.1, 14.12, 14.14, 14.17, 14.18, 22, 25, 36
13-16	1, 12, 14.3, 22, 25, 26.13
16-18	2, 12, 14.17, 20, 22, 25, 26.11, 26.14, 29, 36
A92.19-	
A93.2	12, 14.1, 14.2, 14.6, 14.13, 25, 26.2, 26.18
2-5	7, 12, 14.6, 25, 26.18, 26.22
5-7	1, 7, 14.1, 18, 20, 25, 26.17, 26.18, 26.22
7-10	1, 7, 12, 14.2, 20, 25, 26.18
10-13	12, 14.4, 14.7, 20, 25, 26.11, 26.18
13-16	12, 14.1, 14.4, 14.6, 25, 26.18, 26.20
16-18	7, 12, 20, 25, 26.2, 266.9
18-21	7, 12, 14.2, 14.4, 20, 25, 26.2, 26.9
21-23	7, 12, 14.2, 14.4, 25, 26.2, 26.9
5-7	7, 12, 14.2, 14.10, 20, 25, 26.2, 26.9
7-10	25, 26.2, 26.13
10-13	7, 12, 14.2, 14.4, 20, 25, 26.2, 26.9
B127.9-20	7, 12, 14.2, 14.10, 14.21
20-23	1
B128.1-5	1, 9
17-20	7, 10, 12, 13.3, 14.2, 14.6, 36
B129.2-6	7, 10
A94.14-18	1, 7, 9, 25, 26.9, 26.10, 26.13
18-21	7, 25, 26.10, 26.14, 29, 36
21-23	7, 25, 26.9, 26.10, 26.14

The A Priori *Grounds Of The Possibility of Experience*

A95.3-7	1, 7, 25, 26.9, 26.13
7-8	1, 25, 26.13
8-10	1, 12, 14.1, 14.6, 25, 26.13
10-13	7, 25, 26.9, 26.13
14-15	1, 25, 26.13
15-16	7, 25, 26.9, 26.13
16-17	1, 25, 26.9, 26.13
A95.18-	
A96.3	7, 11
3-6	7, 25, 26.9, 26.13
A96.14-19	1, 7, 14.2, 14.14, 25, 26.1, 26.9, 26.13
19-21	1, 12, 25, 26.9, 26.13

A96.21-
A97.3	7, 11, 12, 14.1
3-10	7, 11, 12, 14.27
11-13	1, 22, 25, 26.13, 25.21
13-14	7, 9, 22, 25, 26.9, 26.21
14-15	25, 26.22
16	9, 25, 26.22
16-17	1, 25, 26.14, 33.2
18-22	9, 25, 26.8, 26.14, 33.2

A97.22-
A98.2	7, 9, 23, 25, 26.8, 26.9

1. The Synthesis of Apprehension in Intuition

A98.16-
A99.1	7, 22, 25, 26.8, 26.20, 26.21, 36
1-3	7, 25, 26.9
3-4	7, 25, 26.9, 26.14, 29, 31.1, 36
7-9	7, 9, 22, 25, 26.8, 26.9, 26.22
10-11	2, 7, 9, 22, 25, 26.9, 26.21, 26.22
11-14	7, 25, 26.9, 26.14, 26.17, 29, 36
14-18	9, 22, 25, 26.14, 29, 36

A99.21-
A100.2	7, 25, 26.14, 29, 36
2-3	7, 25, 26.14, 29, 36

2. The Synthesis of Repreduction in Imagination

4-9	1, 22, 25, 26.13
9-13	7, 20, 25, 26.9
A101.9-11	7, 25, 26.9, 26.14, 29, 36
11-14	17, 18, 22, 36
15-20	1, 7, 20, 25, 26.9, 26.14, 29, 36
20-22	7, 25, 26.9, 26.14, 29, 31.2, 36

A101.22-
A102.1	7, 25, 26.9, 26.14, 29, 36
1-6	9, 22, 25, 26.14
6-11	7, 22, 25, 26.9, 26.14, 29, 36
11-13	1, 25, 26.13, 26.14
14-21	7, 36

3. The Synthesis of Recognition in a Concept

A103.1-3	7, 25, 26.13, 26.14, 29
3-6	7, 25, 26.9, 26.14, 29, 36
6-8	7, 22, 25, 26.9, 26.14, 29, 36
8-12	7, 25, 26.9, 26.14, 29, 36
12-14	25, 26.12
15-18	2, 7, 9, 11, 22, 25, 26.12, 26.14, 29, 33.3, 36

A103.18-
A104.2	9, 25, 26.14, 29, 33.3, 36
2-3	7, 25, 36.14
3-5	7, 25, 26.17
6-7	12, 14.17, 25, 26.21
7-11	12, 14.17, 14.22, 14.28, 18, 20, 22, 25, 26.13, 26.21
A104.11-16	7, 12, 13.1, 14.7, 25, 26.1, 26.9

A104.17-
A105.2	7, 11, 12, 13.1, 14.2, 14.7, 14.10, 25, 26.9, 26.17, 26.19
3-9	1, 7, 11, 12, 13.1, 14.10, 14.17. 17, 18, 21, 25, 26.13, 33.3, 33.5, 33.6
9-11	25, 26.17
11-18	6, 7, 25, 26.14, 29, 31.4, 33.4, 36
18-20	6, 7, 25, 26.13, 33.5, 33.6
20-22	7, 12, 13.1, 14.2, 14.10, 14.17, 22, 25, 26.9, 33.5, 33.6
A106.1-2	7, 25, 26.17
2-4	7, 25, 26.14
4-6	7
6-9	6, 7, 11, 25, 26.14, 26.17, 33.3
10-12	25, 26.14, 26.17, 36
13-19	7, 8, 11, 12, 14.10, 25, 26.9, 26.16, 26.17, 33.1, 33.2, 34, 35.3B, 35.4E
19-21	7, 12, 13.1, 14.10, 25, 26.1, 33.1, 33.2

A106.22-
A107.1	7, 11, 25, 26.1, 26.16, 26.20, 33.1, 33.2, 34, 35.4E
1-3	1, 9, 25, 26.15
3-6	1, 9, 25, 26.15
6-8	1, 2, 7, 11, 22, 25, 26.9, 26.17, 33.1, 33.2
8-11	2, 7, 8, 11, 25, 26.9, 26.17, 33.1, 33.2
12-17	2, 7, 11, 12, 14.17, 14.224, 22, 32, 33.1, 33.2, 34, 35.4E
17-21	2, 7, 8, 11, 25, 26.9, 26.16, 34, 35.4E
21-24	2, 7, 11, 25, 26.9, 26.16, 33.1, 34, 35.4E
A108.1-4	2, 7, 11, 22, 25, 26.14, 26.16, 31.1, 33.2, 34, 35.4E, 36
4-7	2, 7, 25, 26.15, 26.16, 26.20, 33.8, 34, 35.4E, 35.7, 36
7-14	2, 7, 12, 13.1, 14.2, 14.10, 14.21, 25, 26.1, 26.9, 26.12, 26.16, 26.17, 26.20, 32, 33.5, 33.8, 34, 35.4E, 35.6
14-20	2, 7, 22, 25, 26.1, 26.9, 26.14, 26.16, 26.20, 33.3, 33.6, 33.8, 34, 35.3D, 35.4E, 35.7, 36
22-23	11, 12, 14.17, 22, 25, 26.1, 26.20

A108.23-
A109.1	12, 14.1, 18, 25, 26.1, 26.20, 26.21

A108.23- (Continued)

1-3	12, 14.1, 14.6, 14.18, 25, 26.1, 26.20, 26.21
3-7	1, 12, 13.1, 13.2, 14.1, 14.6, 14.17, 14.18, 17, 18, 20, 21, 22, 25, 26.1, 26.20, 26.21
8-11	12, 13.1, 13.2, 14.2, 14.7, 25, 26.1, 26.9
12-15	7, 11, 12, 13.1, 13.2, 14.6, 14.7, 14.18, 25, 26.1, 26.9, 26.20, 33.3, 33.5
15-18	7, 12, 13.2, 14.7, 14.10, 14.17, 14.21, 25, 26.1, 26.9, 26.12, 26.14, 26.17, 31.3, 32, 33.3, 33.5, 34, 35.4E, 35.6

A109.18-

A110.6	2, 7, 12, 13.1, 13.2, 14.1, 14.7, 14.10, 14.21, 25, 26.9, 26.17, 26.19, 26.20, 33.3
6-9	1, 2, 7, 11, 18, 25, 26.9, 26.16, 26.17, 34,
35.4E	
9-10	7, 8, 25, 26.9, 26.16, 26.17

4. Preliminary Explanation of the Possibility of the Categories, as Knowledge a priori

11-15	2, 7, 11, 25, 26.9, 26.16
15-17	2, 7, 11, 25, 26.16
17-18	2, 7, 11, 25, 26.16
19-20	2, 7, 11, 25, 26.16
A111.1-3	1, 2, 7, 11, 25, 26.16
5-7	7, 12, 14.2, 25, 26.16
7-10	31.1
11-13	7, 8, 32
13-16	7, 25, 26.16
16-18	7, 12, 13.3, 14.2, 25, 26.1, 26.9
20-23	7, 8, 25, 26.9, 26.16, 33.1, 33.5, 33.6, 34, 35.7

A111.23-

A112.4	2, 7, 11, 33.1, 33.5, 33.6, 34, 35.4E, 35.7
4-6	2, 7, 25, 26.9, 26.14, 29, 31.5, 36
6-10	7, 11, 25, 26.9, 26.14, 26.16, 33.5, 33.6, 34, 35.4E, 35.7
10-13	1, 12, 25, 26.16
16-18	1, 7, 25, 26.9, 36
19-22	1, 25, 26.9
A113.4-6	30
10-12	7, 8, 18, 22, 33.2, 34, 35.4E
12-15	7, 22, 32, 33.2, 34, 35.4E, 35.6
15-20	7, 11, 25, 26.9, 26.16, 29, 33.2, 36
20-23	7, 25, 26.14, 30
23-26	7, 30
A114.4-13	2, 7, 18, 21, 22, 30, 34, 35.4E
13-15	2
15-19	1, 2, 7, 11, 25, 26.16
19-24	1, 2, 12, 14.2, 25, 26.14

Section 3
The Relation of the Understanding to Objects in General and the Possibility of Knowing them *a priori*

A115.3-6	7, 9, 25, 26.8, 34, 35.4E
6-9	7, 25, 26.9
9-13	35.4E, 36
A115.14-	
A116.3	1, 7, 11, 25, 26.16, 29, 33.2, 34, 35.4E, 35.7,
36	
4-9	2, 7, 11, 25, 26.16, 29, 33.2, 34, 35.4E, 35.7,
36	
9-11	1, 7, 25, 26.16
11-12	7, 8, 25, 26.16
12-16	2, 7, 8, 22, 33.1, 33.2, 34, 35.4E, 35.7
16-18	2, 7, 11, 25, 26.14, 26.16, 29, 34, 35.3B, 35.4E,
	36
19-21	2, 7, 11, 25, 26.16, 33.1, 33.2, 34, 35.3B
A116.21-	
A117.2	2, 7, 11, 25, 26.16, 29, 33.2, 34, 35.3B, 35.4E,
	36
2	
ftnt a	
2-3	7, 25, 26.16
3-5	1, 25, 26.16
6-10	2, 7, 33.2, 34, 35.4E, 35.6, 35.7
10-14	2, 7, 11, 25, 26.16
14-17	2, 7, 11, 25, 26.9, 26.16, 29, 34, 35.3B,
	35.4E, 35.7, 36
17-25	2, 7, 8, 22, 32, 34, 35.4D, 35.4E, 35.6, 35.7
A118.1-3	2, 7, 9, 11, 25, 26.9, 26.14, 26.16
3-6	2, 7, 8, 11, 25, 26.9, 26.14, 26.16, 29, 33.2,
	34, 35.4E, 35.7, 36
6-7	7, 25, 26.9, 26.14, 29, 36
7-8	1, 7, 25, 26.14
8-11	1, 2, 7, 11, 25, 26.9, 26.14, 26.16, 29, 33.6, 34,
	35.3B, 35.4E, 35.7, 36
12-14	7, 25, 26.14, 29, 34, 35.4E, 36
14-17	2, 7, 11, 22, 25, 26.9, 26.14, 26.16, 33.6, 34,
	35.4E
17-20	2, 7, 8, 11, 25, 26.9, 26.14, 26.16, 29, 33.6, 34,
	35.3B, 35.4E, 35.7, 36
20-21	7, 12, 14.2, 14.17, 25, 26.9, 26.14, 26.16
A119.1-4	7, 32, 33.2, 34, 35.4E, 35.6
4-8	2, 11, 25, 26.9, 26.14, 26.16, 29, 33.3, 36
8-11	2, 7, 25, 26.14
11-13	7, 25, 26.14, 29, 36
13-15	7, 18, 25, 26.14
15-19	7, 25, 26.14, 29, 36

A119.20-	
A120.1	7, 25, 26.14
1	9, 25, 26.20
1-2	9, 20, 25, 26.20
2-5	1, 18, 20, 25, 26.20
5-7	20, 25, 26.11
7-10	1, 7, 25, 26.14, 29, 31.2, 36
10-14	8, 25, 26.10, 29, 31.2
14-16	25, 26.10, 29, 31.2, 36
A121.1-7	7, 25, 26.14, 29, 36
8-12	1, 25, 26.14, 29, 36
12-17	7, 22, 25, 26.14, 30
18-23	7, 12, 14.21, 25, 26.9
A121.23-	
A122.2	25, 26.9, 30
2-6	25, 26.9, 30
6-9	7, 26.9, 34, 35.3B, 35.4E
9-16	10, 12, 14.21, 25, 26.9, 26.19, 30, 31.5, 33.2, 33.7
17-23	6, 7, 12, 14.21, 25, 26.9, 30, 31.5, 33.2, 33.7
23-25	6, 7, 12, 14.21, 25, 26.9, 26.17, 33.7
A123.1-6	7, 8, 12, 14.24, 25, 26.9, 26.12, 26.16, 26.17, 30, 31.2, 31.5, 33.3, 34, 35.4E, 35.7
7-8	7, 25, 26.14, 29, 36
8-11	7, 11, 25, 26.14, 29, 36
11-19	7, 12, 14.2, 20, 30, 31.2
20-22	7, 8, 22, 32, 34, 35.4D, 35.4E, 35.6, 35.7
A123.23-	
A124.2	2, 7, 11, 25, 26.16, 34, 35.4E
2-4	7, 25, 26.9, 26.16, 34, 35.4E
4-7	7, 25, 26.14, 29, 31.1, 36
7-11	2, 7, 11, 25, 26.14, 33.1, 34, 35.4E, 36
12-14	7, 25, 26.10
14-16	2, 7, 11, 25, 26.14, 31.3, 34, 35.3C, 35.4E, 36
16-22	2, 7, 11, 25, 26.9, 26.16
A124.22-	
A125.4	7, 25, 26.14
7-11	2, 7, 11, 25, 26.14, 29, 36
11-13	7, 25, 26.14
14-19	7, 18, 20, 21, 25, 26.9, 26.14, 26.17
A125.19-	
A126.2	2, 7, 12, 14.7, 14.18, 14.27, 25, 26.9, 26.17
3-7	7, 9, 25, 26.10
8	25, 26.10
8-10	7, 25, 26.10
10-11	7, 25, 26.10, 31.1
11-13	5, 7, 25, 26.10
13-15	5, 7, 25, 26.20
15-18	5, 7, 25, 26.9, 26.20
A126.18-21	1, 7, 25, 26.9, 26.14, 26.17

Section 2
Transcendental Deduction Of The Pure Concepts
Of The Understanding

The Possibility of Combination In General

B130.22- (Continued)
　1
　ftnt a
　1-7　　　　　　　　　　　　22
B131.2-5　　　　　　　　　　22
　5-6　　　　　　　　　　　　1, 2, 7, 11
　6-9　　　　　　　　　　　　2, 7, 11
　9-10　　　　　　　　　　　7, 33.4
　10-14　　　　　　　　　　2, 7, 11, 27

The Original Synthetic Unity of Apperception

B131.15-
　B132.4　　　　　　　　　　8, 22, 34, 35.4D
　4-15　　　　　　　　　　　1, 2, 7, 22, 29, 32, 33.8, 34, 35.3A, 35.4D,
　　　　　　　　　　　　　　 35.4E, 35.6
B132,17-
　B133.2　　　　　　　　　　2, 7, 22, 31.4, 31.5, 34, 35.4E, 35.7
　4-7　　　　　　　　　　　　2, 8, 22, 29, 33.6, 34, 35.C, 35.4E, 35.7
　7-12　　　　　　　　　　　22, 29, 31.4, 33.2, 34, 35.3C, 35.4E, 35.7
　13-18　　　　　　　　　　1, 7, 8, 22, 29, 33.6, 34, 35.3C, 35.4E, 35.7
　18
　ftnt a
　12-15　　　　　　　　　　2, 7, 11, 33.2, 34, 35.4E
　15-16　　　　　　　　　　2, 7, 11, 32, 33.2, 34, 35.4E, 35.6
B134.16　　　　　　　　　　22, 29, 31.5, 32, 34, 35.4E, 35.6, 35.7
　6-8　　　　　　　　　　　　7, 29, 34, 35.4E, 36
　8-10　　　　　　　　　　　1, 2, 7, 11
　10-13　　　　　　　　　　6, 7, 29, 33.6, 34, 35.4E, 35.7
　13-16　　　　　　　　　　12, 14.21, 29, 31.4
B134.16-
　B135.3　　　　　　　　　　7, 22, 29, 31.4, 33.2, 34, 35.3C
　3-5　　　　　　　　　　　　2, 7, 11, 34, 35.3B, 35.4E
　6-10　　　　　　　　　　　1, 7, 29, 33.6, 34, 35.3B, 35.4E, 35.7
　10-14　　　　　　　　　　7, 22, 34, 35.3A, 35.4D, 35.7
　14-16　　　　　　　　　　1, 7
　16-17　　　　　　　　　　1, 7
　17-21　　　　　　　　　　9, 22, 31.4, 32, 33.6, 34, 35.4E
B135.21-
　B136.1　　　　　　　　　　7, 9, 22, 29, 32, 33.8, 34, 35.4E, 35.7

The Principles of the Synthetic Unity is the Supreme Principle of All Employment of the Understanding

　2-8　　　　　　　　　　　　7, 8, 31.1, 31.4, 34, 35.3B, 35.4E, 35.7
　8
　ftnt a
　1-3　　　　　　　　　　　　7, 22
　3-5　　　　　　　　　　　　22
　5-8　　　　　　　　　　　　22
　8-10　　　　　　　　　　　2, 7, 11

B136.8-10	7, 31.1, 31.4
B136.10-	
B137.1	7, 29, 31.4, 36
1-5	7, 22, 29, 32, 33.2, 34, 35.3C, 35.4D, 35.4E, 35.6, 35.7
6-7	
7-10	2, 12, 13.1, 14.7, 14.17, 22
10-11	7, 22, 33.2
11-15	7, 12, 13.1, 14.17, 14.24, 20, 22, 32, 33.2, 34, 35.3E, 35.4E, 35.6
15-16	7, 33.2
17-21	2, 7, 131.4, 34, 35.3B, 35.4E
21-24	1
B137.24-	
B138.1	9, 20, 29, 31.4
1-2	20, 29, 31.4, 36
2-4	9, 29, 31.4, 33.6, 34, 35.3C, 35.6
4-5	9, 12, 14.7, 14.24, 20, 31.4, 34, 35.3C
6-7	7, 12, 14.7, 144.21, 34, 35.3B, 35.6, 35.7
7-10	7, 11, 12, 31.4, 34, 35.7
10-12	7, 34, 35.4E, 35.7
13-20	7, 22, 31.4, 34, 35.3B, 35.4D, 35.4E, 35.7
21-24	7, 32, 34, 35.3A, 35.4D, 35.4E
B138.24-	
B139.4	2, 7, 11, 36
4-11	1, 7, 29, 31.4

The Objective Unity of Self-Consciousness

12-14	7, 12, 13.1, 14.21, 14.24, 31.4, 33.2, 34, 35.3E, 35.4E
14-18	7, 34, 35.3E, 35.4E
18-20	31.1
B139.20-	
B140.3	1, 31.1
3-9	7, 22, 31.4, 33.2, 34, 35.3C, 35.4D, 35.4E
9-10	1, 7, 34, 35.3E, 35.4E

The Logical Form of all Judgments Consists in the Objective Unity of the Apperception of the Concepts which they contain

B140.17-	
B141.7	38.2
8-14	2, 7, 11, 31.4, 34, 35.4E, 36, 38.2
B141.14-	
B142.3	2, 7, 34, 35.3E, 38.2
3-14	7, 22, 33.2, 34, 35.3B, 35.3E, 35.4E, 38.2
14-19	7, 38.2
119-21	1
22-26	7, 12, 14.7, 14.21

The Application of the Categories to Objects of the Senses in General

*Transcendental Deduction of the Universally Possible Employment
in Experience of the Pure Concepts of the Understanding*

8-10	31.1, 36
12-14	2, 31.1
B160.19-	
B161.5	2, 31.1, 31.4
6-10	2, 31.4, 33.3, 33.8, 34, 35.4E, 34.6
10-11	7, 33.3, 33.8
11-14	2, 5, 7, 12, 14.2, 14.4
B162.1-4	31.1, 31.4
4-6	29, 31.3, 31.4, 36
6-9	7, 31.3, 31.4
10-11	7, 31.3, 31.4
11	
ftnt a	
1-4	7, 19, 31.3, 31.4, 31.5, 34, 35.4E, 35.7
4-7	29, 31.3, 31.4, 31.5, 36
B162.12-	
B163.5	7, 31.4, 31.5
5-11	7, 29, 31.4, 36
11-14	31.4, 36
16-18	7, 20
18-24	2, 7, 20, 29, 36
B164.1-5	7, 20, 29, 36
5-9	7, 18, 21
9-11	7, 17
11-13	1, 18, 20, 22
13-15	7, 20, 22, 31.4
15-16	29, 31.3, 36
16-18	7, 31.3
18-21	7, 31.4
B164.21-	
B165.2	7, 31.4
2-5	7, 20
5-9	1, 7, 14.2
9-13	2
13-16	1, 7, 12, 14.4, 14.7

Outcome of this Deduction of the Concepts of Understanding

17	1, 7, 12
17-19	1, 7, 12, 14.6
19-20	1, 7, 14.18
B165.20-	
B166.1	1
1	32
1-3	1, 7, 12
3	
ftnt a	
5-6	12, 14.7
B166.4-5	1, 20
8-11	7

Book II
The Analytic of Principles

Chapter I
The Schematism Of The Pure Concepts Of Understanding

Chapter II
System of All Principles of Pure Understanding

Section 1
The Highest Principle Of All Analytic Judgments

Section 2
The Highest Principles Of All Synthetic Judgments

Section 3
Systematic Representation Of All The Synthetic Principles
Of The Pure Understanding

1. Axioms Of Intuition

2-10	7, 12, 14.1, 14.2, 14.6, 14.14, 14.17, 14.18, 14.21, 18, 22, 29, 36
A162.21	
163.3	22, 29, 36
3-6	6, 29, 36
6-11	18, 29, 36
10-12	7
15-17	29, 36
A164.24-	
A165.3	7
15-18	7, 20
A165.24-	
A166.3	7, 12, 14.7, 14.19, 14.21, 14.23, 20
3-6	7, 12, 14.10, 14.21, 20

2. *Anticipations Of Perception*

B207.10-11	12, 14.15, 14.18
12-13	32
13-16	1, 12, 14.1
B207.16-	
B208.1	12, 13.3, 14.3, 14.15, 14.17, 14.18, 14.19, 14.23, 22
5-8	6, 36
8-11	12, 14.17, 14.18, 22
11-14	29, 36
14-18	12, 12.12, 36
A167.1-6	1, 6, 31.1
19-24	2, 22
A168.1-4	7
4-11	7
11-16	7
17-19	7
20-21	7
21-24	18, 36
A168.24-	
A169.3	7
5-9	7
13-15	7
A169.15-	
A170.2	1, 30.1
A170.2-6	7
7-9	7, 18
9-14	36
A171.4-20	2, 4, 5, 6, 7, 31.1, 36
A171.21-	
A172.2	1, 4, 5, 31.1
A175.11-16	31.4
A175.23-	
A176.2	20

A175.23- (Continued)
6-13	31.1, 31.4
13-18	7

3. Analogies Of Experience

B218.12-14	7
15-16	12, 14.4, 14.7
16-19	29
B218.19-	
B219.2	7, 12, 14.4, 14.6, 14.7, 14.18, 14.21
2-5	1, 31.1
5-8	22, 29, 31.1, 36
9-12	12, 14.3, 14.4, 14.7, 14.23, 14.29, 22, 31.1, 31.4
12-16	7, 12, 14.3, 14.23, 29, 31.1, 31.4
16-18	7, 22
A177.3-8	7
9-12	7
12-15	7
15-18	7, 22, 34, 35.4E, 35.7
18-19	7, 29, 34, 35.4E, 36
19-23	7, 34, 35.4E, 35.7
A177.23-	
A178.3	7, 31.4
4-7	1
8-12	7, 36
12-17	1, 6
A179.5-10	1
10-15	31.4, 31.5
A179.20-	
A180.2	7
2-4	7, 23
4-6	7
6-7	1
8-9	1, 12, 14.1
A180.20-	
A181.3	1, 18
10-12	7
12-13	7
13-16	7
16-19	7
19-23	7

A. First Analogy–Principle of Permanence of Substance

Proof

B224.14-16	18
B224.16-	
B225.3	7

4	1
4-6	12, 14.1, 14.17, 14.23, 18
12-15	18
A182.4-7	12, 14.4
A182.10-	
A183.1	8
1-3	22
16	1
16-20	8
20-22	10
22-23	12, 14.1, 16, 18
A184.15-20	18
A185.14-18	18
18-22	18
A185.22-	
A186.1	7
8-11	7, 20
11-14	7
14-16	20, 22
A186.17-21	14.3
A186.21-	
A187.1	14.3
A187.2-4	14.3
A189.3-5	7

B. Second Analogy–Principle of Succession in Time, in accordance with the Law of Causality

Proof

B232.11-12	36
B233.10-12	18
12-13	29, 36
13-16	31.3
16-18	29, 31.3, 36
18-20	1, 29, 31.3
20-22	9, 29, 31.3, 31.5, 36
B233.22-	
B234.2	1, 31.5
3-7	29, 31.5, 36
7-9	7, 36
10-14	29, 36
14-19	7, 12, 14.1, 18, 20, 29, 36
A189.9-10	36
11-13	18
13-15	12, 14.17, 22
15-17	12, 14.17, 22
A189.17-	
A190.3	12, 14.1, 14.17, 14.28, 18
3-7	12, 14.1, 14.17, 18, 20, 22
7-9	18, 29, 36

A190.9-12	12, 14.1, 14.17, 14.21, 14.22, 14.28, 18, 20, 22
12-15	1, 17, 22
15-22	1, 17, 18, 22
A190.24-	
A191.2	12, 13.2, 14.1, 14.2, 14.17, 17, 18, 20, 22
2-4	17, 18, 20
5-8	12, 14.1, 14.17, 18, 20, 21, 22
8-10	12, 14.2, 14.17, 14.28, 22
10-17	7, 12, 14.1, 14.10, 14.17, 14.21, 14.28, 20, 21, 22
17-19	7, 12, 14.1, 14.10, 18
A191.20-	
A192.5	1, 7, 18
A192.9-13	7, 18
13-18	7, 18
19-21	7
A193.3-6	7, 20
7-11	18, 21
11-13	12, 14.21
13-17	7, 12, 14.1, 14.10, 20
17-19	18
20-21	1, 20, 29, 36
22-24	7, 36
A193.24-	
A194.2	1, 36
2-5	1, 7, 18
5-7	7, 36
7-10	7, 36
11-12	36
13-22	7, 12, 14.10, 22
A194.22-	
A195.3	7, 12, 14.10
3-5	12, 14.7, 14.10
6-8	7, 31.4, 31.5
8-12	7, 12, 14.10, 31.4, 31.5
12-17	7, 12, 14.10, 31.4, 31.5, 36
A196.1-7	1, 7
9-14	5, 20, 31.4, 36
14-17	7, 18, 20
A196.18-	
A197.1	7, 12, 14.10, 14.17, 31.4, 31.5
1-2	7, 12, 14.10, 14.14, 22, 31.4, 31.5
3-10	12, 14.17, 14.23, 22
10-16	12, 14.8, 14.17, 22
16-20	7, 12, 14.8, 14.10, 14.17, 22, 23, 29, 31.4, 31.6, 36
20-23	7, 12, 14.8, 14.10, 14.17, 14.23, 22
A198.1-4	12, 14.1, 14.17, 14.21, 18, 22, 31.4, 31.5
4-8	12, 14.10, 22, 31.4, 31.5
8-11	12, 14.10, 14.23, 31.4, 31.5, 36

A205.1-4 (Continued)

13-17	18, 36
17-20	36

A205.23-

A206.4	18, 36
10-13	1, 36
13-17	1, 18, 36
17-24	1, 15, 16, 17, 18, 21, 36

A206.25-

A207.7	1, 18, 36
7-13	7, 36
14-16	36

A207.16-

A208.2	36
3-6	36
6-11	18, 36
11-13	36
14-15	36
15-17	36
17-21	36
21-23	36

A208.23-

A209.1	36
2-6	18, 36
6-8	18
9-12	36

A210.4-7	18, 36
7-9	31.4, 36
9-10	29, 31.4
10-11	31.4
11-17	6.2, 7, 29, 31.4, 36
17-18	7
19-21	7

A210.22-

A211.7	7, 12, 14.1, 14.7, 14.23, 14.24, 14.27, 18, 31.4, 31.5, 36

C. *Third Analogy–Principle of Coexistence, in accordance with the Law of Reciprocity or Community*

B256.14-15	36

Proof

B256.16-

B257.3	1, 36
4-6	9
6-7	12, 14.3
9-12	1

12-15	12, 14.3, 14.21, 31.2
15-18	31.2
18-23	12, 14.2, 31.4, 31.5
B257.23-	
B258.2	36
2-5	36
5-7	31.4, 31.5, 36
7-9	8
A211.8-9	36
A212.1-7	12, 14.3, 14.14, 18, 36
7-13	36
14-18	36
18-20	36
20-24	36
A212.24-	
A213.2	36
2-4	7, 12, 14.10, 14.14, 31.5
5-7	7, 31.5, 36
8-12	36
12-14	12, 14.18, 14.19, 36
15-17	36
17-20	7
20-23	7, 36
A213.23-	
A214.5	7, 12, 14.1, 14.17, 14.19, 14.23, 22
11-16	7, 12, 14.3, 14.17, 14.21, 22, 36
16-23	7, 12, 14.14, 14.18, 36
A214.23-	
A215.2	36
2-6	
6-8	7
9-15	7
16-17	1, 14.1
17-20	1, 7, 12, 14.18, 14.23
20-25	7, 31.4, 31.5, 36
A216.1-3	7
3-5	7, 20
5-7	5, 7
8-13	7, 31.4, 31.5
13-16	7
A217.5-8	1, 12, 14.4
8-12	14.13
12-17	7, 31.4, 31.5
17-19	7
A218.1-6	7
6	
ftnt a	
5-8	7, 36
8-12	7

4. The Postulates of Empirical Thought in General

A218.7-9	8
12-14	7

Explanation

A219.1-3	12, 14.2
3-4	
8-12	12, 14.27
13-15	7
15-18	1
18-22	7
A220.1-3	7, 8
3-5	7
5-11	1, 12, 14.2, 14.4, 14.21, 29
11-12	
13-16	7, 8, 12, 14.2, 14.7, 14.14, 14.21, 23, 29
16-18	7, 8, 38.6
18-20	8, 12 ,14.2, 14.15
A221.1-3	1, 7, 8, 12, 14.4, 14.15, 14.19, 31.1
3-6	7, 8, 31.1
8-11	1, 8
11-16	1, 8
16-22	1, 8
A221.22-	
A222.5	7, 8, 12, 14.2, 14.4, 14.15, 14.21
6-13	1, 8
13-19	1, 2, 8
A222.19-	
A223.2	8
A223.3-6	8
A223.7-8	1
8-11	1
A223.12-14	8
15-18	1, 8
19-23	8, 12, 14.2
A223.23-	
A224.2	1, 8, 12, 14.14
2-5	7, 8
5-11	7, 8, 29, 31.1, 31.2, 36
12-16	7, 8, 12, 14.2, 14.4, 14.14
16-19	8, 12, 14.4, 14.13
19-23	7, 8, 12, 14.4, 14.7, 14.14
23-24	1, 8
A225.1-4	12, 14.3, 14.7, 14.18
4-8	7, 12, 14.4, 14.7, 14.18
9-15	1, 23
15-16	23

16-17	23
18-22	7
A226.3-7	1
7-10	1
10-12	1
12-14	1

Refutation of Idealism

B274.17-21	20

Thesis

B275.11-13	12, 14.3, 14.18, 20, 34, 35.2, 35.3D
14-15	9, 12, 20, 34, 35.2
16-19	12, 20, 34, 35.3A, 35.3D
19-21	2, 12, 20, 22
B275.21-	
B276.1	2, 12, 220, 34, 35.4A, 35.3D
2-4	7, 12, 20, 34, 35.2, 35.3D
4-6	2, 12, 20, 34, 35.3D
B276.17-	
B277.3	8, 12, 20, 34, 35.2, 35.3A, 35.3D
1	
ftnt a	
5-10	12, 20, 29
B277.3-5	7, 12, 20, 22, 34, 35.2, 35.4D
5-6	12, 20, 34, 35.2, 35.4D
6-8	1, 12, 20, 34, 35.3A, 35.4D
11-12	12, 20, 14.10, 14.19
12-14	8, 12, 20
17-20	1, 12, 20
B278.2-7	7, 12, 20
7-10	1, 9, 12, 20, 22, 34, 35.3A, 35.4B, 35.4D
10-14	1, 12, 20, 34, 35.3A, 35.4D
15-20	1, 12, 20, 22, 34, 35.3A, 35.3D
20-23	12, 14.14, 14.15, 14.18, 14.19, 20, 22
B278.23-	
B279.1	1, 7, 12, 20

(Kant returns to his treatment of the Postulates)

A226.23-	
A227.1	12, 14.3, 14.7, 14.18
1-4	1
4-7	1, 7
7-10	1, 7
10-12	1, 36
12-15	1, 7, 36
15-18	1, 7, 36

18-23	1
23-24	1
A227.24-	
A228.4	1, 7, 18, 36
4-8	7, 36
8-12	7, 36
12-17	7, 18, 36
A230.15-19	7, 18, 20
19-23	1
23-25	1
A231.1-4	1, 4
4-5	1, 29
5-8	8
8-12	8
12-16	8
16-18	8
18-21	8
21-23	8
A231.23-	
A232.2	8
2-4	8
4-6	8
6-8	8
A232.11-15	1, 7, 8, 11
A232.19-23	1, 12, 14.2, 14.17, 22
A233.23-	
A234.3	1, 7
4-6	7, 12, 14.4, 14.14
6-9	12, 14.3, 14.18
9-10	7, 12, 14.2, 14.10, 14.18
11-13	6, 29
13-17	6, 12, 14.21, 29
17-19	6, 7, 29
A234.20-	
A235.2	1
A234.21	
ftnt a	
2-3	1
4-5	7

General Note on the System of the Principles

B288.1-4	1, 12, 14.2, 14.6, 14.14, 14.15, 14.18, 14.27
4-12	1
15-18	1, 12, 14.2, 14.6, 14.7, 14.18
18-21	1, 7
B289.1-2	1
2-5	1
5-7	1
8-11	1

11-16	1
16-20	12, 14.4, 14.14, 36
20-23	7, 12, 14.6, 14.7, 14.13, 14.18
B289.23-	
B290.2	7, 36
2-8	36
8-11	36
B290.11-	
B291.2	8, 36
2-4	36
4-6	36
7-11	7, 12, 14.2, 14.6, 14.15, 14.18, 14.19
16-17	1
18-20	36
20-23	1
B291.23-	
B292.1	36
1-4	1, 36
8-14	7
14-17	1
17-21	1, 12, 14.2, 14.6, 14.15, 14.18, 14.19
B292.21-	
B293.4	36
4-6	7
11-14	8, 18, 36
14-17	7, 36
18-22	12, 14.6, 14.15, 14.18, 14.19
B294.4-8	1

Chapter III
The Ground Of The Distinction Of All Objects
In General Into Phenomena And Noumena

A235.3-6	7
6-7	7
18-21	7
A236.21-	
A237.1	7
1-5	7, 29, 31.3, 31.5
6-7	18, 31.3, 31.5
7-15	7, 8, 12, 14.4, 14.7, 14.13
A238.9-12	1, 7
A238.21-	
A239.1	12, 14.1, 14.4, 14.14, 17, 18
3-6	7, 12, 14.2, 14.13, 14.14
6-9	1, 12, 14.2, 14.8, 14.13
9-11	1, 12, 14.6, 14.13, 14.18
11-14	12, 14.6, 14.18
14-19	1, 12, 14.2, 14.6, 14.18

A239.23-
   A240.3   1, 6, 7, 12, 14.1, 14.8, 14.17, 18
   3-7   1, 12, 14.2, 14.6, 14.18
   7-13   29, 36
   13-15   7, 8
   15-18   7, 8, 12, 14.2, 14.4
A240.19-
   A241.1   1, 7, 12, 14.1, 14.2, 14.14, 14.15, 14.18,
                      14.27
   1-5   1, 12, 14.8

(The following is material omitted in B)

   18-19   1
A241.19
   ftnt a
   1-15   12
A241.19
   ftnt a
   5-8   12, 14.2
A241.19-
   A242.9   1, 7, 12, 14.2, 14.14

(End of material omitted in B)

A242.15-
   A243.2   1, 22, 34, 35.4D
   2-7   1, 12, 14.2, 14.8, 14.18
   7-11   1, 7, 12, 14.4, 14.18, 14.23, 36
   11-15   1, 12, 14.18, 14.23, 36
A244.4-7   1, 12, 14.3, 14.14
   7-12   1, 12, 14.2
   12-14   8
   14-19   8
A244.19-
   ftnt a
   1-5   1

(The following material omitted in B)

A244.20-33   1
A244.22-
   A245.1   1, 12, 14.2, 14.8, 14.18, 31.1, 31.2
   1-3   1, 31.1, 31.2
   4-7   1, 12, 14.2, 14.18, 31.1, 31.2
   8-10   31.1, 31.2
   10-15   1, 7, 12, 14.2, 14.6, 14.7, 14.18, 14.27
   15-20   1, 11
A245.20-23   1, 7, 22
A246.6-10   1, 12, 14.2, 14.18

(End of Material omitted in B)

11-17	1, 12, 14.2, 14.4, 14.14, 14.18
18-21	1, 7
A246.21-	
A247.1	1, 12, 14.1, 14.4, 18
7-8	12, 14.6, 14.18, 14.27, 29
8-11	1, 7, 12, 14.6, 14.18
11-14	1, 12, 14.2, 31.1
14-15	12, 13.2, 14.2, 31.1
16-19	12, 14.2, 14.6, 14.18, 31.1, 31.2
19-22	1, 31.1, 31.2
A247.22-	
A248.2	1
A248.2-6	1
8-14	1
14-18	1, 12, 14.2, 14.18
18-22	1, 7, 12, 13.3, 14.2, 14.8, 14.27

(The following material omitted in B)

A248.23-	
A249.1	12, 14.1, 14.2, 14.27, 16, 18
1-6	12, 14.6, 14.11, 14.13, 15, 17, 19
7-19	1, 12, 14.1, 14.2, 14.11, 14.15, 14.28, 15, 16, 18, 19, 21
19-22	12, 14.1, 14.6, 14.11, 14.17, 14.18, 14.22, 14.28, 17, 18, 21, 22
22-24	12, 14.14, 14.15, 14.18
A249.24-	
A250.1	12, 14.11, 14.17, 18, 21, 22
2-7	1
10-14	21
15-16	12, 13.2, 14.17, 14.27, 22, 29
16-18	12, 13.1, 13.2, 14.1, 14.7, 14.17, 14.27, 17, 18, 20, 22
18-22	1, 12, 13.1, 13.2, 14.7, 31.5, 31.5, 34, 35.3E
22-24	7, 12, 13.1, 13.2, 14.7, 14.18, 14.24, 31.4, 31.5, 34, 35.3E
24-25	12, 14.2, 14.6, 14.7, 14.21, 14.27,29, 31.4, 31.5
A250.25-	
A251.1	1, 12, 13.2, 14.7, 14.18, 14.27, 22
1-5	1, 12, 13.2, 13.3, 14.1, 14.2, 14.7, 14.17, 22
6-11	1, 12, 13.2, 13.3, 14.1, 14.2, 14.7, 14.13, 14.17, 14.18, 14.27, 14.22, 31.5
12-17	1, 15, 16, 17, 18
17-21	17, 18
A251.21-	
A252.1	18, 20, 22
1-7	14.17, 15, 17, 18, 22, 23

A251.21- (Continued)
   8   15
   8-10   1, 15, 23
   10-12   1, 15, 23
   12-15   12, 14.6, 14.11, 14.18, 14.27, 15, 16, 23
   15-17   12, 14.6, 14.11, 14.13, 15
   17-18   1
   18-20   12, 14.11
   20-21   1, 12, 14.11
A252.22-
   A253.3   12, 14.2, 14.6, 14.11, 14.14, 14.18, 15
A253.4-6   7, 12, 13.2, 13.3, 14.1, 15, 18
   6-7   1, 7, 12, 13.2, 13.3, 14.11, 15
   7-10   1, 7, 12, 13.2, 14.1, 14.6, 14.18, 18
   10-12   1, 12, 13.2, 13.3, 14.2
   14-16   1, 12, 14.2, 14.6
   16-18   1, 12, 14.2, 14.13

(End of material omitted in B)

B305.18-22   1, 3, 12, 14.2, 14.18, 31.1, 31.4, 31.5
B305.22-
   B306.1   1, 7, 31.1, 31.4, 31.5
   1-3   1, 31.1, 31.4, 31.5
   3-7   1, 12, 14.13, 14.18
B306.7-8   12, 14.1, 14.6, 14.28, 16, 18
   8-11   12, 14.6, 14.28, 18, 21
   11-17   12, 13.4, 14.5, 14.6, 14.11, 14.14, 14.18,
                          14.27, 14.28, 15, 18, 19, 21
B306.22-
   B307.2   12, 13.16, 14.2, 14.11, 14.17, 14.22, 14.27,
                          16, 17, 22
   2-5   1, 7, 12, 13.6, 14.2, 14.11, 14.22, 14.27
   5-10   17
   11-14   12, 14.6, 14.11, 14.18, 15, 17, 21
   14-18   12, 14.6, 14.11, 14.22, 15, 19
   19-23   1, 7, 15, 17, 18, 21
B307.23-
   B308.2   1, 21, 31.1
   3-6   1, 20, 31.1, 31.4, 31.5
B308.6-9   1, 15, 31.1, 31.4, 31.5
   9-10   1
   13-16   8
   16-20   12, 14.1, 14.2, 14.6, 14.11, 14.18, 14.28, 15,
                          17
   20-24   1, 12, 14.2, 14.4, 19
B308.24-
   B309.1   2, 21
   1-3   1

Appendix
The Amphiboly of Concepts of Reflection
Arising from the Confusion of the Empirical with the
Transcendental Employment of Understanding

A260.4-5	1, 12, 14.2, 14.26
6-8	7
8-10	9, 22
10-12	1, 7, 9
A261.2-8	9
8-10	7, 9, 29
10-15	9, 22, 29
15-19	7, 9
19-22	7, 9
22-24	9
A262.1-6	9
6-8	9
8-15	9
15-18	1, 7, 9, 22
18-23	1, 9
23-28	1, 9, 22
A262.28-	
A263.1	1, 8, 9, 12, 14.14, 14.17, 14.26, 22
1-2	1, 9
A263.12-17	12, 14.18, 14.19, 18
A263.17-	
A264.3	12, 14.19
A264.20-	
A265.2	15
13-15	16
15-19	12, 36
A265.21-	
A266.3	7, 12, 14.15, 14.27
9-11	7, 9
17-20	38.2
A267.17-20	7, 12, 14.1, 14.18, 18
20-22	7, 18, 31.1
A268.1-9	7, 18, 31.1

Note to the Amphiboly of Concepts of Reflection

10-12	7, 9
12-15	7, 9
15-19	9
19-21	7, 9
A269.4-6	1, 7, 9
6-10	1, 7, 9, 12, 14.2, 14.17, 22

11-15	9, 22
19-23	9, 12, 14.2, 1.26
A269.23-	
A270.5	1, 9
A274.10-14	7
A274.14-19	19
A275.14-17	9
A275.17-21	36
A276.14-17	1, 17, 22
17-20	1, 9
20-21	1, 17, 18
A277.1-3	1, 17, 18
5-8	16, 18
8-11	1
11-13	1
13-17	1, 12, 13.2, 14.1, 14.27, 18
19-23	1
A277.23-	
A278.5	1
8-11	1
11-13	1, 9, 34, 35.3A, 35.3B
13-14	9, 11, 35.3B
14-22	1, 9, 12, 14.18, 18, 34, 35.3A, 35.4A
23-26	1, 9, 18
A278.26-	
A279.6	1, 12, 14.1, 14.7, 14.22, 14.27, 17, 18
13-18	1, 12, 13.3, 14.2, 14.6, 14.18, 14.27
18-21	1, 12, 13.3, 14.17, 14.18, 22
21-24	1, 12, 14.6, 14.18, 14.27
A279.24-	
A280.1	1
1-2	1, 12, 13.6, 14.1, 14.22, 18
2-5	1
A282.4-7	1
10-15	8
A283.1-6	7
6-11	7
11-12	1, 7
12-17	1, 7
A284.4-8	1, 18
8-12	1, 7
12-17	1
17-21	1, 7
22-25	1, 7
A284.25-	
A285.3	17, 18
3-7	1, 12, 14.13, 18
8-11	12, 13.8, 14.1, 14.2, 18
11-12	1, 12, 13.4, 13.8, 14.2, 14.11, 14.14, 15

A284.25- (Continued)

13-14	18
14-15	1, 18
16-17	12, 14.18
17-21	1, 7, 36

A285.21-

A286.2	1, 36
3-5	1, 12, 13.4, 14.2, 14.5, 14.27, 19
5-9	1, 7, 12, 14.2, 14.6, 14.13, 14.14, 14.18
9-12	1
12-17	1, 12, 14.2, 14.18, 15
17-22	1, 12, 14.6, 14.18, 14.22

A286.22-

A287.1	1, 15
1-4	1
4-9	1, 12, 13.4, 14.18, 14.22, 14.28, 15, 18
9-13	1, 12, 14.2, 14.18, 14.27, 17
13-15	1
15-17	1, 12, 14.18, 14.27
17-20	1, 12, 14.2, 14.6, 14.11, 15

A287.20-

A288.1	1, 12, 13.6, 14.2, 14.6, 14.11, 14.15, 14.18, 15
1-4	1, 12, 14.6
4-8	1, 12, 14.27
9-10	1
10-15	1, 2, 12, 13.2, 14.1, 14.3, 14.7, 14.11, 14.27, 15, 17, 18, 36
15-18	1, 12, 13.2, 14.2, 14.3, 14.7, 14.11, 14.18, 15
18-19	1, 4, 12, 13.2, 14.3, 14.7, 14.11, 14.19, 15
19-21	1, 4, 12, 13.2, 14.3, 14.7, 14.11, 14.18, 15
21-23	12, 13.2, 14.3, 14.11, 14.18, 15

A288.23-

A289.3	1, 12, 14.2, 14.17, 14.27, 15, 22
4-7	1, 12, 14.1, 18, 19
7-8	1
8-14	1, 12, 14.2, 14.6
14-16	7, 12, 33.2, 33.3, 34, 35.4E, 35.7
16-20	12, 13.5, 14.3, 14.6, 14.17, 14.18, 14.27, 15
20-24	3, 12, 13.5, 14.3, 14.6, 14.27, 14.18, 14.27, 15

A290.7-10	13.3
10-14	13.3
15-18	1, 7, 12, 14.2, 14.6
18-21	1, 12, 14.11, 15
A291.13-15	8
A292.12-16	8

SECOND DIVISION. Transcendental Dialectic

Introduction
I
Transcendental Illusion

A293.12-15	3
A293.15-	
A294.1	7
3-4	7
4-6	2, 7
6-8	7, 36
8-9	7
9-11	1
11-16	1, 3
A295.7-12	2, 3, 7, 9, 11, 36
17-20	3
A295.23-	
A296.2	1, 3
2-8	3
8-11	3, 7
11-14	1, 3
14-16	3, 7
16-21	1, 3, 9, 11
A297.2-6	3, 7
6-10	3, 7, 12, 14.1, 14.16
10-13	3
13-16	3, 7
19-22	3, 9, 11
A297.22-	
A298.1	1, 3, 7, 11
1-4	3, 7, 12, 14.16
7-11	3, 7

II
Pure Reason as the Seat of Transcendental Illusion

A. Reason in General

A298.15-	
A299.1	7
5-8	7
12-16	9
16-20	7
22	7

B. The Logical Employment of Reason

C. The Pure Employment of Reason

Book I
The Concepts of Pure Reason

A310.1-4	1
4-8	1, 5, 7
9-10	1
11-12	1, 7
13-16	7
A310.17-	
A311.2	7, 11
2-3	9
4-6	9
6-12	1, 7, 10, 11
12-14	11
14-18	1, 3

Section 1
The Ideas in General

A314.1-8	1
9-12	7, 10, 37
12-17	1, 7, 37
A314.18-	
A315.2	7, 37
2-8	1, 37
8-12	1, 7, 37
12-15	1, 7, 37
15-18	1, 37
18-20	7, 37
20-21	7, 37
21-24	1, 37
A316.10-15	7, 37
A316.22-	
A317.4	7, 37
8-13	7, 10, 37
17-19	7, 37
19-23	2, 29, 36, 37
A317.23-	
A318.1	2, 7, 10, 36
4-6	1, 7, 37
6-8	2, 7, 36
8-9	2, 36
9-11	7
16-21	1, 7, 10, 37
A318.24-	
A319.1	3, 5, 7, 37
1-4	1, 7
13-16	7, 11

Section 2
The Transcendental Ideas

A321.1-6	7
6-8	7
8-25	7
A321.26-	
A322.1	7, 11
17-19	7, 11
19-25	7, 11
A323.1-3	7
3-7	7
8-14	7
14-18	7, 11
18-23	1, 7, 10
A324.14-19	7
A324.19-	
A325.2	7
2-4	8
4-8	1, 8
8-10	1, 7
10-13	7, 8
13-16	1, 7
16-20	1, 7
A236.1-4	1, 7
5-8	7, 11
8-11	1
11-15	7, 11
A326.17-	
A327.1	1, 7
1-6	1
7-9	1, 7
9-12	7, 10
13-15	7
15-18	1
18-24	1
A327.24-	
A328.6	1
6-8	1, 3, 7, 18
8-12	7, 37
12-13	7, 37
13-16	1, 7, 37
16-18	7, 37
19-20	2, 29, 36, 37
22-25	7, 37
A329.1-3	1
3-7	1
7-10	1
10-15	7, 10, 37

A330.1-4	7
14-16	1, 7, 11
A331.4-9	7
10-16	7, 11
16-20	7, 10, 11
20-21	7, 10, 11
A331.21-	
A332.3	7
3-6	7, 10, 11
6-11	9
11-14	7, 10, 11
17-22	7, 11
22-26	7, 11

Section 3
System Of The Transcendental Ideas

A333.4-9	1, 7, 9, 11
9-18	1, 7, 9, 11
A333.19-	
A334.3	7, 22, 34, 35.3B
3-7	7, 22, 34, 35.3B
8-12	7, 11, 22
12-14	2, 7, 11, 34, 35.4E
14-15	2, 7, 11
15-16	2, 7, 11
19-21	7, 8
A335.2-8	1
8-10	7, 11
14-16	1
16-21	7, 11, 34, 35.4E
21-23	7, 11
A335.23-	
A336.3	7, 11
4-6	1
6-8	1
8-10	7, 9, 11
11-14	7, 10, 11
14-15	1
15-17	7, 11
17-21	7
21-23	1
A337.1-4	1
4-8	1
8-10	8
13-16	7, 11
20	
ftnt a	
B 1-4	7

A337.1-4 (Continued)
B 4-6	1, 7
B 6-8	1
A338.6-10	1, 7

Book II
The Dialectical Inferences Of Pure Reason

12-15	1, 7, 12, 14.2, 14.16, 35.4G
A338.15-	
A339.3	1, 12, 14.2, 14.16, 14.27, 35.4G
3-7	1, 12, 14.16, 35.4G
8-10	7, 12, 14.16, 35.4G
10-14	1, 3, 7, 12, 14.16, 35.4G
14-18	3, 7, 35.4G
18	3
19-22	3
A339.23-	
A340.2	3
2-5	1, 7, 34, 35.3A, 35.4E, 35.4G

Chapter I
The Paralogisms Of Pure Reason

A341.2-4	1, 3, 7, 35.4G
4-5	3, 7, 35.4G
5-7	3, 7, 35.4G
8-12	2, 7, 34, 35.4G
12-15	7, 34, 35.4D, 35.4G
15-17	7, 34, 35.4D, 35.4G
A341.17-	
A342.3	7, 12, 14.17, 14.28, 22, 35.4G
3-4	12, 14.18, 14.20, 14.27, 34, 35.2, 35.4D, 35.4G
4-5	12, 35.4G
22-23	35.2, 35.4G
23-24	35.3A, 35.4G
A342.24-	
A343.2	35.3A, 35.4G
2-5	7, 8, 22, 33.1, 34, 35.3A, 35.4D, 35.4E, 35.6, 35.4G
5-12	11, 35.4G
A345.15-	
A346.1	1, 7, 34, 35.4D, 35.4G
1-2	1, 34, 35.4D, 35.4G
2-3	1, 34, 35.4D, 35.4G
3-5	1, 22, 34, 35.4B, 35.4D, 35.4G
5-8	1, 34, 35.3A, 35.4D, 35.4G
8-10	11, 22, 34, 35.3A, 35.4D, 35.4G

10-14	1, 11, 12, 14.7, 14.17, 14.20, 22, 34, 35.1, 35.3A, 35.4E, 35.4G
16-18	7, 34, 35.3A, 35.3B, 35.4D, 35.5A, 35.4G
18-19	34, 35.3B, 35.4D, 35.5A, 35.4G
21-23	7, 34, 35.3B, 35.5A, 35.4G
A346.23-	
A347.2	7, 34, 35.3B, 35.5Q, 35.4G
2-4	1, 7, 9, 22, 34, 35.3A, 35.3B, 35.5A, 35.4G
4-5	7, 9, 34, 35.3B, 35.5Q, 35.4G
5-6	9, 12, 14.20, 22, 34, 35.3B, 35.5A, 35.4G
7	1, 7, 22, 34, 35.3B, 35.5A, 35.4G
8-11	1, 34, 35.3A, 35.4D, 35.4G
11-13	1, 34, 35.3A, 35.4D, 35.4G
14-24	1, 34, 35.3A, 35.4G
24-25	1, 34, 35.3A, 35.4G
A348.1-3	7, 34, 35.4D, 35.4G
3-5	1, 34, 35.3A, 35.4D, 35.4G

(The following omitted in B)
First Paralogism: Of Substantiality

A348.18-	
A349.2	1, 12, 14.2, 35.4G
2-4	1, 35.4G
6-8	7, 34, 35.4D, 35.4G
8-9	1, 7, 34, 35.3A, 35.4D, 35.4G
9-11	7, 35.4G
12-15	1
15-17	1
18-21	1
21-23	1
A349.23-	
A350.2	1
2-4	1
4-6	1, 7, 12, 14.6, 14.17, 14.20, 14.24, 22, 34, 35.3A, 35.4D, 35.4G
7-10	1, 7, 22, 34, 35.3A, 35.4D, 35.4G
11-15	1, 35.4G
15-16	1, 34, 35.3A, 35.4D, 35.4G
16-18	7, 22, 34, 35.1, 35.4D, 35.4G
18-19	7, 34, 35.1, 35.4B, 35.4D, 35.4G
19-21	1, 34, 35.4B, 35.4D, 35.4G
21-22	2, 34, 35.4B, 35.4D, 35.4G
A350.22-	
A351.4	1, 13.7, 34, 35.3A, 35.4G

Second Paralogism: Of Simplicity

A351.18-	
A352.4	36

A351.18- (Continued)

15-18	22, 34, 35.3A, 35.4E, 35.4F, 35.4G
18-19	1, 34, 35.3A, 35.4F, 35.4G
A353.1-3	34, 35.3A, 35.4F, 35.4G
3-8	7, 22, 34, 35.3A, 35.4F, 35.4G
8-11	1, 34, 35.3A, 35.4F, 35.4G
11-13	1, 34, 35.3A, 35.4F, 35.4G
16-18	1, 35.4G

A353.23-

A354.1	1, 7, 12, 14.17, 14.20, 14.24, 14.27, 22, 34, 35.3A, 35.4G, 35.5A
1-2	1, 34, 35.3A, 35.4G, 35.5A
2-4	1, 7, 22, 34, 35.4D, 35.4F, 35.4G
4-7	1, 7, 34, 35.4D, 35.4F, 35.4G
7-8	7, 34, 35.4D, 35.4G, 35.7
12-13	1, 7, 34, 35.3A, 35.4D, 35.4E, 35.4G, 35.7
14	7, 32.2, 34, 35.4E, 35.4G, 35.7
14-17	1, 7, 34, 35.4D, 35.4G, 35.7
17-19	1, 12, 14.2, 14.7, 14.14, 14.20, 14.27, 34, 35.4G, 35.5A
19-22	1, 7, 9, 22, 34, 35.4G, 35.5A
23-25	1, 7, 34, 35.3A, 35.4D, 35.4G

A354.25-

A355.1	7, 34, 35.3A, 35.4D, 35.4G
1-4	34, 35.2, 35.3A, 35.4D, 35.4E, 35.4G
4-7	1, 7, 22, 34, 35.3A, 35.4D, 35.4G
8-10	7, 22, 34, 35.3A, 35.4D, 35.4G
10-14	1, 7, 34, 35.3A, 35.4B, 35.4D, 35.4G
14-15	7, 22, 34, 35.4B, 35.4D, 35.4G
15-17	1, 22, 34, 35.3A, 35.4D, 35.4G
17-19	1, 22, 35.4G
19-21	1, 22, 34, 3.3A, 35.4D, 35.4G
21-24	1, 34, 35.3A, 35.4D, 35.5A, 35.4G
A356.1-3	34, 35.4D, 35.4G
3-4	1, 34, 35.3A, 35.4D, 35.4G
4-9	1
9-13	1
13-15	1

A356.15-

A357.10	1
11-13	1
13-17	1, 12, 14.1, 14.17, 14.18, 14.19, 14.20, 14.27, 22, 34, 35.4D, 35.4E
17-20	1, 34, 35.3A, 35.4D, 35.4E, 35.5A, 35.4G
A358.4-7	1, 12, 14.18, 14.18, 14.27, 34, 35.4D, 35.4G, 35.5A, 35.4G
7-12	2, 12, 13.2, 14.1, 14.11, 14.17, 14.19, 14.27, 14.28, 15, 17, 22, 34, 35.3C, 35.3D, 35.4B, 35.4C, 35.4G

12-15	1, 22
15-19	1, 2, 12, 14.6, 14.7, 14.18, 17, 34, 35.3D, 35.4B, 35.4G
A358.19-	
A359.2	1
2-4	7, 34, 35.4B, 35.4G
10-12	1, 18, 35.4G
12-15	2, 17, 34, 35.3C, 35.3D, 35.4B, 35.4G
15-18	17, 22, 34, 35.4B, 35.4G
18-21	21, 34, 35.4B, 35.4C, 35.4G, 35.5B
21-22	18, 34, 35.4G
A359.22-	
A360.4	1, 17, 18, 21, 34, 35.4C, 35.4G
13-17	1, 17, 18, 34, 35.3A, 35.3D, 35.4B, 35.4D, 35.4G
18-20	1, 34, 35.3A, 35.4B, 35.4G
A360.24-	
A361.4	1, 7, 12, 13.2, 17, 34, 35.3A, 35.4G
6-10	1, 7, 35.4G
10-13	1

Third Paralogism: Of Personality

A361.18-	
A362.4	12, 14.1, 14.4, 14.7, 18, 35.4G
4-5	12, 14.20, 14.23, 34, 35.3A, 35.3D, 35.4G
6-8	7, 34, 35.4E, 35.4G
8-11	34, 35.3B, 35.4F, 35.4G
12-14	7, 9, 34, 35.4E, 35.4F, 35.4G
14-16	7, 32, 34, 35.4F, 35.4G
17-18	9, 34, 35.4F, 35.4G
18-20	12, 14.1, 14.16, 14.17, 14.19, 14.20, 14.23, 22, 35.4G
20-21	12, 14.1, 14.6, 14.17, 14.19, 14.20, 14.23, 22, 34, 35.4E, 35.4G
A362.21-	
A363.3	1, 7, 12, 14.17, 14.20, 14.23, 14.24, 22, 34, 35.4D, 35.4F, 35.4G
3-8	1, 2, 34, 35.4F, 35.5A, 35.4G
9-12	1, 7, 34, 35.4F, 35.4G
12-14	1, 7, 34, 35.4D, 35.4F, 35.4G
14-18	1, 7, 34, 35.4D, 35.4F, 35.4G
18	
ftnt a	
4-15	22, 34, 35.4F, 35.4G
A364.5-6	1, 34, 35.3A, 35.4F, 35.4G
6-8	1, 34, 34.4F, 35.4G
8-9	2, 7, 34.4F, 35.5A, 35.4G
10-11	1, 34, 35.3A, 35.4F, 35.5A, 35.4G
11-16	1, 18, 22, 34, 35.4D, 35.4F, 35.4G

A365.8-9	34, 35.4F, 35.4G
9-12	7, 34, 35.3A, 35.4E, 35.4F, 35.4G
15-20	1, 34, 35.3A, 35.4D, 35.4F
21-26	1, 7, 34, 35.4D, 35.4F, 35.4G
A365.26-	
A366.1	7, 13, 34, 35.4F, 35.4G, 37
1-4	1, 34, 35.3A, 35.4F, 35.4G
4-6	11, 34, 35.3A, 35.4G
6-9	1, 12, 13.2, 14.1, 14.17, 14.18, 14.19, 14.22, 17, 18, 21, 22, 35.4G
10-13	1, 22, 34, 35.3A, 35.4D, 35.4F, 35.4G
13-17	11, 34, 35.3A, 35.4G

Fourth Paralogism: Of Ideality
(In Regard To Outer Relations)

A368.8-10	36, 35.4G
A369.6-11	17, 18, 20, 22, 35.4G
11-14	2, 35.4G
A370.1-4	20, 22, 35.4G
4-5	20, 22, 35.4G
5-7	1, 18, 35.4G
7-8	1, 18, 20, 35.4G
8-9	1, 12, 13.6, 14.6, 14.17, 14.19, 22, 35.4G
10	12, 13.6, 14.6, 14.19, 20, 35.4G
12	20, 34, 35.2, 35.4G
15-17	20, 34, 35.2, 35.4G
17-19	20, 35.4G
19-22	9, 22, 34, 35.2, 35.3D, 35.4G
22-23	1, 13, 14.1, 14.17, 14.19, 18, 20, 22, 35.4G
23-24	1, 12, 14.1, 14.17, 14.19, 18, 20, 22, 35.4G
24-25	1, 12, 14.3, 14.17, 20, 22, 35.4G
A370.25-	
A371.1	1, 20, 35.4G
1-3	34, 35.2, 35.3D, 35.4G
3-6	1, 22, 34, 35.3D, 35.4G
6-9	12, 14.15, 14.19, 14.23, 14.27, 35.4G
9-12	1, 12, 14.17, 20, 22, 35.4G
A371.24-	
A372.3	1, 20, 22, 35.4G
8-13	12, 14.1, 14.3, 14.7, 14.17, 14.19, 14.22, 18, 20, 22, 35.4G, 36
13-15	1, 35.4G, 36
15-17	2, 12, 13.2, 14.6, 14.12, 14.17, 14.19, 17, 22, 35.4G, 36
17-19	1, 12, 13.2, 14.6, 14.19, 20, 22, 35.4G, 36
19-20	1, 18, 20, 22, 35.4G, 36
20-22	20, 35.4G, 36
A372.22-	
A373.1	1, 12, 13.2, 14.7, 17, 35.4G

A379.23- A380.5	1, 2, 12, 13.2, 14.1, 14.7, 14.19, 14.23, 14.27, 17, 18, 34, 35.3A, 35.4A, 35.4B, 35.4G
6-11	1, 13.6, 14.4, 14.18

Consideration of Pure Psychology as a Whole
in view of these Paralogisms

A381.1-9	1, 34, 35.3A, 35.4G
9-13	7, 18, 35.4G
13-17	1, 7, 12, 14.17, 14.23, 34, 35.3A, 35.4G
17-19	1, 34, 34, 35.4D, 35.4F, 35.4G
19-20	1, 12, 14.17, 14.20, 14.24, 22, 23, 34, 35.4D, 35.4G
A381.20- A382.2	1, 12, 14.17, 14.20, 14.24, 22, 34, 35.4D, 35.4G
2-6	1, 34, 35.3A, 35.4D, 35.4G
6-8	1, 12, 14.2, 14.20, 14.25, 34, 35.4D, 35.4G
8-12	1, 7, 12, 14.6, 14.17, 14.20, 14.24, 22, 34, 35.4D, 35.4G
12-18	1
A383.5-12	20, 35.4G
13-18	1, 34.1, 35.3A
18-22	35.4F
A384.4-13	35.4G
14-21	1, 3, 20, 35.4G
A384.21- A385.4	20
4-7	18, 35.4G
7-9	14, 35.4G
9-12	18, 35.4G
12-19	18, 35.4G
22-24	35.4G
A385.24- A386.6	35.4G
9-16	35.4G, 36
16-19	35.4G, 36
19-21	35.4G, 36
A386.21- A387.3	35.4G, 36
3-5	35.4G, 36
5-7	35.4G, 36
7-9	35.4G, 36
9-10	35.4G, 36
10	35.4G, 36
11-12	35.4G, 36
12-13	35.4G, 36
21-24	35.4G, 36
A389.12-22	35.4G

A391.1-4	1, 2, 22, 34, 35.3Q, 35.4G, 36
4-11	1, 17, 18, 22, 35.4G, 35
18-22	1, 18, 35.4G
22-23	17, 35.4G
A392.3-10	1, 17, 18, 20, 35.4G
14-20	1, 20, 34, 35.4G
A392.23-	
A393.4	34, 35.4G
4-6	4, 34, 35.3A, 35.4G
6-8	2, 18, 22, 34, 34,3A, 35.4G, 35
8-10	1, 34, 35.3A, 35.4G, 36
10-13	1, 12, 13.6, 14.1, 35.4G
13-15	12, 13.6, 14.2, 35.4G
A394.3-10	1, 11, 17, 18, 34, 35.4F, 35.4G
10-12	12, 14.7, 14.14, 34, 35.4F, 35.4G
17-19	1, 36, 35.4G
A394.19-	
A395.2	1, 35.4G
A395.3-7	1, 35.4G
A395.7-21	1, 35.4G
16-17	1, 35.4G
17-20	1, 35.4G
20-22	1, 35.4G
A395.22-	
A396.2	1, 35.4G
4-15	1, 3, 12, 14.7, 14.27, 35.4G
15-18	1, 11, 35.4G
A396.18-	
A397.4	3
5-7	3
7-11	3
13-18	1, 12, 14.21, 14.27, 29, 34, 35.3A, 35.4G
A398.3-6	7, 11, 12, 14.20, 14.24, 14.27, 34, 35.4D, 35.4G
6-8	1, 7, 34, 35.4D, 35.4G
8-9	12, 14.17, 14.24, 22, 34, 35.4D, 35.4G
10-12	1, 34, 35.3A, 35.4G
12-15	1, 35.3A
15-16	14.6
16-18	1, 35.3A
18-21	1
A398.21-	
A399.1	35.4D
1-6	1, 35.3A
6-9	35.3A
13-16	1, 35.3A
16-17	1
17-19	14.6
A399.19-	

A399.19- (Continued)

A400.1	14.6
1-4	14.1
14-15	35.3A
A400.4-8	1, 12, 13.3, 14.2, 14.6, 14.7, 18, 35.4G
8-11	1, 35.4G
11-14	7, 12, 14.2, 14.6, 14.20, 14.24, 34, 35.4D
14-17	7, 14.2, 14.6, 14.20, 14.24, 35.3A, 35.4G
17-21	1, 35.3A
A401.1-9	1, 35.3A
9-11	35.3A
11-15	35.3A
15-21	35.3A
21-22	7, 8, 33.1, 34, 35.4E, 35.7, 35.4G, 35
23-25	7, 22, 34, 35.4E, 35.4G
25-27	7, 22, 34, 35.3A, 35.4E, 35.4G, 35.6, 35.7
A401.27-	
A402.6	1, 7, 34, 35.4D, 35.4E, 35.4G
6-8	1, 11, 12, 14.7, 14.19, 3, 35.3A, 35.4G
8-11	1, 12, 14.20, 14.27, 34, 35.4D, 35.4G, 36
11-14	1, 3, 7, 34, 35.3A, 35.4G
15-16	3, 34, 35.3A, 35.4G
A402.24-	
A403.4	1
4-8	1
8-10	1
11-19	7, 34, 34.3A, 35.4E, 35.4G
19-21	7, 22, 34, 35.3A, 35.4G
A403.21-	
A404.2	34, 35.4G
3-4	34, 35.4G
5-7	34, 35.4G
8-11	34, 35.4G
A405.7-11	7, 22, 34, 35.4D, 35.4G, 35.5A
11-14	3, 7, 34, 35.3A, 35.4D, 35.3G

(End of material omitted in B)

B406.14-18	1, 7, 34, 35.3A, 35.4D
26-29	1, 12, 14.6, 14.7, 14.27, 34, 35.3A, 35.4E
29-32	1, 9, 34, 35.3A, 35.4D
B406.32-	
B407.1	1, 12, 14.2, 14.20, 14.24, 14.27, 34, 35.4E
2-4	1, 12, 14.7, 14.24, 14.27, 34, 35.4E
4-8	1, 7, 12, 14.6, 14.20, 14.21, 14.23, 14.24, 14.27, 14.28, 29, 34, 35.4D, 35.4E
9-10	34, 35.4D
10-13	12, 14.20, 14.24, 14.27, 34, 35.3B, 35.4D
14-15	1, 12, 14.20, 14.24, 14.27, 34, 35.3A 35.4D
15-19	1

20-24	1, 34, 35.3B, 35.4D, 35.4E, 35.4F
B408.1-2	1, 34, 35.3A, 35.4D
B408.2-5	1
13-15	34, 35.3B, 35.4D, 35.4F
16-18	1, 12, 14.6, 14.17, 14.20, 14.24, 22, 34, 5.3A, 35.4F
18-22	1, 34, 35.3A, 35.4F
B409.3-5	34, 35.3B, 35.4E, 35.5A
5-6	34, 35.3D, 35.3E
6-11	1, 34, 35.3A, 35.3D, 35.4G
12-14	1, 12, 14.7, 14.20, 14.27, 34, 35.3A
14-16	3, 12, 14.27, 34, 35.3A
17-23	1, 34, 35.3A, 35.4F
23-25	1, 15
B410.4-10	1, 34, 35.3A
10-18	1, 14.4, 17, 20, 35.3A
B411.11	
ftnt a	
1-3	12, 13.3, 14.6, 14.13, 14.20, 14.24, 14.27, 14.28, 22
3-4	12, 13.3, 14.6, 14.20, 14.24, 14.27, 14.28, 22
4-5	1, 12, 14.20, 14.24, 14.27, 22
5-7	14.20, 14.24, 22
7-8	7, 14.20, 14.24
8-11	7, 12, 1.20, 14.24, 14.27
11-12	1
12-14	1, 7, 34, 35.4D
14-15	1, 34, 35.3A
B412.1-7	1, 35.3A
7-11	1, 35.3A
B412.11-	
B413.1	1
1-2	1
2-3	1, 34, 35.4D
3-6	1, 35.3A
6-11	1, 35.3A

Refutation Of Mendelssohn's Proof Of The Permanence Of The Soul

B414.17-	
B415.2	35, 35.1
2-4	1, 12, 14.18, 14.23, 34, 35.3A, 35.4F
4-6	12, 14.18, 14.19, 14.23, 34, 35.4F, 35.4G
B418.4-8	1
9-11	34, 35.3A, 35.3B
11-17	34, 35.3A, 35.3B, 35.3C
B418.17-	
B419.1	7, 34, 35.3A, 35.3B

B418.17- (Continued)

B419.19-

B420.22-

B421.21-

B423.1-

2-5	1
5-13	1
14-23	1, 37
B424.23-	
B425.3	37
B425.3-9	2, 7, 10, 11, 37
9-18	7, 10, 37
B425.19-	
B426.6	7, 10, 37
6-11	7, 10

Conclusion, In Regard To The Solution Of the Psychological paralogism

15-18	1, 34, 35.3A, 35.4D
B426.18-	
B427	3, 31.1, 34, 35.2, 353A, 35.4D
2-6	1, 3, 34, 35.2, 35.3A, 35.4D
7-9	7, 34, 35.3A, 35.4E
B427.23-	
B428.3	17, 21

General Note On The Transition From Rational Psychology To Cosmology

10-11	12, 14.2, 14.3, 14.6, 14.20, 14.24, 14.27, 34, 35.2, 35.4D
11-14	1, 12, 14.6, 14.20, 14.24, 14.27, 34, 35.2, 35.3D, 35.4A
18-20	1, 7, 29, 34, 35.4D
B428.20-	
B429.1	1, 18, 34, 35.3A, 35.4A, 35.4D
1-3	1, 34, 35.3A, 35.4D
5-5	1, 34, 35.4A, 35.4B, 35.4D
5-6	12, 13.3, 14.6, 14.20, 14.27, 34, 35.4D
6-9	1, 22, 34, 35.3A, 35.4D
9-11	1, 7, 34, 35.3A
12-16	9, 18, 34, 35.4D
16-18	34, 35.2, 35.4D
19-20	34, 35.2, 35.4D
20-22	34, 35.4D
22-23	1, 34, 35.3A, 35.4D
B429.23-	
B420.1	18, 34, 35.3A, 35.4A
1-3	34, 35.3C, 35.4D
3-4	34, 35.4D
4-8	1, 12, 13.6, 14.6, 14.8, 14.11, 14.20, 14.24, 14.27, 21, 34, 35.3A
8-9	12, 13.6, 14.6, 14.7, 14.11, 14.20, 14.24, 14.27, 15, 34, 35.4B

B429.23- (Continued)

9-13	1, 12, 14.1, 14.3, 14.6, 14.7, 14.11, 14.14, 14.18, 14.20, 14.23, 14.24, 18, 34, 35.3A, 35.4B
14-22	34, 35.4B, 37

B430.22-

B431.3	9, 13, 15, 19, 34, 13.2, 35.4B, 35.4D, 37
5-8	9, 19, 37
8-11	1, 35.4D
11-17	1
17-21	34, 35.4B, 37

B431.21-

B432,5	1, 7, 34, 35.4B, 36, 37

Book II

Chapter II
The Antinomy Of Pure Reason

A405.15-

A406.2	3, 7, 11
2-7	3, 7, 11
8-11	3, 7, 11
11-14	3, 7, 11
16-19	1, 3
19-24	3

A406.25-

A407.6	3, 9, 11
7-10	3, 7, 11

A407.24-

A408.5	3, 7
5-9	7, 11
10-13	3, 11
15-18	3, 11

Section I
System Of Cosmological Ideas

A408.21-

A409.1	1, 7, 9
1	1
1-5	1, 3
5-10	3, 7, 11
10-12	3, 7, 11
12-13	1
14-17	3, 7, 11, 36

17-21	3, 7, 11, 35
21-24	1, 34
A409.24-	
A410.1	1, 36
2-6	1
6-12	1
13-16	7, 11, 36
A411.21-22	7, 11, 36
A411.24-	
A412.5	7, 11, 35
5-7	1
7-11	7, 36
11-14	1
A412.14-	
A413.3	1
3-7	1
7-10	1, 7
14-17	7
17-20	7
20-21	7
A413.22-	
A414.2	1
2-3	1
3-5	1
6-8	1
8-9	1, 12, 13.3, 14.2
10-15	1, 12, 13.13, 14.2
15-17	1
17-21	1
21-25	7, 36
A415.1-7	7, 23, 36
8-23	1, 7, 11
A416.1-5	1, 7, 11, 13.3
5-6	7
6-8	7, 11
8-11	7, 11
12-14	7, 10, 11
14-16	7, 10, 11
16-18	7, 11
18-19	1, 7
19-21	7, 11
A416.26-	
A417.3	1, 7, 11
3-7	7, 11
7-14	7, 11
14-16	1
17-21	7
21-24	7
24	
ftnt a	

A416.26- (Continued)
  1-3   7
  3-7   1, 7, 10, 11
A417.24-
  A418.3   10
  3-9   7, 10
  10-14   7
A418.14-
  A419.1   7
A419.1
  ftnt a
  1-3   7, 36
  3-6   7, 36
  6-8   7
  8-9   7
A419.1-4   7, 36
  4-5   7, 36
  5-6   7, 36
  6-8   36
A421.1-6   3, 9, 11
  6-10   1, 3
  11-12   3, 7
  13-14   3
  15-20   3, 11
A421.21-
  A422.3   3, 7, 11
  3-9   3, 7, 11
  10-12   3, 7, 11
  12-13   7, 11
  13-15   7, 11
  15-17   1, 3, 7
  17-18   1, 3, 7
  18-19   3, 7
A425.8-11   3, 13.37
  11-16   1
  16-18   1, 3, 7, 11

First Conflict Of The Transcendental Ideas

                                   Thesis

A426.11-14   1
A426.27-
  A428.8   1, 7
A426.29
  ftnt 2
  1-5   7
A428.8
  ftnt a
  1-2   1, 7
  2-6   1

A428.8-18	1
18-23	1

Observation

A430.33-36	1
36-42	1
	1
18-23	1
23	
ftnt 2	
1-3	1
A432.52-57	1
57-61	1
61-63	1

Antithesis

A427.14-23	1, 36
A429.14	
ftnt b	
1-2	1, 20
2-7	1, 20
7-9	1, 20
9-11	1, 20
11-17	1, 20

Observation

A431.23-24	1, 20
25-26	1, 20
26-29	1, 20
A431.30-35	1, 20
35-41	20
41-47	1
A431.47-	
A433.3	1, 20
A431.48	
ftnt a	
1-6	1
A433.13-34	19
34-41	1, 20
51-61	1, 19, 20

Second Conflict Of The Transcendental Ideas

Thesis

Observation

A438.1-12	7
12-17	1, 7
17-27	1
27-29	1

A438.20-	1
A440.2	1
2-10	1
14-15	1
A442.1	1

Antithesis

A435.8-15	7
15-17	1
18-19	7
23-28	7
28-33	1, 7
34-37	1
A437.2-6	1
7-11	1
11-15	1
34-37	1, 12, 14.13

Observation

A439.8-16	7
20-24	1
24-28	1
A441.6-11	1
11-17	1
18-21	7
41-43	1, 7
43-47	1, 7
A443.21-30	1
30-38	1
38-46	1, 7, 21

Third Conflict Of The Transcendental Ideas

Thesis

A446.5-9	36
9-17	1, 3, 36
18-29	36
30-35	36
A448.1-6	1, 36
6-10	36
17-22	3, 36
22-27	36
38-44	1
44-50	36
A450.3-15	1, 36
15-27	36
27-31	36
43-48	1, 36
48-51	1, 36

51-54	36
54-58	36

Antithesis

A445.5-27	36
28-30	3
30-38	3, 36
38-40	3, 36
A445.40-	
A447.4	3, 36

Observation

A449.36-42	1, 36
A451.1-10	1, 36
11-23	36
23-36	1, 36

Fourth Conflict Of The Transcendental Ideas

Thesis

A452.5-12	1, 36
12	
ftnt 2	
1-2	7, 20
2-4	22
A452.13-16	7, 36
16-22	7
22-27	7, 36
A452.27-	
A454.3	1, 35
3-14	1, 36
A454.14-19	36
20-21	20
21-25	1, 36

Observation

A458.59-62	1, 7
A460.32-35	1
35-41	1
45-51	1, 36
52-54	36
54-59	36

Antithesis

A455.5	
ftnt 2	
1-5	36

	Observation
A469.23-30	3, 7, 36
A459.31-	
A461.3	3, 36
3-7	7
7-11	3, 21
11-19	21
19-29	21
29	

Section 3
The Interest Of Reason In These Conflicts

A462.1-3	1
3-5	1
5-6	7
6-10	7, 11
11-12	7
12-15	1, 7
A462.26-	
A463.1	1
1-3	9
3-9	7
9-11	7, 10, 11
A463.12-22	7
A463.22-	
A464.2	1, 2, 10
2-8	7
8-13	7
14-19	2, 3, 10, 11
19-21	1, 2, 3, 10, 11
21-24	3, 9, 11
A464.24-	
A465.3	1
7-14	3, 10
19-22	3, 9
A465.22-	
A466.4	3
4-7	3, 7, 19
7	3, 7
7-10	3, 7, 19
11-15	3, 10, 36
15-21	7, 10, 37
21-23	3
24-25	7, 10
A466.25-	
A467.3	7
3-4	7
4-5	1

Section 4
The Absolute Necessity Of A Solution Of The Transcendental Problems of Pure Reason

A476.14-	
A477.1	1, 7, 11
1-5	1, 4, 5
15-18	7, 9, 11
18-21	7, 9, 11
21-24	1, 7
A478.9-	
A479.1	1
1-4	1, 13.2
ftnt a	
4-6	13.2, 35.3A
6-11	1, 12, 14.1, 14.13, 14.20, 14.23, 14.24, 18, 34, 35.3A, 35.4A
A479.1-4	14.13
4-8	1
8-11	1
14-17	1
A480.5-8	9, 11
16-19	7, 37
21-23	12, 14.1, 14.2, 14.13, 18, 31.1
A481.8-22	3, 4
22-25	1, 7, 12, 13.7, 14.16
A482.2-4	1, 12, 13.7, 14.16
4-5	1
5-7	1, 3, 12, 14.16
A483.4-7	1
14-18	1
23-25	1
A483.25-	
A484.2	1
2-4	3
5-8	1, 3
8-13	1, 3, 12, 14.16
A484.13-14	1, 3
14-17	3, 7

Section 5
Sceptical Representation Of The Cosmological Questions In The Four Transcendental Ideas

A486.8-16	1
16-17	1
A486.21-	
A489.15	3
15-18	1, 12, 14.16
18-21	1, 12, 14.16

Section 6
Transcendental Idealism As The Key To the Solution
Of The Cosmological Dialectic

A490.16-	
A491.3	1, 13, 14.1, 14.4, 14.17, 18, 20, 22
4	
ftnt a	
1-4	18, 20
A491.4-7	20
13-18	18, 20
19-21	12, 14.6, 14.15, 14.17, 14.18, 14.19, 14.23, 20, 22
A491.21-	
A492.3	12, 14.7, 14.19
3-6	12, 14.1, 14.17, 14.22, 17, 20
6-11	1, 12, 13.2, 14.3, 14.6, 14.17, 14.18, 14.20, 14.23, 17, 18, 20, 22, 34, 35.3A, 35.4A
12-14	1, 17, 18, 20, 21, 34, 35.4A
19-20	1, 12, 14.3, 14.4, 14.13, 20, 21
A493.4-9	1, 17
10-11	1, 20
11-14	18, 20, 21, 22
14-17	18, 20
17-20	2, 17
20-22	1, 17, 18
A493.22-	
A494.3	17, 18, 21, 22
4-6	22, 36
6-7	20, 22
8-10	1, 12, 14.4, 14.17, 14.19, 14.21, 14.23, 22
10-12	1, 2, 12, 13.2, 14.6, 14.7, 14.14, 14.17, 22, 36
12-15	1, 12, 13.2, 14.17, 14.10, 14.23, 20, 22
15-17	10, 12, 13.2, 14.1, 14.5, 14.18, 18, 19, 36
17-18	10, 13.2, 14.18, 19, 36
19-20	2, 12, 13.2, 14.14, 14.18, 36
20-21	12, 13.2, 14.4, 14.13
21-23	1, 2, 12, 13.2, 14.1, 14.17, 18, 20, 22
A494.23-	
A495.3	1, 7, 12, 14.15, 14.18, 14.27
3-4	12, 13.2, 14.4, 14.15
4-12	12, 14.14, 14.15, 14.17, 14.23, 22
A495.21-	
A496.1	1, 12, 14.4, 14.14, 14.17, 20, 22
4-8	2, 6, 17, 36
8-11	2, 12, 14.1, 36
17-21	2, 12, 14.1, 36
A496.21-	
A497.3	1, 3, 14.15

Section 7
Critical Solution Of The Cosmological Conflict Of Reason With Itself

4-7	3
7-11	3
11-13	3
A497.16-	
A498.2	7, 10
2-6	7, 10
6-7	7
7-10	7
11-14	3
14-18	3
18-22	3
A498.22-	
A499.3	17, 18, 20, 22
6-9	18, 20
9-12	1, 3
12-13	1, 3
13-16	10
17-21	3
A500.1-5	3, 7
5-7	7
7-9	3
9-14	3, 7, 12, 14.1, 14.13, 14.22, 14.27, 14.28
16-19	1
19-25	1, 7, 18, 22
A500.25-	
A501.2	3
A504.11-14	3
15-20	3
A504.20-	
A505.3	1, 3, 20
3-5	1, 3, 20
5-7	1, 3, 18, 20
7-11	1, 3
14-17	1, 3
17-19	1
19-22	1, 3, 18, 20
A506.1-2	1
3-5	17, 20, 21, 22
6-12	3, 7, 18, 20, 21, 22
A506.12-	
A507.1	1, 18, 20
1-4	18, 20, 21, 22
5-9	18, 20
9-13	1, 3, 20

Section 8
The Regulative Principle Of Pure Reason In Its Application To The Cosmological Ideas

A508.1-5	1, 10, 20
5-11	1, 3, 10, 20
11-13	7, 20
13-14	1, 12, 13.6, 14.1, 14.17, 18, 20, 22
14-15	1, 12, 13.6, 14.1, 14.17, 20, 22
15-17	1, 12, 13.6, 14.1, 14.17, 20, 22
A508.18-	
A509.4	1, 10
4-6	1
6-8	1
8-10	1
10-12	10
12-15	10
15-19	10
19-24	1, 3
A509.24-	
A510.3	1, 10
3-5	1
5-7	1
7-10	1
10-12	1, 10, 20
12-14	1, 10
14-16	10
17-18	1
19-21	1
A510.23-	
A511.3	1
15-17	7, 36
18-19	7
A512.18-20	1
A512.20-	
A513.1	1
1-3	1, 7
3-4	7
5-12	7
12	7
12-17	7
18-23	7
A514.1-3	1, 14.13
3-5	1, 18, 20
5-9	10, 20
9-12	7
12-15	7
15-17	1
17-20	1

A514. (Continued)
20-21	7
21-22	7

A514.22-
A515.2	7, 10
2-5	1
5-9	1

Section 9
The Empirical Employment Of The Regulative Principle Of Reason, In Respect Of All Cosmological Ideas

12-14	1

A515.14-
A516.2	3, 7, 11
2-9	1, 3, 10
10-12	1, 7, 10
12-14	1
14-16	1, 3
16-20	1, 3

I   Solution of the Cosmological Idea of the Totality of the Composition of the Appearances of a Cosmic Whole

A517.7-11	1
11-15	1

A517.16-
A518.6	1
12-15	1
16-17	1
17	

ftnt a
1-3	1
3-6	1
6-7	1

A518.17-
A519.1	1
1-4	1
4-7	1
7-10	1
10-12	1
12-13	1
13-18	1
18-20	1
20-22	1
22-24	1, 10

A519.24-
A520.3	1, 10

3-6	1
7-8	1
8-11	1
11-14	1
14-16	1
16-17	1
17-20	1, 10
21-24	1
A520.25-	
A521.2	1
2-8	1, 18
8-9	1
10-12	1
A521.13-	
A522.1	1, 10, 36
2-5	10
6-11	1, 10
11-12	10
12-16	18
17-18	7
18	1
19-21	1
A522.22-	
A523.1	1
3-5	1
5-9	1, 10

II Solution of the Cosmological Idea of the Totality of Division of a Whole given in Intuition

A523.10-12	7
12-13	7
13-15	1
15-18	1, 7
A523.18-	
A524.3	7
3-8	1
8-10	1
10-13	1, 7
13-15	7
15-19	1
20-29	1, 7
A525.1-5	1, 7
5-6	1, 7
7-13	1
13-19	1, 7
19-21	18
A525.22-	
A526.2	1, 18, 20

A525.22- (Continued)

3-7	1
8-11	1
11-12	1
12-14	7
14-18	7
18-19	1
19-22	1

A526.22-

A527.4	1
4-7	1
7-8	1
8-9	7
9-12	7
12-13	1
13-16	7
16-19	1
19-22	7, 10

Concluding Note on the Solution of the Mathematical-Transcendental Ideas, and Preliminary Observation on the Solution of the Dynamical-transcendental Ideas

A528.1-6	3
6-8	3
8-10	3
10-12	7
12-16	7

A528.16-

A529.1	7
1-6	3
7-10	1
10-12	7
12-17	7
17-21	3
21-22	3

A529.22-

A530.5	3
5-6	1
7-10	3, 7
10-14	1, 7
14-17	2, 7, 36
18-20	1

A530.20-

A531.1	2, 7, 11, 18, 19
1-5	2, 7, 10, 11, 18
5-9	2, 7, 18, 19
9-10	3
11-14	2, 7, 19

14-16	10
16	
ftnt a	
1-2	1
2-8	2, 7, 18, 19
A531.16-	
A532.3	3
3-5	1
5-7	1, 7

III Solution of the Cosmological Idea of Totality in the Derivation of Cosmological Events from their Cause

8-9	1, 36
9-10	2, 36
10-12	36
12-19	7, 36
A533.1-3	2, 36
3-5	2, 36
5-8	2, 36
8-10	7, 36
10-12	7, 36
12-14	7
14-15	1, 36
15-18	10, 36
19-20	3, 36
20-22	3, 36
A534.1-2	2, 36
2-3	9, 36
4-5	9, 36
5-6	36
6-7	2, 34
7-9	2, 29, 36
10-12	2, 36
12-14	36
14-16	36
16-18	36
18-20	2, 36
20-24	2, 36
A535.1-4	3
4-7	3
11-14	3, 18, 36
14-16	3
16-20	1, 36
A535.20-	
A536.1	1, 36
1-3	3, 36
3-5	3, 36
5-7	36

Possibility of Causality through Freedom, in Harmony with the Universal Law of Natural Necessity

Explanation of the Cosmological Idea of Freedom in its Connection with Universal Natural Necessity

A542.7-8	7, 36
8-13	36
13-14	7, 36
14-16	7, 36
16-18	7, 36
A542.18-	
A543.2	7
9-15	2, 21, 36
16-18	1, 36
19-20	36
A543.21-	
A544.1	36
1-2	36
2-3	36
3-5	1, 36
6-8	36
8-14	2, 19, 36
14-17	2, 18, 19, 21, 34, 35.4B, 35.4C, 36, 36
17-19	18, 19, 21, 36, 36
20-23	36
A544.23-	
A545.3	10, 36
4-8	2, 19, 21, 34, 35.4B, 35.4G, 36
9-11	36
11-18	2, 15, 16, 18, 19, 34, 35.4A, 35.4B, 35.4C, 35.4G, 36
18-23	1, 18, 19, 34, 35.3A, 36
A545.23-	
A546.1	2, 19, 34, 35.4B, 35.4C, 36
1-5	2, 18, 19, 34, 35.4B, 36
5-10	1, 2, 18, 19, 21, 23, 34, 35.3A, 35.4B, 36
11-14	34, 35.4A, 35.4G, 36
14-15	23, 34, 35.4A, 35.4G, 36
15-16	9, 23, 29
16-19	9
19-21	2, 34, 35.3B, 35.4E
21-23	2, 34, 35.3B, 35.4E
A546.23-	
A547.2	2, 12, 13.4, 14.5, 14.18, 14.28, 15, 16, 19, 21, 29, 34, 35.4A, 35.4B, 35.4G
2-8	12, 14.2, 14.16, 14.27, 19
9-12	2, 22, 36, 37
12-14	2, 36, 37
14-15	1
15-17	1, 37
17-18	1, 37
18-22	1, 37

A547.23-

A548.2	2, 36, 37
2-3	7, 36, 37
3-6	1, 36, 37
6-9	1, 36, 37
9-11	7, 37
14-20	7, 18, 37
20-22	2, 29, 36

A548.23-

A549.1	2, 29, 36
1-2	21
2-10	18, 36
11-17	19, 21, 36

A549.17-

A550.1	18, 23, 36
1-5	18, 36
5-6	18, 23, 36
6-10	9, 18, 23
11-17	2, 18, 21, 29, 36, 37
17-19	13, 21, 36, 37
20-25	2, 9, 36, 37
A551.1-5	2, 18, 21, 29, 36, 37
5-6	2, 18, 19, 29, 36
6-7	1
7-8	2, 18
8-10	1
10	
ftnt a	
1-2	1, 4, 37
10-12	2, 13, 18, 36, 37
A551.12-14	18, 36, 37
14-16	11, 19, 36
A551.12-14	18, 36, 37
14-16	11, 19, 36

A551.16-

A552.1	2, 19, 36
1-4	36
5-8	2, 18, 36
8-9	2, 36
9-12	36
12-16	17, 18, 19, 36
17-18	17, 18, 21
18-20	18, 21, 34, 35.4A, 35.4G, 36
20-24	18, 23, 36

A552.24-

A553.2	1, 18, 36
2-4	1, 18, 36
4-9	1, 2, 18, 34, 35.4G, 36
10-11	18, 34, 35.3A, 35.4A, 36
11-13	21, 36

IV Solution of the Cosmological Idea of the Totality of the Dependence of Appearances as regards their Existence in general

Concluding Note on the Whole Antinomy of Pure Reason

Book II

Chapter III
The Ideal of Pure Reason

Section 1
The Ideal in General

Section 2
The Transcendental Ideal (Prototypon Transcendentale)

A571.18-
    A572.3   1, 7, 8, 38.1
    3-8   7, 8, 11
    8-11   7, 8
    11
    ftnt a
    1-9   8, 30
    11-12   7, 8
    13-14   7, 8
A572.16-
    A573.3   7, 8
    4-10   8
    10-13   8
    13-15   1, 7, 8
    15-16   7, 8, 11
    17-18   7, 8, 11
A573.19-
    A574.2   7, 8, 11
    2-3   7, 8, 11
    3-6   7, 14.16
    7-11   7, 8
    11-15   1, 7
    18-21   7
A574.21-
    A575.3   7
    4-5   1, 7, 38.1
    10-13   7, 38.1
A575.14-
    A576.4   7, 10, 17
    5-6   7, 17, 32
    6-10   7, 8, 38.1
    10-12   7, 8
    12-16   7, 8
    16-17   1, 7, 8, 11
    17-19   1, 7, 8
A576.20-
    A577.2   7, 38.1
    2-5   1, 5, 38.1
    5-8   7, 10, 38.1
    8-10   7, 38.1
    10-16   7, 8, 38.1
    16-19   7, 8, 38.1
    19-22   7, 38.1
A577.23-
    A578.5   1, 7, 10, 11, 22
    5-9   1, 7, 8, 10
    10-14   7, 8, 10
    19-22   7, 8
A578.22-
    A579.1   1, 7, 12

Section 3
The Arguments of Speculative Reason in Proof Of The Existence Of A Supreme Being

Section 4
The Impossibility Of An Ontological Proof Of The Existence of God

3-6	7, 14.3
6-12	1, 7, 14.3
13-22	7, 14.3
23-24	1, 7, 8, 14.3
24-26	1, 7, 8, 14.3, 38.1, 38.3
A593.26-	
A594.1	1, 7, 8, 14.3, 38.1, 38.3
1-17	3, 7, 8, 14.3, 39.1, 38.3
18-22	8, 14.3, 38.1
A594.22-	
A595.8	7, 8, 14.3, 38.1
8-14	7, 8, 14.3, 38.1
15-18	7, 8, 14.3, 38.1
18-23	7, 8, 14.3
A595.24-	
A596.2	1, 7, 8, 14.3, 38.1
2-3	1, 7, 8, 14.3, 38.1
4-11	7, 8, 14.3, 14.14, 38.1
12-14	7, 8, 14.3, 14.14, 38.1
14	
ftnt a	
1-10	7, 8, 14.3, 14.14, 38.1
A596.14-	
A597.6	1, 7, 8, 14.3, 14.14, 38.1, 38.3
7-18	1, 8, 14.3, 14.14, 38.1, 38.3
A597.18-	
A598.1	1, 8, 14.3, 14.14, 38.1, 38.3
1-7	1, 8, 14.3, 14.14, 38.1, 38.3
8-13	1, 3, 8, 14.3, 14.14, 38.1, 38.3
13-15	1, 8, 14.3, 14.14, 38.1, 38.3
15-18	1, 8, 14.3, 38.1
19-21	1, 8, 14.3, 38.1
21-23	1, 8, 14.3, 38.1
23-25	8, 14.3, 38.1
A598.25-	
A599.1	1, 8, 14.3, 38.1
1-6	1, 8, 14.3, 38.1
6-10	1, 8, 14.3, 14.14, 38.1
10-11	1, 8, 14.3, 14.14, 38.1, 38.3
11-19	1, 8, 14.3, 14.14, 38.1, 38.3
19-21	1, 8, 14.3, 14.14, 38.1, 38.3
22-24	1, 8, 14.3, 14.14, 38.1, 38.3
A600.1-4	1, 8, 14.3, 14.14, 38.1, 38.3
4-7	1, 8, 14.3, 14.14, 38.1, 38.3
7-12	1, 8, 14.3, 14.14, 38.1, 38.3
12-18	1, 8, 14.3, 14.14, 38.1, 38.3
A600.18-	
A601.2	1, 8, 14.3, 14.14, 38.1, 38.3
2-6	1, 8, 14.3, 14.14, 38.1, 38.3
6-8	1, 8, 14.3, 14.14, 38.1, 38.3

A600.18- (Continued)

9-11	1, 8, 14.3, 14.14, 38.1, 38.3
11-13	1, 8, 14.3, 14.14, 38.1, 38.3
13-16	1, 8, 14.3, 14.14, 38.1, 38.3
16-23	1, 8, 14.3, 14.14, 38.1, 38.3
A601.24-	
A602.1	1, 8, 14.3, 14.14, 38.1, 38.3
1-3	1, 8, 14.3, 14.14, 38.1, 38.3
3-5	8, 14.3, 14.14, 38.1, 38.3
6-12	1, 8, 14.3, 14.14, 38.1, 38.3
12-15	1, 8, 14.3, 14.14, 38.1, 38.3
16-21	1, 8, 14.3, 14.14, 38.1, 38.3
A603.1-3	1, 8, 14.3, 14.14, 38.1, 38.3

Section 5
The Impossibility Of A Cosmological Proof Of The Existence of God

A603.3-7	7, 10
7-12	7, 10
12-15	3, 7, 10
16-17	3, 7
A609.16-18	1, 36
18-19	1, 36
19-21	1, 36
21-23	1, 36
A610.1-6	1, 36
6-11	1, 8
11-17	8
A611.21-	
A612.3	7, 8
3-9	1, 14.3
10-13	10
16-18	7
A612.19-	
A613.3	1, 7, 8
4-6	7
19-21	4
A613.21-	
A614.1	1, 3, 4, 12, 13.2, 14.1, 14.7, 17, 18, 36
2-3	1, 3, 12, 13.2, 17
3-7	1, 3, 7, 10
7-9	1, 3, 12, 14.2, 14.13, 14.16, 14.27
9-11	3, 7, 10
11-15	3, 7, 9, 11

Discovery And Explanation of the Dialectical Illusion in all Transcendental Proofs of the Existence of a Necessary Being

A615.3-5	3, 7

A615. (Continued)

5-6	3
6-9	7
14-16	3, 7
16-18	7
18-22	1, 22

A615.22-

A616.1	1, 7, 10, 12
1-3	1, 10, 12
4-8	1, 7, 10, 12
8-9	1, 12, 14.10, 12
17-19	10
19-22	10
22-24	10

A616.24-

A617.5	10
5-8	1, 8
9-11	7, 10, 11
12-16	10
23-24	1
24-25	1
25-26	1, 7
A618.1-2	7, 10
2-3	7, 10
3-4	7, 10
5-6	10
6-11	8
12-14	8
15-17	8
17-21	1, 10
A619.3-6	10
6-9	7, 10
9-10	1, 10
10-13	1, 3, 7, 12, 22
13-18	1, 7, 12, 14.3, 14.10, 14.13, 14.19, 20
18-2	7, 10

A619.21-

A620.2	3, 7, 10, 12, 14.2, 14.3, 14.10, 14.15, 14.17, 22
2-5	3, 7, 12
5-6	1, 7, 12
6-8	1, 7, 11, 12
8-9	1, 12

Section 6
The Impossibility Of The Physico-Theological Proof

A621.23-

A622.2	12, 14.18, 14.21, 36
3-5	2, 5, 7, 10

Section 7
Critique Of All Theology Based Upon Speculative Principles Of Reason

A634.25-	
A635.3	1
4-7	1, 36
7-13	1, 36
13-16	1, 36
17-19	1, 36
19-22	1, 36
A635.22-	
A636.1	1
1-6	1, 14.4, 36
6-10	1, 36
11-15	1
15-17	1, 37
17-21	1
A636.21-	
A637.1	36
1-7	36
7-17	1
18-21	1
A637.21-	
A638.1	1, 14.1
2-6	7, 14.1, 14.4
6-8	1
9-18	1
A638.18-	
A639.1	1
1-16	1
17-19	1, 14.3
A639.19-21	12, 13.6, 14.3, 14.7
22-25	1
A639.26-	
A640.6	1, 13.4
7-11	1
11-21	7, 37
A640.21-	
A641.11	1
12-15	1, 7
15-17	1
17-23	1, 37
A641.23-	
A642.5	7, 38.1
6-10	1

Appendix To The Transcendental Dialectic

The Regulative Employment Of The Ideas Of Pure Reason

A642.10-12	2, 3, 7, 11
12-14	2, 7

A662. (Continued)
   8-11   30
A662.11-
   A663.15   5.2, 10, 30
   16-23   10, 12, 14.2, 14.16
   23-25   10
A663.25-
   A664.2   1, 10
   3-9   1, 7, 9
   9-12   1, 10, 12, 14.10, 14.15, 14.16
   12-16   1, 10
   17-18   12, 14.16, 14.27
   18-22   7, 10
A664.22-
   A665.4   1, 2
   4-7   1, 7
   7-9   7
   9-12   7
   12-13   7, 12
   13-18   1, 7, 12, 13.6, 14.2, 14.7, 14.10, 14.16, 14.18,
                          14.27

A665.18-
   A666.2   1, 7, 10, 12, 14.4, 14.10, 14.15, 14.16, 14.27
   2-5   7
   6-9   7, 10, 12, 14.7, 14.10, 14.16
   9-12   7, 10, 12, 14.10, 14.16
   13-15   1, 12, 14.10
   15-18   1
   18-21   1, 7, 10
A666.22-
   A667.1   1
   4-7   1, 7, 10
   7-18   1
   19-23   7
A667.23-
   A668.5   1
   6-19   1, 7, 30
   20-28   1, 7, 10

The Final Purpose Of The Natural Dialectic Of Human Reason

A669.1-2   1, 3, 7, 11
   2-3   1, 3, 11
   3-4   2, 7, 11
   4-6   1, 3, 7, 11
   6-9   7
   17-18   1
   19-20   1

A675.22- (Continued)
1-4	7, 10
5-10	7, 10
11-14	10
14-16	1, 10
17-20	1, 4, 7, 10
20-21	10

A676.22-
A677.3	1, 10, 12, 14.2, 14.3, 14.27
3-7	1, 12, 14.2, 14.7
7-9	1, 12
9-11	1, 12, 14.2, 14.4, 14.14, 14.19
11-14	1, 10, 12, 14.2, 14.3, 14.18
14-20	7, 10
21-22	10, 12, 14.2, 1.15
22-24	1, 10, 12, 14.7, 14.15, 17

A677.24-
A678.3	10
3-6	10, 12
6-7	10, 11, 12, 36
8-9	10, 12, 36
9-13	1, 7, 10, 12
13-15	10, 12
15-18	10
18-20	10
29-22	1, 2
22-24	12, 14.2, 14.7

A678.24-
A679.5	1
5-10	7, 10
11-15	1, 12, 13.2, 14.2, 14.15
16-17	1, 10, 36
17-18	7, 10
18-20	1, 10, 13.7, 17
20-23	1, 7, 10

A679.24-
A680.2	10
2-3	3
4	1, 7, 9, 11
4-5	1, 7, 10
5-10	7, 12, 14.2, 14.13, 14.6
10	2, 7, 10, 12, 14.10, 14.16
11-14	1, 7, 10, 12, 14.10, 14.16
14-17	7, 10, 12, 14.16, 14.27
17-19	1, 10, 12, 14.16, 14.27
19-21	1, 10, 12, 14.10
21-23	1, 10, 12
23-26	1, 10
A681.1-2	1, 10, 12, 14.2, 14.16, 14.27
2-5	1, 10, 12, 14.2, 14.4, 14.13

5-8	1, 10, 12, 14.2, 14.15
8-12	1, 10, 12, 13.7
12-13	7, 10
13-16	1
17-20	1
20-22	1
A681.22-	
A682.1	7, 10
1-4	7, 10
5-6	10, 12, 14.2, 14.20, 14.24, 14.27
6-8	34, 35.3A, 35.4A
8-10	1, 34, 35.3A
10-11	1, 34, 35.3A, 35.4A
12-19	10, 11, 19, 34, 35.3A, 35.4F, 35.4G
A682.19-	
A683.2	10, 34, 35.3A, 35.4F, 35.4G
2-7	10, 11, 34, 35.3A, 35.4F, 35.4G
7-11	1, 4, 10, 34, 35.3A, 35.4F
12-14	1, 34, 35.3A
14-15	1, 34, 35.3A
15-17	1, 10
17-20	1, 10, 34, 35.3A, 35.4F
20-22	34, 35.3A
24-26	35.3A
A683.26-	
A684.1	7, 10, 34, 35.3A, 35.4F
1-2	1, 10, 34, 35.3A, 35.4F
2-3	10, 34, 35.3A, 35.4F
3-4	1, 10, 34, 35.3A, 35.4F
4-6	34, 35.3A, 35.4A
6-10	12, 14.2, 14.27
10-11	1, 12, 14.2, 14.8
12-15	10, 12, 14.10, 14.16
16-21	1, 8
A684.21-	
A685.1	7, 10, 34, 35.4D
1-3	10
3-8	1, 10
8-11	10, 18
11-15	10, 12, 14.10, 14.16, 14.18, 14.27, 36, 37
15-17	13, 37
17-19	10, 13, 19, 36, 37
19-22	1, 10
25-27	10, 36
A685.27-	
A686.2	1, 12, 14.2
6-7	1, 10
7-13	7, 10
13-15	1, 7, 10
15-16	1

A685.27- (Continued)

16-19	1
20-21	7, 12
21-24	7, 10, 12

A686.24-

A687.4	7, 10, 12

A687.13-

A688.2	1
2-4	1
4-5	1, 7
8-10	1
11-17	1, 10
17-18	1
18-24	10, 19, 36
A689.1-7	1, 10

A689.8-

A690.3	1, 10
3-9	1, 10, 34, 35.3A, 35.4A
9-12	34, 35.3A
15-22	34, 35.3A, 35.4A

A690.22-

A691.1	1
1-12	1, 10
12-19	10
19-22	7
22-24	10

A691.24-

A692.6	2, 5, 10
9-12	1, 5, 10
12-15	1, 10
15-16	1, 10
16-18	1
18-24	1, 5, 10

A692.24-

A693.3	1, 10
4-9	5, 7, 10, 12
9-13	7, 10, 12
13-17	1, 12

A693.20-

A694.2	1, 10
2-9	1, 2, 5, 7, 10, 12, 36
9-12	2, 7, 12
12-15	1, 10
16-17	7, 12
17-23	1, 7, 12, 36
23-25	10, 11, 12

A694.25-

A695.1	10, 11, 12
1-2	7, 10, 11, 12
2-3	3, 7, 10, 11, 12

II
TRANSCENDENTAL DOCTRINE OF METHOD

Chapter 1
The Discipline Of Pure Reason

Section I
The Discipline Of Pure Reason In Its Dogmatic Employment

7-10	1, 7
10-14	7, 12
A714.21-	
A715.1	1, 7
1-2	1
3-4	1
4-7	1
7-9	7
9-11	1
11-13	1, 36
20-21	1
A715.21-	
A716.4	1, 7
9-13	1
A717.1-3	7
18-22	1, 7
A718.8-12	7
15-17	1
18-24	7
A718.25-	
A719.2	1
2-7	7, 17
7-11	1, 12
20-21	12, 14.6, 14.7, 14.14
21-25	7
A719.25-	
A720.4	1
5-6	1, 7
6-10	7
10-13	1, 18, 22
13-14	1, 12, 17, 22
15-17	1, 12, 13.3, 14.6, 14.7, 14.15, 14.21, 17
17-19	1, 12, 13.3, 14.6, 14.7, 14.15, 14.21
20-22	1, 12, 14.13, 17
22-24	1
A720.24-	
A721.1	1, 7, 22
1-5	1
6-8	7
A722.5-9	1
9-13	1
12	
ftnt a	
1-5	36
5-9	1
A722.13-17	1, 7
A723.4-8	12, 14.1, 14.6, 14.13, 18
8-10	12
11-15	1, 7, 12
15-26	12, 14.16, 14.21

Section 2
The Discipline Of Pure Reason In Respect Of Its Polemical Employment

The Impossibility Of A Sceptical Satisfaction Of Pure Reason In Its Internal Conflicts

A759.14- (Continued)

1-3	1
8-15	1, 36
15-18	1, 36
A761.5-10	1, 7, 9, 11
10-16	1, 7, 11
A762.1-7	1, 7, 11
7-8	1
8-12	1
13-15	7
A762.15-	
A763.2	1, 7, 9
7-11	7, 11
15-17	3
A765.20-22	1, 36
A766.1-4	1, 36
4-10	1, 7
10-17	1, 36
17-19	36
19-23	36
A766.23-	
A767.3	30, 36
8-11	7, 36
11-14	1
A768.16-20	1, 3, 9, 11

Section 3
The Discipline Of Pure Reason In Regard To Hypotheses

A769.17-19	1
A769.20-	
A770.9	1, 8, 14.14
10-16	1, 8, 14.14, 36
A770.16-	
A771.2	1, 8
2-7	1, 8, 12, 14.2, 14.4, 14.14
8-9	1, 10, 12, 14.2, 14.4, 14.6
10-12	1, 8
12-15	1, 10, 12
15-19	1, 10, 13.7
19-24	1, 10, 34, 35.3A
A771.24-	
A772.3	1, 34, 35.3A
3-6	1
7-12	1, 12, 19, 34, 35.3A, 35.4B
13-17	1, 19
17-19	1
A772.25-	
A773.1	2, 7, 10

9-14	36
14-18	1
A773.18-	
A774.5	1
6-8	7
A774.8-	
A775.3	10
13-17	1, 7
17-25	1
A776.9-13	1
17-20	1, 36
A776.20-	
A777.14	37
15-18	1
18-20	3, 11
A777.25-	
A778.1	3, 7, 11
A781.14-19	1
19-21	1, 7
21-22	1

Section 4
The Discipline Of Pure Reason In Regard To Its Proofs

A782.9-14	1
17-19	1
A782.19-	
A783.1	7
2-4	7
4-7	1, 36
7-10	7, 36
10-13	7
20-25	1
A784.8-17	1
A785.5-6	1
6-10	1, 34, 35.3A, 35.4D
A786.14-17	1, 7, 36
18-22	1, 3, 7, 10
A788.14-17	1, 7, 36
18-22	1, 3, 7, 10
A788.3-10	7, 12, 14.2, 14.10, 14.14, 14.23, 36
10-13	1, 36
A789.22-24	7, 9
A792.7-11	1, 3
11-13	1, 3
18-24	1, 7, 8, 14.10
A792.24-	
A793.5	1, 3
5-14	1

Chapter II
The Canon Of Pure Reason

A795.17-	
A796.4	3, 7, 10, 11, 37
A796.4-5	10, 12, 14.16, 37
10-12	7, 11
12-14	7
14-17	7
17-23	1, 8

Section I
The Ultimate End Of The Pure Employment Of Our Reason

6-11	2, 3, 7, 10, 11
13-15	37
A798.1-4	7, 11
5-8	7, 11, 12, 14.16, 37
15-16	2, 19, 36, 37
16-22	7, 16, 18
A798.22-	
A799.5	1
5-12	1, 10
12-16	1
16-22	1
A799.23-	
A800.2	37
3-4	36, 37
4-7	10
7-11	10, 37
11-14	7, 10, 37
14-15	1, 37
15-19	2, 7, 10, 11, 13, 37
19-21	1, 7, 37
A800.22-	
A801.1	2, 7, 10, 11, 37
1-5	2, 7, 10, 11, 37
7	
ftnt a	
1-3	12, 14.2
3-5	1, 22, 37
5-8	7
A801.15-	
A802.2	37
2-4	36
5-7	22, 36, 37
8-9	36, 37
9-10	36, 37

Section 2
The Ideal Of The Highest Good, As A Determining Ground Of The Ultimate End Of Pure Reason

5-6	7, 10
6-7	7, 37
7-12	2, 7, 10, 37
12-14	7, 10, 37
14-17	2, 7, 36
18-19	10
20	2, 7, 37
20-21	1, 10, 37
A816.21-	
A817.1	1, 7, 12, 14.2, 14.10, 14.16
1-2	1, 7, 14.2
2-4	1, 14.2
4-5	2, 7
5-8	2, 7
8-11	1, 2, 7, 36, 37
12-20	7, 10, 37
20-24	37
24-27	37
A818.1-5	2, 7, 37
4-9	7, 20, 37
9-12	2, 10, 37
13-19	1, 37
19-22	2, 7, 10, 36, 37
A818.22-	
A819.2	1, 37
2-6	7, 37
6-8	2, 7, 10, 37
8-11	7, 37
11-13	37
13-14	1
14-16	2, 7, 10, 37
16-20	1, 37
20-23	1, 7, 10, 37

Section 3
Opining, Knowing, Believing

A820.1-4	2, 12, 36, 38.4
4-7	12, 14.16
9-11	1, 3, 12
11-12	1, 38.4
16-20	38.4
A820.20-	
A821.5	38.4
6-8	38.4
8-15	38.4
16-23	3
A821.24-	
A822.3	1, 38.3

A821.24- (Continued)

4-9	1
9-11	1, 12
18-25	1

A822.3-

A823.5	1, 7
5-10	1, 37
11-15	1
15-20	1, 38.4
21-23	1, 14.28, 37
23-26	10, 14.28, 37

A823.27-

A824.8	7, 10, 37
13-15	37

A824.16-

A825.8	37
9-23	1, 37

A826.1-7	1, 10, 37
7-10	2, 5, 7, 10
10-13	2, 7, 10, 36
13-16	2, 10, 36
16-21	10
21-22	10, 37

A826.22-

A827.3	1, 7, 10, 37
3-7	37
8-16	1, 37
16-19	1, 37
19-24	1

A827.25-

A828.2	1
3-5	7, 37
5-6	2, 7, 10, 37
6-9	7, 10, 37
10-12	1, 2, 7, 10, 37
12-15	7, 37
15-17	7, 37
17-18	37

A828.19-

A829.6	1, 37, 38.4
6-7	37
7-10	1, 37
10-13	7, 37
14-15	1, 37

A829.16-

A830.1	37

A830.1

ftnt a	
1-3	7, 37
4-8	37

A830.1-14	1, 37
A830.15-	
A831.2	37
12-15	7, 37
15-19	2, 7, 10, 37

Chapter III
The Architectonic Of Pure Reason

A832.1-2	7
2-4	7
4-6	7, 11
7-9	7
9-10	2, 7, 10, 11
10-11	7
12-15	7, 11
15-17	7, 10, 11
A832.17-	
A833.3	7, 10, 11
4-5	7
5-10	7, 10
11-14	7, 10
14-18	10, 11
18-21	7, 10, 11
A833.21-	
A834.6	7, 11, 30
6-9	7, 10, 11, 30
10-11	1
11-16	1, 7
16-27	1, 7, 10
A834.28-	
A835.3	7, 10
4-7	7
7-9	2, 7, 11
9-16	7
16-19	2, 7, 11
19-21	7
21-23	7
A835.24-	
A836.3	7
3-24	1
A836.24-	
A837.3	1, 7
4-6	7
9-13	1
13-26	3, 7
26-30	1, 7
A838.1	7
2-12	1, 7

A838. (Continued)

12-19	1, 7
20-25	1, 7

A838.25-

A839.6	2, 7, 10, 11
6-8	1, 7
9-13	1
13-15	7, 10

A839.16-

A840.2	1, 2, 7, 10, 11
1	
ftnt a	
1-5	7, 10
3-5	1, 2, 7, 10, 11
5-7	7, 10, 36
9-16	37
17-21	2, 7, 11, 12, 14.16, 37
21-22	7, 37
23-26	7
A841.1-7	7, 14.9
8-14	1, 7, 14.9, 37
15-22	1, 7, 14.9, 37
22-24	1, 7, 37

A841.24-

A842.6	1, 7, 14.9, 37
6-8	1
9-18	1

A842.18-

A843.8	1, 7, 14.9
8-12	1, 14.9

A843.13-

A844.7	1, 7
7-17	1, 7, 14.9
17-27	1
A845.1-5	2, 7, 11
5-9	14.9, 37
10-18	7, 9, 13.3, 14.9

A845.18-

A846.1	14.9
1-8	1, 7, 14.9, 37
9-16	7, 14.9, 36.3A
16-21	1, 7, 14.9, 35.3A

A846.22-

A847.2	14.9, 35.3A
2	
ftnt a	
1-3	1
3-13	1, 14.9
A847.3-7	2, 7, 10, 11
7-8	1, 7

A847.12-	
A848.7	1, 7, 14.9, 35.A
7-11	1, 14.9
12-21	1, 35.3A
A848.21-	
A849.9	1, 14.9, 35.3A
10	7, 14.9
10-14	1, 14.9
14-23	1, 3, 7, 14.9, 37
A849.23-	
A850.7	1, 7, 10, 14.9, 37
8-12	1, 7, 14.9, 37
12-15	7, 14.9
15-18	1, 7, 10, 37
18-21	1, 7, 14.9, 37
22-23	7, 11, 14.9
A850.23-	
A851.5	8, 10, 14.9
5-12	1, 10, 14.9, 37

Chapter IV
The History Of Pure Reason

A852.1-7	7
8-12	7, 37
A852.12-	
A853.1	37
1-7	14.9, 37
A854.20-	
A855.4	1
5-7	1
A856.4-19	10

PART TWO

TOPICAL INDEX

Section I

Limits

1. Limits

Abbreviations

R	Reason
R i	Ideas
R il	Ideals
R p	Principles of Reason
R tel	Finality, Ends, Interests of Reason (see Topic 10.)
U	Understanding
U a	Analysis
U d	Division
U c	Categories
U p	Principles
U s	Synthesis
U pa	Analogies
U pm	Modals
U sch	Schemata
Im	Imagination
I	Intuition
S/T	Space and/or Time
K	Knowledge
E	Subject
O	Object

Avii.1-5	R tel
Aviii.10-13	R p
Bxiii.8-11	R tel
Axviii.4-7	U
Bxviii.2-9	R
Bxviii.9 ftnt a 3-6	R
Bxviii.9 ftnt a 6-12	U c U p
Bxix.10-Bxx.1	K
Bxx.1-6	K
Bxxi.1-9	K
Bxxii.8-9	K

Bxxiv.1-5	R p
Bxxiv.16-20	R p
Bxxv.19-Bxxvi.5	U c, K, S, T, I
Bxxvi.11 ftnt a 7-11	U c, K, I
Bxxvii.14-Bxxviii.4	U c, O, U p
Bxxviii.4-6	K
Bxxviii.7-9	K
Bxxviii.9-12	K
Bxxviii.16-18	K, U e
Bxxviii.12-16	K
Bxxx.9	K
Bxxxi.13-15	R, K
Bxxxi.19-Bxxxii.5	R, K
A1.8-10	K
A1.10-11	K
A1.11-A2.2	R, K
A2.2-4	K
A2.11-20	K
A2.21-A3.4	K, O
B1.8-10	K
B2.3-6	K
B2.24-B3.1	K
B3.5-8	K
B3.9-10	K
B3.10-12	K
B3.16-B4.2	K
B4.2-5	K
B4.5-7	K
B4.8-10	K
B4.10-12	K
B4.12-18	K
B4.19-22	K
B5.2-10	C
B5.13-16	K
B6.1-7	C
A3.5-7	K, R
A4.15-22	K, I
A6.6-11	U s, R, K
B11.19	K, U s
B12.3-7	K, U a
B12.20-22	K, U s

B12.22-25	K, U a, U s	B16.3-5	U a
A9.9-15	U c	B16.5-6	U a, U s
A9.16-20	U c	B16.6-10	U a
A9.21-25	U s, I, U c	B16.11-12	U a
A9.25-A10.2	K	B16.12-13	U a, U s
B14.5-6	K	B16.13-17	U a
B14.10-15	U a	B16.17-B17.1	U a, U s
B14.15-19	U a, U s	B17.1-5	U a

B17.5-7	U a		A25.19-20	S/T
B17.7-9	U a		B40.4-5	U c, U d
B17.9-13	U a		B40.7-8	S/T, U c
B16.1-3	U a		B41.3-5	S/T, I
B16.3-B17.3	U a		B41.8-11	S/T, K
B17.3-6	U a		A26.1-3	S/T, O
B18.3-7	U a, U s		A26.3-6	S/T, O, I
B18.14-19	U a, U s		A26.6-9	I
B19.8-17	U a, U s		A26.21-22	S/T, E
B22.6-12	R		A26.22-25	S/T, E
B22.23-B23.3	R		A27.1-2	S/T, E
B23.9-14	R		A27.7-9	S/T, E, O
B23.15-17	K		A27.9-12	S/T, E, O
B23.17-21	K, U a		A27.12-15	S/T, I
B23.21-23	K, U a		A28.13-15	S/T, E
B23.23-B24.2	K		A28.21-24	E, O
B24.2-6	K, R		A28.25-A29.2	O, K
A11.17-A12.2	K		A29.2-4	E, K
A12.11-13	K		A29.4-7	K
A12.13-16	R tel		A29.7-8	K
A14.23-A15.9	R p		B44.16-18	E, K, S/T
A15.9-10	R		B44.19-26	S/T, I, K
A15.11-13	R		A29.15-20	S/T
A15.19-22	U, I, K		A29.20-A30.2	S/T, E
A15.22-23	O, I		A30.2-9	E, U s, K, O
A15.23-24	O, U		A30.9-12	K
A16.1-5	O, I		A30.13-14	S/T, K
A19.1-10	I		A31.2-4	S/T
A19.11-14	U c, I		A31.5-7	S/T
A20.8-10	S/T		A31.10-11	S/T
A22.15-17	S/T, I, E		A31.11-12	S/T
A23.4-6	S/T, I		A31.13-15	S/T, I
A23.18-19	S/T		A31.15-16	S/T, K
A23.25-27	S/T		A31.20-21	T, U c, I
A23.27-28	S/T, K		A32.1-2	I, O
A24.2-4	S/T, O		A32.3-4	S/T, U c
A24.4-6	S/T, O		A32.5-6	S/T, U c, U s
A24.10-13	S/T, K		A32.8-10	S/T, U d
A24.13-14	K		A32.18-21	S/T, O
A24.15-17	K		A32.33-36	T
A24.17-19	K		A33.4-6	S/T, I
A24.19-21	S/T		A33.9-10	S/T, I, E
A24.20-A25.1	S/T, U c, I		A33.10-11	S/T
A25.1-2	S/T		A33.11-13	S/T
A25.2-4	S/T		A33.13-14	S/T
A25.4-6	S/T, U s		A35.19-22	S/T, I, O
A25.6-7	S/T		A35.22-A36.2	S/T, I
A25.8-9	S/T		A36.3-4	O, I
A25.9-11	S/T, I		A37.17-18	S/T
A25.11-16	S/T, I, U c		A39.5-9	K

A95.7-8	U c, I		B142.19-21	U s
A95.8-10	I, O, K		B145.10-15	U c, I
A95.14-15	U c		B145.15-22	K, I
A95.16-17	U c, O, K		B146.5-6	U c, O, K
A96.14-19	U c, K, O		B146.9-12	U c, O, K, I
A96.19-21	U c		B146.12-14	U c
A97.11-13	K		B146.14-B147.1	I
A97.16-17	K, U s, I		B147.4-6	U c, O, K, I
A99.19-21	U s		B147.11-14	O
A100.4-9	Empirical		B147.19-B148.2	U c, O
	association		B148.3-7	U c, I
A101.15-20	I, K, U s		B148.7-12	S/T
A102.11-13	S/T, U s		B148.15-B148.2	U c, I
A105.3-9	O, K		B149.3-6	9, I
A107.1-3	E		B149.6-9	O, I
A107.3-6	E		B149.9-11	O, I, K
A107.6-8	U c		B149.11-16	U c
A109.3-7	I, O		B149.16-20	U c
A110.6-9	K		B149.20-23	I, U c, O
A111.1-3	U s		B150.1-4	U c, I
A112.10-13	U c		B150.4-6	U c, K
A112.16-18	I		B150.6-9	K
A112.19-22	I		B151.1-3	O, I
A114.15-19	I		B151.19-23	I
A114.19-24	I		B152.12-17	Im
A115.14-A116.3	U c		B153.13-17	I, U c
A116.9-11	I		B156.14-20	I, K
A117.2 ftnt a 3-5	I		B158.1	
A118.7-8	U s		ftnt a 7-11	I, E
A119.8-11	U, U s, O, I		B158.1	
A120.2-5	O, I		ftnt a 13-14	I, U c
A120.7-10	I, U s		B158.3-5	K
A121.8-12	U s		B158.5-9	K
A126.18-21	U c		B159.1-6	U s, I
A128.18-A129.2	U c		B159.6-9	K, I
A130.6-10	U c		B164.11-13	K
A130.10-12	U c, U s		B165.5-9	U, U c
B130.6-11	U s		B165.13-16	K
B130.11-13	U s		B165.17	U c, O
B132.4-15	E		B165.17-19	U c, O, I, K
B131.5-6	U c		B165.19-20	I
B133.12-18	E		B165.20-B166.1	K, I
B134.8-10	E		B166.1-3	K, I
B135.6-10	E		B166.4-5	K
B135.14-16	U, I		B166.11-B167.4	U c, I
B135.16-17	U, I		A131.14-17	K
B137.21-24	I, K		A131.10-15	U c, I
B139.4-11	I		A138.13-20	U sch
B139.20-B140.3	U s		A139.16-19	U c
B140.9-10	U s		A139.19-21	U c

B289.8-11	K, U c
B289.11-16	K, U c
B291.16-17	T
B291.20-23	K, U c
B292.1-4	K
B292.14-17	I
B292.17-21	K, U pa
B294.4-8	U p
A238.9-12	U c
A239.6-9	U c
A239.9-11	U c
A239.14-19	U c, U p
A239.23-A240.3	U p
A240.3-7	U c
A240.19-A241.1	U c, U p
A241.1-5	U c
A241.18-19	U c
A241.19-A242.9	U c
A242.15-A243.2	U c
A243.2-7	K, U c
A243.7-11	K, U c
A243.11-15	U c
A244.4-7	K
A244.7-12	U c
A244.19	
ftnt a 1-5	I, U c
A244.20-23	U c
A244.22-A245.1	U c
A245.1-3	U c
A245.4-7	K, U c
A245.10-15	U c
A245.15-20	U c
A245.20-23	U c
A246.6-10	U c
A246.11-17	K, U c
A246.18-21	K
A246.21-A247.1	K, U
A247.8-11	U c
A247.11-14	U c
A247.19-22	K
A247.22-A248.2	U c
A248.2-6	U c, U p
A248.8-14	U c
A248.14-18	U c
A248.18-22	U c
A249.7-19	K
A250.2-7	K
A250.18-22	K
A250.25-A251.1	K
A251.1-5	K

A251.6-11	U c
A251.12-17	I, U c
A252.8-10	K
A252.10-12	K
A252.17-18	U c
A252.20-21	I
A253.6-7	O
A253.7	K
A253.10-12	K, U c
A253.14-16	U c
A253.16-18	U c
B305.18-22	U c
B305 22-B306.1	U c
B306.1-3	I, U c
B306.3-7	U s, U c
B307.2-5	U c
B307.19-23	U
B307.23-B308.2	U, U c
B308.2-3	U c
B308.3-6	U c
B308.6-9	U c
B308.9-10	U c
B308.20-24	I, U c
B309.1-3	I
B309.3-5	U c
A253.19-20	K
A253.21-23	I
A254.3-6+	
A257.6-7	U c
A254.7-10	I, U c
A254.11-15	K, U c
A254.18-19	I, K
A354.22-A255.3	K, U c
A255.3-6	K
A255.6-12	I, K, U c
A255.12-14	I
A255.15-17	I
A255.18-20	O
A255.22-24	U c
A255.25-A256.5	U c
A256.5-8	I
A256.8-11	O
A256.11-14	I, K
A256.15-16	U c
A256.16-17+	
A256.17-19	I
A256.20-22	K, U c
A256.15-22	U c
A257.22-27	K, U c
A258.1-9	K, U c

A309.1-5	R p
A309.5-10	R p
A310.1-4	R p
A310.4-8	U c
A310.9-10	U c
A310.11-12	U c
A311.6-12	R p, O, K
A311.14-18	R p
A314.12-17	R, K, O
A315.2-8	P, K
A315.8-12	R p
A315.12-15	R p
A315.15-18	R p
A315.21-24	R p
A318.4-6	R p
A318.16-21	R p
A319.1-4	R p
A323.18-23	R p
A325.4-8	O, K
A325.8-10	O These texts
A325.13-16	O define "abso-
A325.16-20	O lute possibility"
A326.1-4	O and "bsolute
	necessity"
A326.8-11	R, U, O, Im
A326.17-A327.1	R i, U
A327.1-6	R, U p
A327.7-9	R, P, O, I
A327.15-18	R, P, O, I
A327.18-24	R i
A327.24-A328.6	R i
A328.6-8	R i
A328.13-16	R p
A329.1-3	R i
A329.3-7	R i
A329.7-10	R i
A330.14-16	R, K, U
A333.4-9	R p, U c
A333.9-18	R p, U c
335.2-8	R p, U c
A335.14-16	R p, U c, O
A336.4-6	R p
A336.6-8	R p, O
A336.14-15	R p
A336.21-23	R p
A337.1-4	R p
A337.4-8	R p
A337.20	
ftnt 9(B)4-8	R i
A338.6-10	R i

A338.12-15	R i, U c
A338.15-A339.3	I, R i, U c
A339.3-7	R i
A339.10-14	U c
A340.2-5	U c
A341.2-4	R
A345.15-A346.1	E
A346.1-2	E, U c
A346.2-3	E
A345.3-5	E
A346.5-8	E, K, U c
A346.10-14	Consciousness
A347.2-4	S, U c
A347.7	U c
A347.8-11	E, I
A347.11-13	E
A347.14-24	K, E, R, U c
A347.24-25	K
A348.3-5	E, U c
A348.18-A349.2	U c
A349.2-4	U c
A349.8-9	E
A349.12-15	U c
A349.15-17	U c
A349.18-21	U c
A349.21-23	U c
A349.23-A350.2	U c
A350.2-4	U c
A350.4-6	E, I
A350.7-10	E, I
A350.11-15	E, I, K
A350.15-16	E, K
A350.19-21	E, K
A350.22-A351.4	K
A352.18-19	K, U c
A353.8-11	K
A353.11-13	K
A353.16-18	E, K
A353.18-20	O, K
A353.23-A354.1+	
A354.1-2	U c, E
A354.2-4	E, U i
A354.4-7	E
A354.12-13	E, K
A354.14-17	E, K
A354.17-18	E, U c
A354.19-22	U c, E
A354.23-25	E, K
A355.4-7	E, I
A355.10-14	E, K

A355.15-17	E	A372.22-A373.1	K
A355.17-19	E	A373.6-9	S
A355.19-21	E, K	A373.9-15	S
A355.21-24	E, K	A373.22-A374.1	U c
A356.3-4	E, K	A374.17-19	S
A356.4-9	U c	A374.19 ftnt a	
A356.9-13	U c	1-2	S
A356.13-15	U c	3	S
A356.15-A357.10	U c	3-4	S
A357.11-13	U c	4-5	S
A357.13-17	E, S	5-9	S
A357.17-20	E, S, I	A375.1-4	U c, Im
A358.4-7	E, W	A375.12-14	S, I
A358.12-15	S, I	A375.14-15	S
A358.15-19	E, S	A375.15-A376.6	K, I
A358.19-A359.2	K	A378.4-8	O
A359.10-12	K	A378.13-15	S
A359.22-A360.4	E	A378.19-22	I
A360.13-17	E, K	A379.23-A380.5	O, K
A360.18-20	E, K	A380.6-11	K, O
A360.24-A361.4	E, K	A381.1-9	K
A361.6-10	E, K, U c	A381.13-17	T, K
A361.10-13	U c, K	A381.17-19	T, E
A362.21-A363.3	E, K, U c	A381.19-20	E
A363.3-8	E, K	A381.20-A382.2	E
A363.9-12	E, K, U c	A382.2-6	E, I
A363.12-14	E, K	A382.6-8	E, I, U c
A363.14-18	E, U c	A382.8-12	E
A364.5-6	E, U c	A382.12-18	K, E
A364.6-8	E	A383.13-18	K, E
A364.10-11	K	A384.14-21	I
A364.11-16	E, K, U c	A391.1-4	E, K
A365.15-20	E, U c	A391.4-11	O
A365.21-26	E, U c	A391.18-22	O
A366.1-4	E, U c	A392.3-10	O
A366.6-9	K, S	A392.15-20	O
A366.10-13	E, K	A393.9-10	K
A370.5-7	O	A393.10-13	O
A370.7-8	O	A394.3-10	O, K
A370.8-9	O	A394.17-19	K
A370.22-23	O, S	A394.19-A395.2	K
A370.23-24	O	A395.3-7	K
A370.24-25	O	A395.7-21	K
A370.25-A371.1	O	A395.16-17	K
A371.3-6	E	A395.17-20	K
A371.9-12	O	A395.20-22	K
A371.24-A372.3	O	A395.22-A396.2	K
A372.13-15	K	A396.14-15	K
A372.17-19	O	A396.15-18	K
A372.19-20	O	A397.13-18	K

A398.6-8	K	B413.6-11	U c
A398.10-12	K	B415.2-4	K, E, U c
A398.12-14	K, U a	B418.4-8	K
A398.16-18	I	B419.19-B420.1	S
A398.18-21	K	B420.3-8	K
A399.1-6	K	B420.9-13	E, K, U c
A399.13-16	U c	B420.22-B421.3	E, K, U c
A399.16-17	U c	B422.1-2	E, K, U c
A400.4-8	K, I	B422.2	E, K, U c
A400.8-11	K	B422.2-4	E, K, U c
A400.14-17	K	B422.4-5	E, K
A400.17-21	U c	B422.5-7	E, K, U c
A401.1-9	U c	B422.9-11	E, K, U c
A401.27-A402.6	K, E, U c	B422.11-14	E, K, U c
A402.6-8	K	B422.14 ftnt a	
A402.8-11	K, O	2-3	E, K, U c
A402.11-14	K, E	3-4	E, K, U c
A402.24-A403.4	U c	5-6	E, K
A403.4-8	U c	6-8	E, K, U c
A403.8-10	U c	13-14	E, K, U c
B406.14-18	K, E	14-15	E, U c
B406.26-29	K	15-17	U c
B406.29-32	K, E	19	E
B406.32-B407.1	K, E, U c	21-24	E
B407.2-4	K, E, O	26-27	E, K
B407.4-8	K, E, O	27-29	U
B407.14-15	K, E, O, U c	B423.1-B424.2	K
B407.15-19	K, E	B424.2-5	R, K, O
B407.20-24	E	B424.5-13	K, R
B408.1-2	E, U c	B424.14-23	K, R
B408.2-5	U c	B426.15-18	E, K
B408.16-18	E, I	B427.2-6	E, K
B408.18-22	E, U c	B428.11-14+	
B409.6-11	E, K	B428.20-B429.1	E, K
B409.12-14	E, K	B428.18-20	U c
B409.17-23	U c	B429.1-3	U c
B409.24-25	K, U c	B429.3-5	E, K
B410.4-10	K, E, U c	B429.6-9	E, U c
B410.10-18	K	B429.9-11	E, U c
B411.11 ftnt a		B429.22-23	E, U c
4-5	E, U c	B420.4-8	E, U c
11-12	U c	B430.9-13	E, K, U c
12-14	K	B431.8-11	E, K
14-15	K	B431.11-17	E, K, U c
B412.1-7	U c	B431.21-B432.5	K, U c
B412.7-11	U c	A406.16-19	Illusion
B412.11-B413.1	U c	A408.21-A409.1	U c
B413.1-2	I, U c	A409.1	R
B413.2-3	E	A409.1-5	R, U c
B413.3-6	U c	A409.12-13	R p

A454.21-25	U c, S/T	A485.5-8	O
A458.59-62	U pm	A484.8-13	O, I
A460.32-35	U pm	A484.13-14	O
A460.35-41	U pm	A496.8-16	R i, U c
A460.45-51	U pm	A486.16-17	R i, O
A462.1-3	R i	A489.15-18	U c, O
A462.3-5	R i, U c	A489.18-21	R i, U c, O
A462.12-15	R i	A490.16-A491.3	O, I, S/T
A462.16-A463.1	R, K	A478.9-A479.1	O, K, R i
A463.22-A464.2	U, K	A479.1	
A464.19-21	R	ftnt a 6-11	U c, E
A464.24-A465.3	R, U	A479.4-8	U s, R i
A467.4-5	R, U	A479.8-11	O
A467.5-7	U s	A479.14-17	O, R i
A467.8-14	U s	A492.6-11	E, O, K
A467.23-25	U s	A492.12-14	E, O, K
A468.4-6	R p	A492.19-20	O
A468.6-11	R p	A493.4-9	O
A468.15-20	U p, K	A493.10-11	O
A468.20-24	I, O, Im, U c	A493.20-22	O, S/T
A468.24-A469.3	R i, O, I	A494.10-12	K, O
A469.3-6	U, R, R i	A494.12-15	O, S/T, I
A469.6-8	U	A494.21-23	O
A469.8-10	U	A494.23-A495.3	O, K
A469.13-16	U, R, S/T	A495.21-A496.1	O
A469.16-20	O, I	A496.17-21	O
A469.20-23	U	A496.21-A497.3	O, R i, K
A470.1-3	U c	A499.9-12	U s
A470.3-4	K, O, U c, U p	A499.12-13	U s
A471.1-2	R tel	A500.16-19	U s
A471.2-4	K	A500.19-25	U s
A471.4-7	K, I	A504.20-A505.3	O
A471.8-11	K, I	A505.3-5	O
A471.14		A505.5-7	O
ftnt a 5-14	R i	A505.7-11	O
A474.12-20	R i	A505.14-17	O, U s
A474.20-A475.1	R i	A505.17-19	O
A476.14-A477.1	R p, K	A505.19-22	O
A477.1-4	K	A506.1-2	U s
A477.21-24	K, O	A506.12-A507.1	O, K
A479.1		A507.8-12	
ftnt a 1-4	K, O	A508.1-5	O, R i
4-6	E, K	A508.5-11	R p, R i, U
A481.22-25	O, R i	A508.13-17	O
A482.4-5	R i	A508.18-A509.4	R p
A482.5-7	O, R i	A509.4-6	R p, K, O, I, U
A483.4-7	O	A509.6-8	K, I
A483.14-18	R i, U s	A509.8-10	R p, K
A483.23-25	O, I	A509.19-24	R p
A483.25-A484.2	O, I	A509.24-A510.3	R p, O, U c

A540.10-12	O	A566.2	O, K
A541.4-5	E	A566.4-8	O
A541.5-7	E	A566.12-16	O, K, U c
A541.10-12	E	A566.17-19	O, K
A543.16-18	U c, S/T	A566.21-A567.5	K
A544.3-5	U c, S/T	A567.7-9	U c, O, I
A545.18-23	O, E, K	A567.9-11	U c, O, I
A546.5-10	E, K	A567.16-18	R i
A547.14-15	U, K	A567.18-A568.2	R i
A547.15-17	U, K	A568.16-18	R il
A547.17-18	U, K	A569.1-5	E, K
A547.18-22	U, K	A569.5-7	R p
A548.3-6	O, E	A569.12-15	R il
A548.6-9	R p, U c	A569.21-A570.3	R il
A551.6-7	E, K	A571.6-9	R il, I
A551.8-10	E, K	A571.10-13	U c, R p
A551.10		A571.14-15	R p
ftnt a 1-2	K	A571.15-17	R p, K
A552.24-A553.2	U c	A573.13-15	R il
A553.2-4	E, K, R, U c	A573.19-A574.2	R i
A553.4-9	E, T, R, U c	A574.11-15	R p, K
A553.14-15	E, T	A575.4-5	R p
A554.2-3	R, T	A576.16-17	R il
A554.3-4	R, T	A576.17-19	R il
A555.21-23	R, U c	A577.2-5	R i, K, I
A556.1-2	R, T, U c	A577.23-A578.5	R il
A556.9-12	R, K, U c	A578.5-9	R il
A557.1-3	R, U	A578.22-A579.1	R il
A557.6-9	R, K	A579.2-4	R il, O
A557.15-20	U c, Freedom	A579.4-5	K
A558.2-4	K	A579.18-23	R il
A558.4-6	K	A580.10-11	R il
A558.8-10	K, U c	A580.12-15	R i
A559.13-17	R i	A580.17-18	R il, O
A561.14-16	O	A580.18-21	R il, O, K
A561.17-21	R p	A581.24-25	U c
A561.21-23	R p	A582.7-9	O, K, I
A561.23-26	R p	A582.9-11	O, R i
A562.7-11	R	A582.11-14	O, K
A562.11-16	U	A582.15-18	O, K
A562.21-A563.5	K	A583.4	
A563.5-6	R	ftnt a 5-7	O, K
A563.11-13	K	A583.7-A584.2	O, K
A564.21-23	O, K	A584.4-6	O, K
A565.4-7	R i	A586.4-6	R i
A565.7-11	O, K	A586.6-9	R, K, U c, O
A565.11-14	K	A588.8-10	U pm
A565.14-18	R i	A588.10-14	U pm
A565.18-23	O, K	A588.18-22	U pm
A565.23-A566.1	O, K	A592.4-7	O, R i

A636.15-17	K, R
A636.17-21	R, R p, U, K
A637.1-7	U c, U p
A637.7-17	U c, U p, I, R i
A637.18-21	K
A637.21-A638.1	K, R i
A638.2-6	K, U p, O
A638.6-8	K, R
A639.9-18	K
A638.18-A639.1	K
A639.1-16	K
A639.17-19	U, U a, O, U pm
A639.22-25	K, U c, U pm
A639.26-A640.6	R, K
A640.7-11	R, R i, K
A640.21-A641.11	K, R
A641.12-15	R il
A641.15-17	K
A641.17-23	R
A642.6-10	R, K
A643.2-7	R i
A643.7-14	R i, K, O, U
A643.14-15	R, U
A643.16-18	R, U
A643.19-22	R
A643.23-25	U
A644.1-650.3	R, U c, K, E
A644.1-2	R, U
A644.8-9	R i
A644.9-12	R i
A644.21-23	U c, O
A647.5-11	R, R i, K
A647.12-15	R, K
A647.18-21	R i, K
A647.21-24	R p, U, U p
A648.4-6	R i, U
A648.9-21	R, U
A650.22-A651.1	R p, U p
A651.1-10	R p, R tel
A651.10-13	R p, K
A653.13-17	R i
A654.12-23	U d
A655.1-9	U d
A655.10-16	U d
A655.16-26	U d
A655.26-A656.4	U c, K, U d
A655.5-15	U d
A656.15-19	U, U c, K, I, U d
A655.19-24	U d
A657.1-8	R p, I, U d

A657.8-14	U d
A657.14-20	U d
A657.21-A658.3	U d
A658.3-10	U d
A658.18-21	U d
A659.6-8	U d
A659.8-17	U d
A659.17-22	U d
A659.22-A660.2	U d
A660.3-12	U d
A660.22-24	R p
A661.11-13	R p, R i, O, I, K
A661.13-17	R p, U d
A661.17-22	R p
A662.4-8	R, K, U, I, R i, R tel
A663.25-A664.2	R i
A664.3-9	U p, I
A664.9-12	R p, U c, U sch
A664.12-16	R p
A664.22-A665.4	U, R, U sch
A665.4-7	U sch, I, U c
A665.13-18	U sch, U c, U p, K, U
A665.18-A666.2	U p, R p, U
A666.13-15	U p, R p
A666.15-18	R p
A666.18-21	R p
A666.22-A667.1	R p
A667.4-7	R p
A667.7-18	I, O
A667.23-A558.5	R, R p, R tel, K
A668..6-19	R, R p, R tel, K, I, O
A668.20-28	R, R p, K
A669.1-2	R i
A669.2-3	R i
A669.4-6	R
A669.17-18	U c
A669.19-20	R i
A670.5-7	R i, O
A670.8-10	R sch
A670.10-12	O, R sch
A670.12-16	R i
A672.14-16	U c, K
A673.4-7	U c
A673.7-12	R i, U
A673.13-16	R i
A673.16-18	R i
A673.23-A674.1	U c, R

A701.7-9	R i		A728.16-18	Definition
A701.21-A702.3	R p, U		A728.18-21	Definition
A702.3-7	R p, K		A728.21-A729.2	Definition
A702.8-14	K, R, I		A729.2-6	Definition
A702.19-21	R tel		A729.6-9	Definition
A702.21-A703.4	K		A729.13-14	Definition
A703.10-14	K		A729.14-20	Definition
A703.20-22	R		A729.20-23	Definition
A708.7-15	R p (logic)		A729.23-24	Definition
A709.14-20	K		A730.8-15	Definition
A711.1-6	R p		A730.15-17	Definition
A711.6-14	R, I, U c, K		A730.17-20	Definition
A711.15-24	R, R p		A730.20-23	Definition
A714.2-6	I, Im, U c		A731.1-3	Definition
A714.7-10	K, R		A732.6-11	Definition
A714.21-A715.1	K, Im, I, S/T		A732.11-13	Definition
A715.1-2	I		A732.15-19	U s
A714.3-4	R, U, U c		A732.19-21	R, U c, K
A715.4-7	I, U c, K		A733.2-8	U s, U, U c
A715.9-11	I, Im		A733.8-10	U s, I
A715.11-13	I, Im, U c		A733.10-13	R p, I
A715.20-21	K, U c		A733.13-16	U s, R
A715.21-A716.4	K, U c, I		A733.23-A734.3	K
A716.9-13	K		A734.4-5	K, I
A717.18-22	K, I, Im, U c		A734.5-7	K
A718.15-18	K		A734.7-11	K, I
A718.25-A719.2	K, U		A734.11-14	K, U c, I
A719.7-11	K, O		A735.14-19	K
A719.25-A720.4	K, I, Im		A736.7-11	K
A720.5-6	I, S/T		A736.21-23	R, U s
A720.10-13	I, S/T, O		A736.23-25	U c, R i
A720.13-14	U c		A737.4-7	U p, K
A720. 15-17	K, U s, I		A737.8-10	U c, K
A720.17-19	I		A738.1-4	R
A720.20-22	U s, I		A740.7-22	R, R i
A720.22-24	U c		A741.23-A743.4	R, K
A720.24-A721.1	O, I		A744.25-A745.4	K
A721.1-5	U c, U p, U s, I		A750.25-A751.8	R, S/T, U p, U s
A722.5-9	U c, I, U s		A758.4-5	K
A722.9-13	U s, I, U p		A758.9-13	K
A722.12			A758.19-21	R, K
ftnt a 5-9	U c, Im, I, U p		A759.15-A760.1	K, R i
A722.13-17	U s, K, R, I		A760.1-3	K
A723.11-15	I, U c, K		A760.8-15	U c, K
A725.3-6	R, U c, I		A760.15-18	U c, K
A726.21-A727.1	K, R		A761.5-10+	
A727.5-6	K, R		A761.10-16	R, K
A727.12-A728.1	Definition		A762.1-7	R, K
A728.4-8	Definition		A762.7-8	R, K, O
A728.12-16	Definition		A762.8-12	R, O

A827.25-A828.2	K
A828.10-12	R tel
A828.19-A829.6	K
A829.7-10	K
A829.14-15	K
A830.1-14	K
A834.10-11	K
A834.11-16	R, R i, K, U sch
A834.16-17	K
A836.3-24	K
A836.24-A837.3	K, R, R p
A837.9-13	K
A837.26-30	K, R
A838.2-12	K, R i
A838.12-19	K, R
A838.20-25	K
A839.6-8	K, R i
A839.9-13	K, R
A839.16-A840.2	K
A840.3-5	R tel
A841.8-14	K
A841.22-24	K, R
A841.24-A842.6	K, R
A842.9-18	K
A842.18-A843.8	K, R

A843.8-12	K, R p
A843.13-A844.7	K
A844.7-17	K
A844.17-27	K
A846.1-8	K
A846.16-21	K, R
A847.2	
ftnt a 1-3	K
A847.2	
ftnt a 3-13	K
A847.7-8	K
A847.12-A848.7	K, O, E
A848.7-11	K, O
A848.12-21	K, E
A848.21-A849.9	K, E
A849.10-14	K
A849.14-23	K
A849.23-A850.7	K
A850.8-12	K, R
A850.15-18	K
A850.18-21	K, R
A851.5-12	K
A854.20-A855.4	K
A855.5-7	K

2. Beyond Limits

Abbreviations

R i	Ideas
R p	Principles of Reason
R tel	Finality, Ends, Interests of Reason
U c	Categories
U s	Synthesis
I	Intuition
S/T	Space and/or Time
K	Knowledge
E	Subject

(See Topic 29)

A19.15-16	U c
A44.1-4	K
B72.16-21	K

A64.17-A65.9	K
A65.13-A66.11	K
A67.7-15	K
A87.14-17	S/T, K
A92.8-10	Either O makes R poss. or R makes O poss.
A92.16-18	R determines O
A99.10-11	Each R in a moment an absolute unity (see A772.3-6)
A103.15-18	U c
A107.6-8	U c
A107.8-11	U c, R p
A107.12-17	E, K
A107.17-21	U c, R p
A107.21-24	U c, R p, S/T, I
A108.1-4	E, K, U c
A108.4-7	E, K, U c
A108.7-14	E, K, U c
A108.14-20	E, K, U c
A109.18-A110.6	E, K, U c
A110.6-9	U c, R p, S/T, I
A110.11-15	U c, R p, S/T
A110.15-17	U c, R p
A110.17-18	U c, R p
A110.19-20	U c, R p
A111.1-3	U c
A111.23-A112.4	E, K, U c
A112.4-6	U c
A114.4-13	E, K, U c
A114.13-24	E, K, U c
A116.4-9	U c
A116.12-16	E, K, U c
A116.16-18	U c
A116.19-21	U c
A116.21-A117.2	U c
A117.2 ftnt a 6-10	E, K, U c
A117.2 ftnt a 10-14	U c
A117.2 ftnt a 14-17	U c
A117.2 ftnt a 17-25	E
A118.1-3	U c
A118.3-6	U c
A118.8-11	U c
A118.14-17	U c
A118.17-20	U c
A119.4-8	U c

A123.8-11	U c
A123.23-A124.2	U c
A124.7-11	U c
A124.14-16	U c
A124.16-22	U c
A125.7-11	U c
A125.19-A126.2	E, K, U c
A127.5-11	E, K, U c
A129.18-21	E, K, U c
A130.2-4	U c
A130.4-6	U c
A130.6-10	U c
A148.17-A149.4	
B130.1-6	K, U c, U s
B130.13-14	K, U c
B131.5-6	U c
B131.6-9	U c
B131.10-14	U c
B132.4-15	E, K, U c
B132.17-B133.2	E, K, U c
B133.4-7	E, K, U c
B137.17-21	E, K, U c
B133.18	
ftnt a 12-15	U c
B133.18	
ftnt a 15-16	U c
B134.8-10	U c
B135.3-5	U c, R i
B136.8	
ftnt a 8-10	U c
B138.7-10	U c
B138.24-B139.4	U c
B141.8-14	U c
B142.3-14	E, K, U c
B143.1-3	E, K, U c
B143.7-10	U c
B143.10-12	U c
B144.1-4	E, K, U c
B144.4	
ftnt a 1-5	E, U c
153.17-21	E, U c
B153.21-24	U c
B153.24-B154.2	U c
B154.3-6	U c
B155.1	
ftnt a 1-3	U c
B157.1-5	E
B157.10-B158.3	E, U c

B160.19	
ftnt a 6-8	U c
ftnt a 12-14	U c
B160.19-B161.5	K, U c
B161.6-10	K, U c
B161.11-14	U c
B163.18-24	U c
B165.9-13	Discovery
A167.19-24	S/T, R p
A171.4-20	U c
A222.13-18	Discovery
B275.19-21	K
B275.21-B276.1	K, U c
B276.4-6	K
A288.10-15	U c
B308.24-B309.1	K
B294.4-6	U c
A295.7-12	R i, U c
A305.19-A306.2	U c, R p, R tel
A307.19-22	U c
A317.19-23	U c
A317.23-A318.1	K, U c
A318.6-8	K
A318.8-9	K, U c
A328.19-20	U c
A334.12-14	U c
A334.14-15	U c
A334.15-16	U c
A341.8-12	U c
A350.21-22	K, U c
A358.7-12	U c, K, E
A358.15-19	U c, K
A359.12-15	U c
A363.3-8	E, U c
A364.8-9	U c
A372.15-17	U c
A379.23-A380.5	U c
A391.1-4	U c
A393.6-8	U c
A420.19-22	U c
B421.21-B422.1	U c
B422.11-14	U c
B422.14	
ftnt a 13-14	U c
B425.3-9	R p
A463.22-A464.2	R tel
A464.14-19	R tel
A464.19-21	R tel

A797.6-11	K		A815.10-17	U c
A798.15-16	U c		A815.18-20	R tel
A800.15-19	R tel		A815.21-22	U c
A800.22-A801.1	R tel		A815.22-23	U c
A801.1-4	R tel		A816.7-12	U c, U tel
A803.10-15	U c, K		A816.14-17	K, U c
A807.12-16	U c		A816.20	R tel
A807.16-18	R, K		A817.4-5	R tel
A807.18-19	K, U c		A817.5-8	R tel
(see A644.1-A650.3)			A817.8-11	R tel
A808.5-7	K, U c		A818.1-5	K
A808.11-15	U c		A818.9-12	K
A808.20	U c		A818.19-22	U c
(see A644.1-A650.3)			A819.6-8	U c, U tel
A808.21-33	U c		A819.14-16	R tel
(see A644.1-A650.3)			A819.21-23	R tel
A809.7-12	K		A820.1-4	U c
A810.14-16	U c		A826.7-10	R tel
(see A644.1-A650.3)			A826.10-13	R tel, U c
A811.3-4	K, U c		A826.13-16	U c
A811.5-9	U c		A828.5-6	R tel
(see A644.1-A650.3)			A828.10-12	R tel
A811.15	U c		A831.15-19	R tel
(see A644.1-A650.3)			A832.9-10	R tel
A811.16-18	U c		A835.7-9	K, R
(see A644.1-A650.3)			A835.16-19	U c
A811.22-A812.3	U c		A838.25-A839.6	R tel
(see A644.1-A650.3)			A839.16-A840.2	K
A814.14-17	U c		A840.3-5	R tel
(see A644.1-A650.3)			A840.7-9	R tel
A814.19-24	U c		A840.17-21	U c
A815.3-9	U c		A845.1-5	U c
A815.9-10	R tel		A847.3-7	R tel

3. Illusion

A6.6-11	A293.12-15
A60.20-A61.5	A294.11-16
A61.6-9	A295.7-12
A61.14-16	A295.17-20
A62.4-7	A295.23-A296.2
A63.11-15	A296.2-8
A63.23-A64.5	A296.8-11
A88.11-17	A296.11-14
B305.18-22	A296.14-16
A289.20-24	A296.16-21

A498.11-14
A498.14-18
A498.18-22
A499.9-12
A499.12-13
A499.17-21
A500.1-5
A500.7-9
A500.9-14
A500.25-A501.2
A504.11-14
A504.15-20
A504.20-A505.3
A505.3-5
A505.5-7
A505.7-11
A505.14-17
A505.19-22
A506.6-12
A507.9-13
A508.5-11
A509.19-24
A515.14-A516.2
A516.2-9
A516.14-16
A516.16-20
A528.1-6
A518.6-8
A528.8-10
A529.1-6
A529.17-21
A529.21-22
A529.22-A530.5
A530.7-10
A531.9-10
A531.16-A532.3
A533.19-22
A535.1-4
A535.4-7
A535.11-16
A536.1-3
A536.3-5
A558.10-16
A558.16-9
A560.16-18
A581.1-5
A582.11-14

A583.4 ftnt a 1-4
A583.7-A584.4
A586.20-23
A594.1-17
A598.8-13
A603.12-17
A614.11-14
A615.3-6
A615.14-16
A619.10-13
A619.21-A620.2
A620.2-5
A642.10-12
A642.16-19
A643.2-7
A644.21-23
A644.24-A645.4
A645.4-7
A669.1-3
A669.4-6
A680.2-3
A695.2-6
A695.20 ftnt a 1-7
A702.3-7
A703.14-16
A703.22-A704.5
A709.14-20
A711.15-24
A712.18-A713.4
A735.14-19
A743.5 (no antithetic)
A744.19-22
A751.9-14
A763.15-17
A768.16-20
A777.18-20
A777.25-A778.1
A786.18-22
A792.7-11
A792.11-13
A792.24-A793.5
A795.17-A796.4
A797.6-11
A820.9-11
A821.16-23
A837.13-16
A849.14-23

4. Agnosticism

A15.19-22
B145.22-B146.4
B141.17-21
B171.4-20
A171.21-A172.2
A231.1-4
A288.18-19
A288.19-21
A393.4-6
A477.1-5
A481.8-22
A551.10 ftnt a 1-2
A556.9-12
A557.5-11
A613.19-21
A613.21-A614.1
A676.17-20
A683.7-11

(See A614.11-15)

5. Laws

1. Constitutive

A126.15-18
A127.24-A128.6
B130.6-11
B156.8-14
B161.11-14
A196.9-14

2. Discovery

Bxiii.11-15
Bxiii.19-Bxiv.5
B12.16-20
A52.22-25
A60.16-20
A114.15-18
A84.5-9
A85.13-16
A85.16-17
A86.16-19
A91.12-15
A91.20-A92.1
A126.11-13
A126.13-15
A126.15-18
A127.20-24
A171.4-20
A171.21-A172.2
A216.5-7
A310.4-8
A318.24-A319.1
A477.1-5
A577.2-5
A622.3-12
A657,8-14
A660.24-A661.4
A662.11-A663.15
A691.24-A692.6
A692.9-12
A692.18-24
A693.4-9
A694.2-9
A699.19-21
A700.22-A701.1
A826.7-10

6. Sensation

1. Can't Be Anticipated

A167.1-6
A171.4-20
A178.12-17
A496.4-8

2. Must Be Generated

A105.11-18
A105.18-20
A106.6-9
A122.17-25
B134.10-13
A143.1-4
A145.7-8
B202.12-B203.2   (?)
A210.11-17
B208.5-8
A234.11-13   (?)
A234.13-17   (?)
A234.17-19   (?)
A239.23-A240.3   (?)

Section II

Basic Models

7. Necessity, *A priorism* and Essentialism

Abbreviations

a	*a priori*
C	complete, whole
c	unconditioned
Po	possible (see Topic 8)
Ip	impossible
K	knowledge, experience
M	meaning
N	nature, interest
n	necessity
P	principle, rule, schema, concept, idea, form, law, ends, categories, space, time
R	reason
S	system
s	synthesis
T	thought
Tg	transcendental ground
Tr	transcendental representation
U	understanding/imagination
u	unity
I	intuition
Trf	transcendental reflection
D	division

(See Topic 37)

Avii.1-5	R, N, Ip, K	Axx.1-7	K, C
Avii.6-8	P, N, n	Axx.7-9	K, R, S
Avii.10-Axiii.1	R, N	Axx.13-18	K, u, C
Axiii.5-6	R, N	Axxi.1-2	R, S
Axiii.13-19	R, P	Axxi.14-16	K, C
Axiv.12-14	R, S, C	Bviii.1-3	K, C
Axiv.20-23	K, N, n	Bviii.7-10	Logic, C
Axv.9-14	K, n, a, c	Bix.1-6	Logic, C

B41.5-8	a, I, n, P	A48.7-15	a, I
B41.21-23	Po, a, K, S, s	A48.19-25	a, I, s
A26.11-12	P, I, Po	A48.25-A49.6	P, a
A26.15-17	P, I, a	A51.11-13	T, N, U
A26.17-20	I, P, S, a	A51.21-22	n, N, T, I
A28.24-25	P, Po, n, I	A52.8-10	n, P, T
A29.8-13	P, I, a	A52.12-15	P, T
A29.13-14	P, Po	A53.9-13	P, a, U, R
B44.16-18	P, a, s, K	A53.22-A54.2	P, a, R
A30.14-17	P, a, Po	A54.5-10	K, P, T
A30.17-19	P, Po	A54.14-16	a, K, S, P, U
A31.1-2	P, n, I	A55.10-12	P, T
A31.2-4	P, n	A55.12-21	P, T
A31.4	P, a	A55.21-A56.1	P, K
A31.4-5	P, Po, K	A59.10-14	P, K, U, C, n
A31.5-7	P, n	A59.14-16	P, U
A31.8-10	P, Po, a, n	A59.16-18	P, T
A31.10-11	P	A59.22-A60.1	P, K
A31.11-12	P	A60.4-6	P, U, R
A31.16-19	P, Po, K	A60.6-11	P, K, C
A31.20-21	P, I, a	A76.17-20	a, P, I
A31.21-A32.1	P, C	A64.17-A65.9	K, U, a, C, S
A32.6-7	I, P, M	A67.7-15	K, P, a, U, u, S, C
A32.10-11	P, n	A69.20-23	U, u, C, P
A32.12-17	P, Po, D, Ip, I	A70.1-4	U, u, C, S, P
B48.12-15	P, Po	A79.3-6	P, s, u
B48.15-20	P, Po, a	A79.6-7	U
B48.20-B48.2	P, Po	A79.8-10	u, s
B49.2-5	P, S, C, a, K, s	A79.12-17	U, s, P, u, I
A33.6-8	P, a, Po, I	A79.17-20	U, P, a
A33.9-10	P, I	A79.21-26	C, a, P, U
A33.15-17	P, U	A80.4-5	U, P, a
A33.17-20	P, C	A80.7-9	U, P, I
A33.20-22	P, I	A80.9-A81.2	T, S
A34.1-2	P, Po, a, C	A81.2-5	T, S
A34.2-4	P, a, I, Po	A81.5-7	U, P
A34.6-9	P, a, Po, I	A81.22-23	U, P
A34.9-11	P, Po	A82.6-9	U, P
A34.11-16	a, P, C, n	B109.17-B110.1	U, C, S, P, a
A35.19-22	I, Po, P	B110.14-15	U, N
A37.16-17	P, Po, K	B109.17-B110.3	P, S, a, P
A38.25-A39.2	P, a, K, s	B111.1	C, u
A39.11-15	P, K, n, I	B111.4-5	u
A42.17-20	a, K, I	B111.20-B112.3	C, P
A42.22-24	c, n, P, I	B113.9-14	a, P, C
A43.20-24	P, M, C, T	B113.14-16	P
A46.26-A47.4	a, P, K, n	B113.23-26	P
A47.13-17	a, K, P	B113.26-B114.3	P, K
A48.1-5	a, I	B114.3-4	P, K
A48.5-6	a, I, s	B114.4-11	P, K, C, M, n

A109.15-18	u, n, s
A109.18-A110.6	u, n, T, a, P, s
A110.6-9	I, P, u, n
A110.9-10	K
A110.11-15	K, u, S, C
A110.15-17	K, u, S, C
A110.17-18	K, u, s, C
A110.19-20	u, s, P
A111.1-3	u, s, Tg
A111.5-7	u, s, P
A111.11-13	a
A111.13-16	T
A111.16-18	P, a
A111.20-23	P, n, I, u
A111.23-A112.4	Tg, n, u, P, S, C
A112.4-6	P, s
A112.6-10	u, P, a, n
A112.16-18	P, n
A113.10-12	C
A113.12-15	Tg, Tr, a
A113.15-20	u, n, s, K, a, P
A113.20-23	P, n, C
A113.23-26	u, n, C, P
A114.4-13	N, Tg, P, u
A114.15-19	u, P, T, s, C
A115.3-6	P, K
A115.6-9	a, P
A115.14-A116.3	a, I, s, u, C
A116.4-9	s, u
A116.9-11	I
A116.11-12	K
A116.12-16	Tg, n, C, u
A116.16-18	u, s
A116.19-21	P, a, Tg, u, C, I
A116.21-A117.2	u, s, P, I
A117.2	
ftnt a 2-3	C, u, n
A117.2	
ftnt a 6-10	Tg, n, C, u
A117.2	
ftnt a 10-14	u, s, a, P
AA17.2	
ftnt a 14-17	u, s, a, P
A117.2	
ftnt a 17-25	Tr, Tg, n
A118.1-3	u, s, N, a
A118.3-6	u, P, s, U, a
A118.6-8	s, U, a
A118.8-11	P, n, u, s, K
A118.12-14	s, Tg, I, a

A118.14-17	Tr, n, a, s
A118.17-20	u, K, s, U
A118.20-21	U, C, K, a
A119.1-4	Tg, u, s, U
A119.8-11	U, C, K, I, s
A119.11-13	U, C, s, I
A119.13-15	K, N, I
A119.15-19	U, P, S, n, K, C
A119.20-A120.1	U, P
A120.7-10	I, s
A121.1-7	s, U
A121.12-17	P, n
A121.18-23	u, s, N
A122.6-9	Tg, n
A122.9-23	Tg, P, n, K, u
A122.23-25	s, u, n
A123.1-6	u, Tg, n, s, a, P
A123.7-8	U, s, a
A123.8-11	U, s, N, u
A123.11-19	P, u
A123.20-22	Tg, n, Tr
A123.23-A124.2	C, u, I
A124.2-4	U, u
A124.4-7	U, s, I, a
A124.7-11	P, U, u, s
A124.12-14	P, U, a
A124.14-16	P, U, s, I, u, n
A124.16-22	U, s, I, n, u, K
A124.22-A125.4	K, P, u
A125.5-7	P
A125.7-11	u, s, U, P
A125.11-13	P, K
A125.14-19	N, u, n, a
A125.19-A126.2	s, a, n, K, P
A126.3-7	U, T, P
A126.8-10	U, P
A126.10-11	U, P
A126.11-13	U, P
A126.13-15	P, N
A126.15-18	P, U
A126.18-12	P, K
A126.21-A127.5	U, P, N, s, u, K, Tg
A127.5-11	Tg, P, u, U
A128.7-9	U, P, s, u
A128.13-15	P, a
A129.7-10	n, a, P, K
A129.11-18	C, u, n, Tg, K
A129.18-21	u, T, K, P
A129.21-A130.1	u, K, P, a, T

A130.2-4	s, U, u, K
A130.4-6	P, U, a, n
A130.6-10	K, u, s
A130.10-12	u, s, I
B129.7-11	P, a
B130.6-11	s, n
B130.11-13	s, n
B130.13-14	u, s
B131.5-6	u, P, a
B131.6-9	P, u, T
B131.9-10	P, s
B131.10-14	u, U
B132.4-15	n, u, Tg, Tr
B132.17-B133.2	u, Tg, Tr, s
B133.18	
ftnt a 12-15	u, U
B133.18	
ftnt a 15-16	u, U, Tg
B134.6-8	s, u
B134.8-10	u
B134.10-13	s, u, Tg, T
B134.16-B135.3	U, s, a, u, Tg
B135.3-5	u, P, C, K
B135.6-10	P, n, u, Tg, s, T
B135.10-14	Tr, u, s, T
B135.14-16	U, I
B135.16-17	U, I
B135.21-B136.1	Tg, u, s
B136.2-8	P, U, Tg, s
B136.8	
ftnt a 1-3	I
B136.8	
ftnt a 8-10	u, s, I
B136.8-10	I, P
B136.10-B137.1	P, I, s
B137.1-5	T, s, n, Tr, Tg
B137.10-11	u, Tg, s, n
B137.11-15	Tg, K, U
B137.15-16	U, Tg, u
B137.17-21	K, U, s, Tg, u
B138.6-7	s, u, K, Tg
B138.7-10	u, s, P, I
B138.10-12	u, s
B138.13-20	s, u, T, n, P, Tr
B138.21-24	U, Tg, Tr
B138.24-B139.4	u, s, I
B139.4-11	U, T, n, P
B139.12-14	Tg, u, s
B139.14-18	u, I

B140.3-9	U, s, P, Tg, u, n, Tr
B140.9-10	u, K
B141.8-14	u, s
B141.14-B142.3	u, s
B142.1-14	Tg, u, n, s, P, K
B142.14-19	u, s
B142.22-26	u, s
B143.1-3	n, u, Tg, s
B143.4-7	U, Tg, s
B143.7-10	u, s, P
B143.10-12	P, s, I
B143.12-14	I, s, P, n
B144.1-4	s, U, n, u, Tg, P
B144.4	
ftnt a 1-5	u, s, Tg
B144.4-8	P, I, s, a
B146.6-9	K, P, I
B144.10-16	U, P, u
B144.16-B145.3	u, P
B145.15-22	P, U, T, s, u, Tg
B145.22-B146.4	U, a, u, Tg, P
B150.6-9	s, u, Tg, a, K, U
B150.10-20	P, a, U, s, u, Tg, n
B151.4-10	s, n, a, T, P, U
B151.13-18	s, u, Tg, T, P
B151.19-23	U, P
B151.23-B152.4	s, a, P, u, Tg
B152.4-6	s, P, N
B153.10-13	U, s, Tg
B153.17-21	U, s, u, Tg
B154.2-6	Tg, u, s, P
B154.6-13	U, s
B154.13-22	T, s
B157.6-9	K, T, u, Tg, S
B158.1	
ftnt a 4-7	P, a
B158.5-9	K, P, s, u, Tg
B158.9-15	K, T, n
B147.1-3	I, P
B147.4-6	I, a, K
B147.8-11	P, K, I
B147.14-19	P, U, a, I, K
B148.12-15	P, U, I
B150.4-6	P, T, K
B159.10-12	a, P, T, u
B159.12-15	P, a, K, I
B159.15-B160.1	K, a, P, I, s, N
B160.1-5	P, a

B160.11-15	P, n, s	A142.7-11	P, U, s, u
B160.15-19	P, a, I, u	A142.11-16	P, s, a, u, Tg
B161.6-10	s, u, Tg, P	A143.1-4	u, s
B161.10-11	s, n, C, P	A145.5-6	P
B151.11-14	K, P, a	A145.10-12	P, s, C
B162.6-9	s, u, U, P	A145.15-16	P, a
B162.10-11	s, n, P	A145.20-24	P, U, s, u, Tg
B162.11		A146.1-5	P, U
ftnt a 1-4	s, Tg, n, P, a	A146.5-10	a, n, u, C, Tg, s, P
B162.12-B163.5	n, s, u	A146.14-17	U, P
B163.5-11	s, u, a, P	A147.7-13	P, u, M
B163.16-18	P, a, N	A147.18-22	P, M, U
B163.18-24	P, a, N	A148.8-13	a, K, U, P, C, S
B164.1-5	P, N, n, U, a, s	A148.14-17	P, a, K
B164.5-9	P, U	A148.17-A149.4	P, K, C
B164.9-11	n, P, U	A149.4-6	K
B164.13-15	P, s, n	A151.1-7	Logic, P
B164.16-18	u, s, U	A151.18-22	P, C, K
B164.18-21	s, P	A151.22-A152.2	P, C, K
B164.21-B165.2	N, P, n	A152.21-23	Logic, P
B165.2-5	P, n	A154.1-10	s, Logic, C, U
B165.5-9	U, P, a, N	A155.10-12	s, u, Tg
B165.13-16	a, P, K	A156.5-6	a, M, P, I, n
B165.17	T, P	A156.16-23	s, u, P, K, n, Tg
B165.17-19	K, I, P	A156.23-A157.4	P, a, C, u, s
B165.19-20	I, C	A157.8-15	K, a, T, n
B166.1-3	K, I	A158.2-5	s, P, u
B166.5-8	P, I, K	A158.6-10	s, a, n, u, Tg, K
B166.8-11	n, P, K	A158.14-A159.2	P, U, C, n
B167.4-8	C, P, K	A159.11-14	P
B167.21-B168.3	n, P, C	A159.21-A160.3	P, a, U
A130.15-17	C, P, U	A162.98-11	P, U
A131.1-4	S, u, U	A162.17	I
A131.5-9	T, R	B203.2-10	s, u
A131.9-13	R, P, N	A163.10-12	C, s
A131.22-24	U, P	A164.24-A165.3	P, U
A132.11-14	U, P	A165.15-18	n, C
A135.16-19	K, P, a	A165.24-A166.3	s, P, C, K
A136.2-5	K, C	A166.3-6	s, P, n
A136.8-11	U, N, n, C	A168.1-4	I, K
A136.11-15	U, P, a, C, K	A168.4-11	I
A138.21-A139.7	P, C, a, U	A168.11-16	I
A139.23-A140.3	a, P, U, n	A168.17-19	I
A140.3-9	P, C, U	A168.20-21	I
A140.11-14	s, u	A168.24-A169.3	I
A140.23-25	P, C	A169.5-9	I
A140.20-A141.1	P	A169.13-15	I
A141.6-8	P, T, S	A170.2-6	I, s, U
A141.8-12	P, C	A170.7-9	I
A141.12-17	P	A171.4-20	I

A219.18-22	T, s, u, K, C	A240.13-15	P, a, s
A220.1-3	P	A240.15-18	P
A220.3-5	s, K, P	A240.19-A241.1	P, n
A220.13-16	s, P, K	A241.19-A242.9	U, M, P
A220.16-18	n, P	A243.7-11	M
A221.1-3	n, s, P	A245.10-15	M, P
A221.3-6	P	A245.20-23	P, T, n
A221.22-A222.5	P, a, C, s, u, K	A246.18-21	U, P, a
A224.2-5	n, T, P	A247.8-11	P, U, u
A224.5-11	P, s	A248.18-22	P, U, T
A224.12-16	P, s, K	A250.22-24	u, Tg
A224.18-23	K, a, P, K	A253.4-10	T, C
A225.4-8	P, C	B305.22-B306.1	P, T, u, s, a
A225.18-22	K, a, P	B307.2-5	U, C, P, T
B276.2-4	n	B307.19-23	T, n, U
B277.3-5	T, C, Tg, Tr	A253.23-A254.3	P, T
B278.2-7	n, a, P	A254.19-22	P, n, K
B278.23-B279.1	n	A255.15-17	n, P
A227.4-7	P, K, C, n	A256.5-8	n, P
A227.7-10	P, K, n	A256.22-23	n, T
A227.12-15	K, P, n	A260.6-8	P, n
A227.15-18	P, C, a	A260.10-12	n
A227.24-A228.4	n, P, a	A261.8-10	n
A228.4-8	N, n, P, C	261.15-19	C, P
A228.8-12	N, n, P	A261.19-22	u, n
A228.12-17	P, N, u, U, s	A262.15-18	S, n, K
A230.15-19	U, n, P, Tg, a	A265.21-A266.3	U, n, T
A232.11-15	U, R, P	A266.9-11	P, U, C, n
A233.23-A234.3	P, s	A266.20-22	U
A234.4-6	P, U	A267.17-20	P, a
A234.9-10	P, s, n	A267.20-22	P, a
A234.17-19	P, n	A268.1-9	P, a, C
A234.21		A268.10-12	P, U, S
ftnt a 4-5	U	A268.12-15	P, S
B288.18-21	P, K, T	A268.19-21	P, S
B289.20-23	P, K	A269.4-6	P, S, C
B289.23-B290.2	P	A269.6-10	C, S, P
B291.7011	n	A274.10-14	C
B292.8-14	n	A274.14-19	P
B293.4-6	S, u	A283.1-6	P
B293.14-17	a, P	A283.6-11	T
A235.3-6	U, C, S	A283.11-12	P
A235.6-7	N, U	A283.12-17	T
A236.18-21	U	A284.8-12	T, n
A236.21-A237.1	P, U, a	A284.17-21	T, P, n
A237.1-7	K, U, s, u, Tg, a	A284.22-25	M
A237.7-15	P, U, a, C, K	A285.17-21	n, P, U
A238.9-12	U	A286.5-9	P, U, n
A239.3-6	T, P, C	A289.14-16	Tg, T, a
A239.23-A240.3	P, C, a	A290.15-18	P, C

A330.14-16	R, K, U, P	A347.2-4	Ip
A331.4-9	R, P	A347.4-5	Tg
A331.10-16	R, P	A347.7	n
A331.16-20	R, P, C, N	A348.1-3	Tr, Tg
A331.20-21	R, P, a	A349.6-11	n, T
A331.21-A332.3	R, P, S, C	A349.9-120	Tr, C
A332.3-6	R, K, C, c	A350.4-6	Tr, C, T
A332.11-14	R, a, C, c	A350.7-10	Tr, C, T
A332.17-22	C, c, n	A350.16-19	n, T, C, Tg
A332.22-26	R, n, K, a, c	A353.3-8	u, T
A333.4-9	R, a, Trf, P	A353.16-18	Ip, n, u
A333.9-18	N, R, P, U, s, C, c	A353.23-A354.1	n, Tr
A333.19-A334.3	C	A354.2-4	n, Tr, T, u, c
A334.3-7	C	A354.4-7	Ip, T, u
A334.8-12	P, s, u, R, c, s	A354.7-8	Tr, T, C
A334.12-14	C, u, c, T	A354.12-13	P, Tg
A334.14-15	C, u, c, T	A354.14	C
A334.15-16	C, u, c, T	A354.14-17	n, P, K
A334.19-21	Tr, T, C, P	A354.19-22	Tr, n
A335.8-10	S, P, R,	A354.23-25	Tr, T, C
A335.16-21	R, n, s, P, u, c	A354.25-A355.1	Tg, P, n, Tr
A335.21-23	R, n, P, u, c	A355.4-7	Tr, c, u
A335.23-A336.3	R, n, P, u, c	A355.8-10	Tr, u
A336.8-10	R, N, P	A355.10-14	Tr, K
A336.11-14	R, C, c, s	A355.14-15	Tr, M
A336.15-17	R, C, c, s, a, U	A359.2-4	N, T
A336.17-21	R, C, c, P	A360.24-A361.4	Tr, K, Ip
A337.13-16	u, S, Tr, P, s, K	A361.6-10	Ip, K
A395.2		A362.8-11	P, a, Tg
ftnt a 1-4	Tr, C, s, S	A362.12-16	C, Tg, u, C
A395.2		A362.21-A363.3	Tr, C, u
ftnt a 4-6	K, Tr	A363.9-12	P, Tg, u, S
A338.6-10	Tr, S, C, R	A363.12-14	Tr, u
A338.12-15	Tr, P, n, R	A364.8-9	n, T, u, Tg
A339.8-10	n, P, R	A365.9-12	u, Tg
A339.10-14	n	A365.21-26	Tr, Tg, K, S, C
A339.14-18	R, n, N	A365.26-A366.1	n, P
A340.2-5	Tr, u	A373.16-19	a, P
A341.2-4	Tg, n	A381.9-13	Tr, s, P
A341.4-5	R, N	A381.13-17	Tr, K
A341.5-7	n	A382.8-12	P, K, Tr
A341.8-12	Tr, C, Tg	A398.3-6	T, C, Tr, R, c
A341.12-15	Tr, P, C	A398.3-8	T, Tr, R, c, n, P,
A341.15-17	C, T		u, C
A341.17-A342.3	N	A400.12-14	Tg, Tr, M
A342.3-5	Tr, Tg, P	A401.21-22	P, Tg
A345.15-A346.1	Tr	A401.23-25	P, U, Tg
A346.16-18	P, T	A401.25-27	Tg, Tr, u, c
A346.21-23	n, C, Tg, N	A401.27-A402.6	Tg, Tr, K, P
A346.23-A347.2	n, a, P, C	A402.11-14	N, u, s, T, Tg

A428.8	
ftnt a 1-2	C, P, s
A438.1-12	C, n, D, s
A438.12-17	C, D, s
A435.8-15	C, D, s
A435.18-19	C, D
A435.23-28	C, D, s
A435.28-33	C, D, s
A439.8-16	I, U
A441.18-31	U, T, n
A441.41-47	U, P, n
A443.38-46	c, n, u
A452.12	
ftnt a 1-2	P
A452.13-16	P
A452.16-22	C, c, n, P
A452.22-27	c, n, P
A458.59-62	Ip
A459.23-30	C, c
A461.3-7	R, N
A462.5-6	n, P
A462.6-10	R, s, n, C, P
A462.11-12	R
A463.12-15	C, a
A463.3	R, P
A463.9-11	R, P, c
A463.12-22	R, P, C, c
A464.2-8	R, N, U
A464.8-13	R, K
A466.4-10	R, c
A466.15-21	R, c, S, u
A466.24-25	R, N
A466.25-A467.3	Tr, c, P, C, a
A466.3-4	c
A467.17-18	U
A468.1-4	R, P, N
A468.15-20	U, P, K
A468.20-24	I, U, P
A469.24-A470.1	N, U, n, P
A474.8-12	R, N, S, C, K
A475.1-4	R, n, S, u, a, N
A476.7-12	K
A476.14-A477.1	K, P
A477.15-18	K, Trf
A477.18-21	K, Trf
A477.21-24	K
A478.1-5	K
A480.16-19	R, P
A481.22-25	O, C, c, s, T
A484.14-17	Trf

A494.8-10	s, u, K, P
A494.23-A495.3	P, u, n, K
A498.2-7	n, M
A498.7-10	R, U
A500.1-5	n, N
A500.5-7	n, P
A500.9-14	N, U
A500.19-25	s, n, C
A506.6-12	C, c, P
A508.11-13	I
A511.15-17	s
A511.18-19	s
A513.1-3	D, C
A513.3-4	D, C
A513.5-12	D, C
A513.12	D
A513.12-17	s
A513.18-23	s, C
A514.9-12	P, D, C
A514.12-15	P, s, C
A514.20-21	n, P
A514.21-22	n, P
A514.22-A515.2	n
A515.14-A516.2	c, C
A516.10-12	R, P
A522.17-18	C, I
A523.10-12	C, P
A523.12-13	C, P
A523.15-18	C, P
A523.18-A524.3	C, P
A524.10-13	D
A524.13-15	C, P, D
A524.20-23	C, P, D, I
A525.1-5	C, P, D
A525.5-6	C, P, D
A525.13-19	C, P
A526.12-14	C, D
A526.14-18	C, D
A527.8-9	C, D
A527.9-12	D
A527.13-16	D
A527.19-22	D, R, P, N
A528.10-12	D
A528.12-16	D, C, T
A528.16-A529.1	D, C
A529.10-12	s
A529.12-17	R, P
A530.7-10	s, D, C
A530.10-14	U, P
A530.14-17	s

A579.8-9	Tr, n, T	A592.14-17	c, n
A579.16-18	Tr, C, c	A592.17-A593.1	c, n, Ip
A580.1-6	Tr, C	A593.1-3	T, Ip, n
A580.6-7	Tr	A593.3-6	Po, P, M
A580.12-15	R, Tr, C	A593.6-12	Po, D, M, c, n
A580.15-17	Tr, s	A593.13-22	c, n, M, K
A580.21-23	Tr, n	A593.23-24	c, n, P
A581.5-6	Tr, N	A593.24-26	c, n
A581.6-11	R, T, C, S, Tr	A593.26-A594.1	c, n
A581.13-19	T, a, n	A594.1-17	c, n, M
A581.19-23	C	A594.22-A595.8	c, n, M
A582.4-7	C	A595.8-14	c, n, M
A582.9-11	C	A595.18-23	c, n
A582.11-14	N, P	A595.24-A596.2	n, M, Ip
A583.4		A596.2-3	a, P, n, Ip
ftnt a 1-4	Tr, N, R, C, u	A596.4-11	C, c, n, Po
A583.4		A596.12-14	Po
ftnt a 5-7	u, S, U	A596.14	
A583.4		ftnt a 1-10	Po
ftnt a 7-10	u, c, C, U	A603.3-7	R, n, C, N, Tg
A584.2-4	n, c, N	A603.7-12	R, n, c, Tr, a
A584.4-8	c, C, P	A603.12-15	R, Tr
A584.9-11	R, N	A603.16-17	R, N
A584.11-19	C, n	A611.21-A612.3	C, Po, a
A584.20-23	n	A612.16-18	K, n, c
A584.23-28	C, n	A612.19-A613.3	C, c, n, P, Tg
A585.1-9	C, n, P, R	A613.4-6	n, c, R
A585.9-11	C, n	A614.3-7	Tr, R
A585.11-15	c, n, P	A614.9-11	R, N, Tr
A585.16-20	C, n, P	A614.11-15	R, N, C
A585.20-23	c, n, P	A615.3-5	R, N, n, Tr
A585.23-A586.3	P, C	A615.6-9	n, Tg
A586.10-12	Tr, c, n	A615.14-16	n
A586.12-14	n	A615.16-18	N
A586.14-16	n	A615.22-A616.1	n
A586.20	R, N	A616.4-8	n, C
A586.20-23	n, c	A617.9-11	n, c, u
A586.23-24	c	A617.25-26	n, c, T
A586.24-A587.2	C, c	A618.1-2	P
A587.2-3	C, u, c	A618.2-3	P
A587.3-4	Tr, c	A618.3-4	U, P
A587.4-6	Tr, c, Tg, n	A619.6-9	u, C, Tr, P, S, n
A587.11-15	c, u, C, P	A619.10-13	n, P, u
A589.2-7	Tr, R	A619.13-18	P, C
A589.7-12	n, Tr, P, R	A619.18-21	s, u, N, R, Tr
A589.14-19	R	A619.21-A620.2	N, Tr, n
A590.8-11	n, c	A620.2-5	Tr, c, n
A590.11-16	N, U	A620.5-6	n, M
A592.1-4	Tr, R	A620.6-8	P, n, R, T
A592.4-7	Tr, C, U	A622.3-5	u, S

A667.4-7	R, N, P	A694.17-23	u, N, P, C, c
A667.19-23	R, N, P, u	A695.1-2	Tr, u, N, R
A668.6-19	R, P, N, I, D, u, Ip, K	A695.2-3	P, n
		A695.3-6	N, Tr, R, S, u
A668.20-28	N, S, P, R, u	A695.7-12	R, K, C, N, Trf
A669.1-2	Tr, R, Ip	A695.12-15	N, R
A669.3-4	Tr, R, N	A697.4-5	Tg, N, U, T
A669.4-6	Ip, R	A699.17-19	R, n, u, N
A669.6-9	R, P, N	A700.22-A701.1	P, n, R
A669.20-A670.3	Tr, R, n, P	A702.8-14	a, K, R, P, Po
A670.16-18	P, R, u, C	A702.14-19	R, P, K, N, u
A670.18-20	R, P, S, u	A707.1-3	C, K, R, S, Tr
A671.6-11	Tr, P, R, S, u	A707.25-A708.2	C, S, R
A671.14-15	P, n, R	A708.7-16	Po, S, P
A674.1-4	P, S, u, N, K	A711.15-24	R, S, C, P, N
A675.7-10	R, P, Tg, n, u, c	A712.14-15	R, a, K, s
A675.10-13	T, n, P, R	A713.10-11	K, R, P
A675.13-14	T, n	A713.11-12	K, R, I
A676.1-5	R, c, u	A713.12-14	a, I, P, M
A676.5-10	R, N, C	A713.14-19	a, I, P, n
A676.17-20	P, n	A713.19-24	a, I, P, U
A677.14-20	R, Tr, S, u, n	A713.24-A714.2	P, a
A678.9-13	S, u, R	A714.7-10	K, a, R
A679.5-10	S, u, P, R	A714.10-14	P, n, T, C, U
A679.17-18	S, u	A714.21-A715.1	P, K, a, I, U
A679.20-23	Tr, n, c	A715.7-9	P, a
A680.4	R	A715.21-A716.4	P, K, a, I, U, C
A680.4-5	R	A717.1-3	P, K, a, I
A680.5-10	R, u, P	A717.18-22	P, K, I, U
A680.10	R, u, S	A718.8-12	T, P, K, s
A680.11-14	S, u, R, K, C	A718.18-24	K, a, I, P, s
A680.14-17	S, u, R, U	A719.2-7	s, Tr, Ip, K
A681.12-13	S, u, R, n	A719.21-25	a, P, I, s, Ip
A681.22-A682.1	Tr, u, n, U	A720.5-6	a, I
A682.1-4	P, R, S	A720.6-10	P, a, I, Ip
A683.26-A684.1	R, S	A720.24-A721.1	P, S, u
A684.21-A685.1	Tg, Tr, a, u, T	A721.6-8	s, P, I
A686.7-13	Tr, R, C, u, P	A722.13-17	P, Tr, s, K, R, u
A686.13-15	R, P	A723.11-15	a, P, s, u, C, I, Po, K
A686.20-21	R, P, u, c		
A686.21-24	R, N, n, P, c	A723.26-A724.4	R, U, a, I
A686.24-A687.4	P, R, S, u	A724.17-23	I, a, P, K, s, R, U
A688.4-5	P	A724.24-A725.3	I, P, R
A691.19-22	N, P	A729.9-13	C, Po, M, P
A693.4-9	P, u, N, Tr, n, c	A729.23-24	Definition
A693.9-13	P, S, u, N, a, c	A729.24-A730.4	a, I, M, P
A694.2-9	P, N, C, Tr, K	A730.8-15	Definition, s
A694.9-12	N, P, c, n	A730.15-17	Definition, s
A694.16-17	C, u	A731.3-7	Definition, s

A815.23-25	u, C, n, P
A815.25-26	u, C
A815.26-A816.4	T, n, Tr, u, R, c
A816.5-6	S, K, N, u
A816.6-7	c, K
A816.7-12	u, N, Tg, a
A716.12-14	c, S, u, P
A816.14-16	c, n, Tg, P, C, N
A816.20	c, P
A816.21-A817.1	N, u, K, Ip
A817.1-2	R, u, N
A817.4-5	u, P, n, N
A817.5-8	u, N
A817.8-11	K, P, P
A817.12-20	R, S, u, P, n
A818.1-5	Tr, R, u, P
A818.5-9	R, u, n, K, T, Ip
A818.19-22	P, n, c
A819.2-6	P, n
A819.6-8	u, P, R
A819.8-11	T, u, P, R, N
A819.14-16	u, S, P, C
A819.20-23	c, P, R
A822.3-A823.5	R, a, K, n, P, C
A823.27-A824.8	n, P, K
A826.7-10	u, R, N
A826.10-13	u, N, c, R, P
A826.22-A827.3	N, n
A828.3-5	c, n, P
A828.5-6	P, n, c
A828.6-9	P, c, C, u, Tg
A828.10-12	u, P, n
A828.12-15	P, R, n
A828.15-17	P, n
A829.10-13	T, Tr, c, n
A829.21	
ftnt a 1-3	R, n
A831.12-15	N
A831.15-19	N, P, U
A832.1-2	S
A832.2-4	S, u, K
A832.4-6	S, K
A832.7-9	R, P, n, P, S
A832.9-10	P, N, R
A832.10-11	S, u, K, P
A832.12-15	P, R, Tr, C, a, S
A832.15-17	P, R, C
A832.17-A833.3	u, P, S, Tr, K, C
A833.4-5	C, S, u
A833.5-10	C, S, u

A833.11-14	P, a
A833.18-21	P, R, a, S, u
A833.21-A834.6	C, P, a, K
A834.6-9	S, u, P, c, C
A834.11-16	K, S, P, R
A834.16-27	N, P, u, Tg, R, S
A834.28-A835.3	P, C, S, R
A835.4-7	S, C
A835.7-9	S, P, R
A835.9-16	S, P, u, K, C
A835.16-19	S, C, K, R
A835.19-21	R, P, D, K
A835.21-23	R, D, K
A835.24-A836.3	R, K
A836.24-A837.3	R, K, a, P
A837.4-6	C, K, R, D
A837.13-26	K, R, a, P, I
A837.26-30	a, K, R
A838.1	C, K, S
A838.2-12	C, S, K, R, P
A838.12-19	R, K, P
A838.20-25	S, K, u
A838.25-A839.6	Tr, K, C, S, P, R
A839.13-15	P, N, R
A839.16-A840.2	P, R, S, u, N
A840.1	
ftnt a 1-5	P, N, K
A840.3-5	P, N, R, S, C, u
A840.5-7	N, P, D, n
A840.7-9	P, c, K
A840.17-21	P, R, N, S
A840.21-22	N, K, n
A840.23-26	K, R, D
A841.1-7	K, R, a, S, u, C
A841.8-14	C, K, a, S, K, D
A841.15-22	D, R, N, P, a, n
A841.22-24	P, a, C
A841.24-A842.6	D, K, R
A842.18-A843.8	R, P, K, D, a
A843.13-A844.7	D, a
A844.7-17	P, K, a, D
A845.1-5	K, a, C, u, S
A845.10-18	K, U, R, S, P, D, N, C, I
A846.1-8	D, K, C, N
A846.9-16	K, C, I, a, D
A846.16-21	K, D, P, a, R
A847.3-7	c, Tr, R, S, n
A847.7-8	D, n
A847.12-A848.7	K, a, N, P

A849.10	P, K	A850.15-18	K, N, n, P
A849.14-23	R, N	A850.18-21	K, R, P
A849.23-A850.7	K, N, n, R, P	A850.22-23	K, C, S, R
A850.8-12	K, N, R	A852.1-7	C, S, Tg, N, R
A850.12-15	K, P	A852.8-12	K, N, Tg

8. Possibility

(See Topics 14.14 and 38.1)

"P" = possibility of

Axxii.8-10	P	Metaphysics
Axvi.20-Axvii.2	P	Understanding
Bxxi.1-9	P	Knowledge of the unconditioned
Bxxv.3-7	P	Concept
B20.14-20	P	Knowledge
B20.21-22	P	Knowledge
B20.22-B21.1	P	Knowledge
A12.22-A13.3	P	System of transcendental knowledge
A24.4-6	P	Appearance
A106.13-19	P	Thinking "Object"
A107.8-11	P	Experience
A107.17-21	P	Unity
A110.9-10	P	Knowledge
A111.11-13	P	Experience
A111.20-23	P	Categories
A113.10-12	P	Self-consciousness
A116.11-12	P	Knowledge
A116.12-16	P	Representation
A117.2 ftnt a 17-25	P	Collective unity of representation
	P	Logical form of all knowledge
A118.3-6	P	Imaginative synthesis
A118.17-20	P	Knowledge
A120.10-14	P	Association
A123.1-6	P	Perception
A123.20-22	P	Representation
A127.11-15	P	Formal Experience
B131.15-B132.4	P	'I think'
B133.4-7	P	Apperception
B133.12-18	P	Apperception
B136.2-8	P	Intuition in relation to understanding
A144.10-12		Schema of P
B143.1-3	P	Unity of intuition
B153.10-13	P	Understanding
A144.12-15		Impossibility
A156.15-16	P	Experience
A157.15-18	P	Experience
B160.6-10	P	Perception

A182.10-A183.1	P	Time-relations
A183.16-20	P	Synthesis of perception
B258.7-9	P	Experience
A218.7-9	P	Possibility
A220.1-3	P	Thing
A220.13-16	P	Objects
A220.16-18	P	Possibility
A220.18-20	P	Objects
A221.1-3		Impossibility
A221.3-6	P	Things
A221.8-11		Impossibility
A221.11-16		Impossibility
A221.16-22		Impossibility
A221.22-A222.5	P	Knowledge
A222.6-13	P	Knowledge
A222.13-19	P	Knowledge
A222.19-A223.2	P	Knowledge
A223.3-6	P	Object
A223.12-14	P	Knowledge, Experience
A223.15-18	P	Knowledge
A223.19-23	P	Object, Knowledge
A223.23-A224.2	P	Object
A224.2-5	P	Object, Experience
A224.5-11	P	Object
A224.12-16	P	Object, Magnitudes
A224.16-19	P	Knowledge
A224.19-23	P	Knowledge
A224.23-24	P	Knowledge
B276.17-B277.3	P	Determining my existence in time
B277.12-14	P	Inner experience
A231.5-8	P	Possibility
A231.8-12	P	Actuality
A231.12-16	P	Possibility
A231.16-18	P	Possibility
A231.18-21	P	Possibility, Actually
A231.21-23	P	Actuality
A231.23-A232.2	P	Experience
A232.2-4	P	Experience
A232.4-6	P	Possibility
A232.6-8	P	Possibility
A232.11-15	P	Absolute Possibility
B290.11-B291.2	P	Events
A237.7-15	P	Experience
A240.13-18	P	Experience
A244.12-14	P	Possibility
A244.14-19	P	Object
B308.13-16	P	Thing
A262.28-A263.1	P	Comparison of Representations
A282.10-15	P	Conflict in reality
A290.4-6		Possibility and Impossibility

A582.9-11	P Object, Knowledge
A582.15-18	P Object, Knowledge
A582.19-A583.4	P Object, Knowledge
A586.16-19	P *ens realissimum* as the necessary being
A587.11-15	P Possibility
A593.23-24	P Predicates
A583.24-26	P Predicates
A593.25-A594.1	P Predicates
A594.1-17	P Predicates
A594.18-22	P Predicates
A594.22-A595.8	P Predicates
A595.8-14	P Predicates
A595.15-18	P Predicates
A595.18-23	P Predicates
A595.24-A596.2	Impossibility
A596.2-3	Impossibility
A596.4-11	P Possibility, P Predicates
A596.12-14	P Possibility, P Predicates
A596.14 ftnt a 1-10	P Possibility
A596.14-A587.6	P Predicates
A597.7-18	P Possibility, P Predicates
A597.18-A598.1	P Predicates
A598.1-7	P Predicates
A598.8-13	P Predicates
A598.13-15	P Predicates
A598.15-18	P Predicates
A598.19-21	P Predicates
A598.21-23	P Predicates
A598.23-25	P Predicates
A598.25-A599.1	P Predicates
A599.1-6	P Predicates
A599.6-10	P Predicates
A599.10-11	P Predicates
A599.11-19	P Predicates
A599.19-21	P Predicates
A599.22-24	P Predicates
A600.1-4	P Predicates
A600.4-7	P Predicates
A600.7-12	P Predicates
A600.12-18	P Predicates, P Knowledge
A600.18-A601.2	P Knowledge, P Experience
A601.2-6	P Perception
A601.6-8	P Possibility
A601.9-11	P Predicates
A601.11-13	P Predicates, P Perception
A601.13-16	P Knowledge
A601.16-23	P Perception, P Predication
A601.24-A602.1	P Knowledge
A602.1-3	P Knowledge
A602.3-5	P Possibility

9. Introspective Description

Abbreviations

L	Limit
Lx	Law
O	Observation
R	Reason
Rep	Representation
S	Self
So	Sources
Sy	Synthesis
TA	Transcendental Analysis
U	Understanding

(See Topics 7, Trf; 26.8; 28.3)

Axvi.20-Axvii.2	TA, U	A97.22-A98.2	So, U
Bxxiii.1-7	TA, R	A99.7-9	Rep
B21.9-13	R, L	A99.10-11	Rep
B23.4-9	TA	A94.14-18	U, Sy
B23.9-14	TA, R, L	A102.1-6	Rep, Sy, U
A11.8-13	O, R, So	A103.15-18	Sy, U
A11.17-A12.2	TA	A103.18-A104.2	Sy
A15.19-22	O, L, So	A107.1-3	O, S
A15.22-23	So	A107.3-6	O, S
A15.23-24	U	A115.3-6	So
B41.5-8	O	A115.9-13	So
A46.26-A47.4	O, So	A118.1-3	Sy
A47.4-6	So, L	A120.1	So
A47.23-25	So, L	A120.1-2	So
A47.25-A48.1	So, L	A126.3-7	U
A55.19-21	So	A129.2-7	U, L, So
A55.21-A56.1	So	B135.17-21	S, O
A56.12-17	TA	B135.21-B136.1	S, O, Sy
A56.19-22	TA	B137.24-B138.1	Sy, O
A57.4-8	So	B138.2-4	S, Sy, O
A57.8-16	L	B138.4-5	S, Sy, O
A62.8-11	L	B154.14-23	Sy, O
A64.6-8	TA, U	B156.20	
A65.13-A66.11	TA, U	ftnt a 1-8	Sy, O
A66.12-17	O	B157.1-5	S, O
A94.14-18	So, L	B158.1	
B128.1-5	So, L	ftnt a 7-11	Sy, O
A97.13-14	Rep	B158.5-9	S, O
A97.16	Sy	B158.15-B159.1	S, Sy, O
A97.18-22	Sy	B159.10-12	So

10. Heuristics, Teleology

Abbreviations

1.

F1	Finality, interests, purposes, motives, as real (See Topic 37, E, M.)
Ne	Needs, demands, seeks
Nr	Necessary to regard as
P	Posit, assume, postulate (See Topic 37, Fa.)
R	Reason
Rp	Principle of reason
Un	Understanding

2.

C	Cause as heuristic
F2	Finality as heuristic
N	Necessity as heuristic
O	Origin as heuristic
U	Ultimate as heuristic
W	Wholes and unities as heuristic

Ax.12-14	F1
Bxviii.9 ftnt a 6-12	F1, R
Bxx.11-24	F1, P
Bxxi.1 ftnt a 3-10	F1, R
Bxxxi.19-Bxxxii.5	F1
Bxxxiii.3-5	F1
Bxxxiii.5-14	F1
Bxxxvii.20-Bxxxviii.3	F1
A3.5-7	F1, R
B7.7-9	F1
B18.11-14	F1
B18.14-19	F1
B21.1-5	F1
B21.6-9	F1
B21.9-13	Ne
B22.1-20	Ne
B23.17-21	F1
B23.21-23	F1
B115.13-15	Kant's theory of hypothesis
B115.16-17	(See A769.17-A782.8)
B115.17-22	
B128.17-20	Nr
B129.2-6	Nr
A122.9-16	Nr
A183.20-22	Nr
A254.19-22	F1
A305.4-8	R, W, Un

A305.11-18	R, W, Un
A305.19-A306.2	R, W, Un, Fl, Ne
A306.5-8	R, W, Un, Fl, U
A307.12-16	R, Fl, W, O, U, C
A307.16-19	R, Fl, W, O, U, C
A307.19-22	R, W, Fl, U, C, Un
A309.1-5	R, W, Fl, Un, C
A309.5-10	R, W, E, Ne
A311.6-12	R, W, U, C
A314.9-12	Ne
A317.8-13	Fl, U
A317.23-A318.1	Fl
A318.16-21	Fl
A323.18-23	R, Fl, W, Un
A327.9-12	R, E
A329.10-15	R, W, Nr
A331.16-20	R, W, Nr
A331.20-21	R, W, Nr
A332.3-6	R, W, Nr
A332.11-14	R, W, Nr
A336.11-14	R, Fl, W
A328.8-13	Nr
B423.1-B424.2	Fl
B425.3-9	R, Fl, W
A425.9-18	R, Fl, W
B425.19-B426.6	Fl, Ne
B426.6-11	Fl, W
A416.12-14	Fl, R, W, Ne, U
A416.14-16	Fl, R, W, Ne, U
A417.24 ftnt a 3-7	W, Nr
A417.24-A418.3	W, Nr
A418.3-9	W, Nr
A463.9-11	Fl, R, U, W
A463.22-A464.2	Fl
A464.14-19	Fl, R
A464.19-21	Fl, R
A465.7-14	Fl, R
A466.11-15	Fl, U
A466.15-21	Fl, W, O, U, C
A466.24-25	R, Fl
A468.1-4	Fl, R
A468.12-15	Fl, R
A470.5-19	Fl, R, Un
A470.19-A471.1	Fl
A471.11-13	Fl, R
A471.14 ftnt a 14-18	Fl, R
A473.24-26	Fl
A475.1-4	Fl, W, R, Ne
A475.5-10	Fl, R
A494.15-18	Fl, R

A497.16-A498.2	F2
A498.2-6	F2
A499.13-16	F2
A508.1-5	F2
A508.5-11	F2
A508.18-A509.4	R, W, F2
A509.10-12	R, W, F2
A509.12-15	R, W, F2
A509.15-19	R, W, F2
A509.24-A510.3	R, W, F2
A510.10-14	R, W, F2
A510.14-16	W, F2, N, C
A514.5-9	W, F2, C
A514.22-A515.2	F2, N
A516.2-9	F2, R, W
A516.10-12	F2, R, W
A519.22-24	F2, Rp
A519.24-A520.3	F2, Rp, W
A520.17-20	F2, Rp, W
A521.13-A522.1	F2, Rp, W
A522.2-5	F2, Rp, W
A522.6-11	F2, Rp, W
A522.11-12	F2, Rp, W
A523.5-9	F2, Rp, W
A527.19-22	E, W
A531.1-5	F1, R, W, Un, C
A531.14-16	F1, R, Un
A533.15-18	R, W, C
A544.23-A545.3	W, F1, Un
A555.9-13	Nr
A555.13-16	Nr
A558.10-12	Nr
A561.11-14	Nr
A561.17-21	Rp
A561.21-23	Rp
A561.23-26	Rp
A564.17-20	R, F1
A565.4-7	F1, W
A568.2-4	F2, W, R
A568.10-16	F1, W, R
A571.3-4	F1, W, R
A571.4-6	R, Nr
A575.14-A576.4	W, R
A577.23-A578.5	R, F1, W
A578.5-9	O, U, E
A578.10-14	W, O
A579.16-25	W, R, O
A580.12-23	W, R
A581.5-6	W, Nr
A581.6-11	R, W, O, Nr

A583.5-7	R, Ne
A583.7-A584.8	R, W, O, Nr
A589.14-19	F1
A590.8-11	U, C, N
A592.1-4	U, N, R, Nr
A592.4-7	W
A577.5-8	Nr
A603.3-7	Ne, R, N
A603.7-12	N, R
A603.12-15	N
A612.10-13	U, C, O, R, N
A614.3-7	Ne, R, N
A614.9-11	Nr
A615.22-A616.1	N, U
A616.1-3	W
A616.4-8	N, Nr
A616.17-19	R, F1
A616.19-22	N, U, C
A616.22-24	F1, W, U, C
A616.24-A617.5	U, C, N
A617.9-16	N, U, W, C, O
A618.1-2	F2
A618.2-6	W
A618.17-21	N, U, O, W
A619.3-6	U
A619.6-9	W, N
A619.9-10	N
A619.18-21	U, C, R, W
A619.21-A620.2	N
A622.3-14	F1
A623.21-22	F1
A623.22-24	W
A625.12-A626.4	F1
A626.5-18	F1
A626.19-26	F1
A626.26-A627.2	F1
A627.2-7	F1
A627.18-A628.13	F1
A629.3-23	F1
A633.22-A634.4	N, C
A644.12-16	N, W
A644.16-19	W
A644.24-A645.4	W
A647.5-11	W, R
A647.12-15	W, R
A647.16-18	R, F1, W
A647.18-21	W
A647.21-24	W
A648.4-6	F1, N
A648.6-9	W, N

A648.9-21	W, Fl, R
A649.24-A650.3	W, R, N
A650.4-9	C, R, W
A650.10-16	W, C
A650.16-21	R, W, N
A650.22-A651.1	R, W, P
A651.1-10	R, Fl, W
A651.10-13	R, Rp, W
A651.13-20	W, R, N
A652.11-22	W, P
A653.13-17	W, P
A653.18-A654.3	Un, Ne, Rp
A654.3-6	P, W, Rp
A654.6-11	P, W, Un, Ne
A654.12-23	R, Fl, Rp, P, W
A654.23-A655.1	Un, Rp
A656.5-15	Un, Rp, Ne
A657.1-8	R, Ne, P, W
A657.8-14	R, Un, P, W
A657.14-20	Un, P, W, Rp
A657.21-A658.3	Rp, Un, P, W
A658.12-18	W
A659.8-17	P, W Rp
A659.17-22	P, W, Rp
A659.22-A660.2	P, W, Rp
A660.3-12	P, W, Rp
A660.13-18	P, W, Rp, Un
A660.18-22	R, Rp, W
A660.22024	P, Rp
A660.24-A661.4	P, Rp
A661.4-10	P, Rp, Fl, W
A661.13-17	R, Rp
A661.17-22	P, Rp, W
A662.11-A663.15	P, Rp, W
A663.16-23	W, R
A663.23-25	Rp
A663.25-A664.2	Rp
A664.9-12	W
A664.12-16	Rp, P, W
A664.18-22	W
A665.18-A666.2	W, R
A666.6-9	R, Fl, W
A666.9-12	R, W, Fl
A666.18-21	R, Fl, W
A667.4-7	R, Fl
A668.20-28	Rp, P, W
A670.5-7	R
A670.8-10	W
A670.10-12	W
A670.12-16	U

A678.15-18	R, U, Un
A678.18-20	W
A679.5-10	W, R
A679.16-18	W, U, C
A679.18-20	
A679.20-23	U, O, C, N
A679.24-A680.2	R, F1
A680.4-5	F1, R
A680.10-14	R, W
A680.14-17	W, R, Un
A680.17-19	W
A680.19-21	C, U, N
A680.21-23	W, R
A680.23-26	W
A681.1-2	R, W
A681.2-5	W
A681.5-12	W, Un, O, C, U
A681.12-13	W, F1, R
A681.22-A682.1	W, R, Un, F1
A682.1-4	W, R
A682.5-6	W
A682.12-19	W
A682.19-A683.2	W, F1
A683.2-7	W
A683.7-11	W
A683.15-17	W
A683.17-20	W, R
A683.26-A684.1	W, R, F1
A684.1-3	P
A684.3-4	W
A684.12-15	W, R
A684.21-A685.1	W
A685.1-3	R, W
A685.3-8	W, C, R
A685.8-11	W
A685.11-15	R, C, Un
A685.17-19	C
A685.19-22	Rp, W, P
A685.25-27	C, W
A686.6-13	W, C, U
A686.13-15	F1, W, R
A686.21-24	F1, R, W, C, U
A686.24-A687.4	W, R, F2
A688.11-17	Rp, F1, F2
A688.18-24	R, W, F2, U, C
A689.1-7	Rp, F2
A689.8-A690.3	Rp, F2
A690.3-9	Rp, F2
A691.1-12	F1, R, F2
A691.12-19	F2, W, U, C

A691.22-24	W, U, C
A691.24-A692.6	W, F1, F2, R
A692.9-12	W
A692.12-15	W
A692.15-16	W
A692.15-16	W
A692.18-24	F1, F2, U
A692.24-A693.3	F2, R, F1, U, W
A693.4-9	F2
A693.9-13	F2, W
A693.20-A694.2	R, C, W, F2
A694.2-9	U, C, F2
A694.12-15	F2, U, W, N
A694.23-25	W, F2, R
A694.25-A695.1	R, W
A695.1-2	W, Nr
A695.2-6	R, U, Nr
A695.20 ftnt a 1-7	W
A696.16-A697.1	P, U, C
A697.1-4	W, F2
A697.4-5	R, W, Nr
A697.5-8	W
A697.8-14	W, U, R, O, F2
A697.14-18	U, O, W, R
A697.19-A698.2	P, U, C
A698.2-6	W, F2
A698.6-10	F2, U, C, R, W
A698.11-12	R, W
A698.19-22	U, O, F1
A698.22-A699.4	F2, U, C
A699.4-11	U, C, F2, W
A699.11-17	U, C, F1, W
A699.19-21	F1
A699.21-A700.1	W, U, C
A700.1-4	W, F2
A700.4-9	U, C, W
A700.10-18	U, C
A700.18-22	W, F2
A700.22-A701.1	R, W, Nr
A701.1-7	U, C
A701.7-9	W
A701.21-A702.3	R, Un, W, F1
A702.14-19	R, F1, W, F2
A734.15-22	M
A735.14-19	F1
A738.1-4	R, W
A743.15-22	R, F1
A744.7-10	F1
A759.15-760.1	U, W
A771.8-15	R, W, Un

A771.15-19	U, W, N
A771.19-24	F2
A772.17-A773.1	F1
A774.8-A775.3	F1
A786.18-22	F1, W, F2
A796.4-5	F1
A795.17-A796.4	F1, R, Ne
A796.4-5	R, F1
A797.6-11	F1, R, W
A799.5-12	F1
A800.4-7	R, W, C
A800.7-11	R, F1, W
A800.11-14	R, F1, W
A800.15-19	F1, R
A800.22-A801.1	F1, R, C
A801.1-5	U, F1, R
A804.19-A805.3	F1, R
A805.25-A806.5	F1
A805.8-12	F1, R
A807.1-11	F1
A809.23-A810.5	W, U, C
A811.5-9	P
A811.16-18	P, R, Nr
A812.21-A813.2	F1
A813.5-8	F1
A814.9-12	F1
A815.3-9	W, C
A815.9-10	F2
A815.18-26	F2, W
A815.26-A816.5	O, W, R, U
A816.5-6	F2, Un
A816.7-14	F1
A816.18-19	F2, Un
A816.20-21	F1, U
A817.12-20	F1
A818.5-9	F1, U, R
A818.9-12	R, F1, U, P, Nr
A818.19-22	P, U, C, W
A819.6-8	R, F1, W
A819.14-16	W, F1
A819.20-23	U, F1, R
A823.23-26	F1
A823.27-A824.8	F1
A826.1-7	Nr
A826.7-10	F1, W, R
A826.10-13	F2, P, Un
A826.13-16	F1, P, U, C
A826.16-21	F1, P
A826.22-A827.3	P
A828.5-6	F1

A828.6-9	F1
A828.10-12	F1
A831.15-19	F1
A832.9-10	F1, R
A832.15-17	F1, W, R
A832.17-A833.3	F1, W
A833.5-10	F1, W
A833.11-14	F1
A833.14-18	F1, U, R
A833.18-21	F2, R, W
A834.6-9	W, O, U, F1
A834.16-27	F1, R
A834.28-A835.3	F1, R
A838.25-A839.6	F1, R, O
A839.13-15	F1
A839.16-A840.2	F1
A840.1 ftnt a 1-5	F1
A840.3-5	F1, U, R, W
A840.5-7	F1
A840.7-9	F1, U
A847.3-7	F1, U, R
A849.23-A850.7	F1
A850.15-18	F1
A850.23-A851.5	F1
A850.5-12	F1
A856.4-19	F1

11. Reflexivity

Abbreviations

I	Illusion, antinomy (See Topic 3.)
K	Knowledge
L	Limits
M	Metaphysics (See Topic 14.19.)
R	Reason
TR	Transcendental Reflection
U	Understanding
W	Whole, system, science, unconditioned

Axi.4-Axii.3	R	Bxxi.1-9	TR, M, L
Axii.5-8	R	B1.1-8	TR, W, K
Axii.13-19	R	B3.12-14	U, K
Axiv.14-17	R	B3.14-16	U, K
Axx.9-12	R	B7.7-9	R, M
Bx.18-Bxi.1	R	B7.9-12	R, M
Bxxiii.1-16	R	A3.15-20	K

A5.18-23	R	B109.17-B110.1	W, U
A6.6-11	R	B110.14-15	U
B22.6-12	R, M, I	A85.11-13	U
B22.12-19	R, M, L	A86.3-4	U
B22.19-21	R, M	A95.19-A96.3	U
B23.4-9	R	A96.21-A97.3	U, W
B23.9-14	R, W, U	A97.3-10	U
A10.19-A11.1	R, TR	A103.15-18	U
A11.1-2	R, M, K	A104.17-A105.2	U, K, W
A11.2-4	R, M, K	A105.3-9	U, W
A11.4-6	R, M, K	A106.6-9	U, W
A11.7-8	R, M, K, W	A106.13-19	U, W
A11.10-13	R, M, W, TR	A106.22-A107.1	U
A11.17-A12.3	R, K, TR	A107.6-8	U
A12.2-3	W, TR	A107.8-11	U, R
A12.8-11	W, TR, U	A107.12-17	U, K, W
A12.11-13	TR, L	A107.17-21	U
A12.22-A13.3	U, R, TR, K	A107.21-24	U, R
B27.3-4	TR, R	A108.1-4	U, K, W
A13.10-12	TR, W, R	A108.22-23	U
A13.12-14	TR, W, R	A109.12-15	U, W
A13.14-15	W, R	A110.6-9	U, R
A13.15-19	W, R, TR	A110.11-15	U, R
A13.19-21	W, R, TR	A110.15-17	U, R
A14.14-15	W, TR, K	A110.17-18	U, R
A14.15-19	W, TR, K	A110.19-20	U, R
A15.9-10	TR, R	A111.1-3	U, R
A24.4-6	TR	A111.23-A112.4	U, W
B40.1-4	U, W, L	A112.6-10	U, R
B40.4-5	U, W, L	A113.15-20	U, R
B40.5-6	U, W, L	A114.15-19	U, R
A53.22-A54.2	TR, R	A115.14-A116.3	U, R
A55.19-21	TR, K	A116.4-9	U, R
A55.21-A56.1	TR, K	A116.16-18	U, R
A56.12-17	TR, K	A116.19-21	U, R
A56.19-22	TR, K	A116.21-A117.2	U, R
A57.1-3	TR, K	A117.2	
A57.8-16	W, K, R, U	ftnt a 10-14	U, R
A59.10-14	U	A117.2	
A62.8-11	TR, U	ftnt a 14-17	U, R
A62.15-19	TR, U, K	A118.1-3	U, R
A63.11-15	TR, U	A118.3-6	U, R
A64.6-8	TR, U	A118.8-11	U, R
A64.17-A65.9	W, K, U	A118.14-17	U, R
A65.13-A66.11	U, TR	A118.17-20	U, R
A67.7-15	TR, U, W	A119.4-8	U, R
A78.22-24	TR, U	A123.8-11	U, R
A79.21-26	W, U	A123.23-A124.2	U, R
A82.24-A83.4	U	A124.7-11	U, R
A83.4-6	U	A124.14-16	U, R

A416.8-11	L, W, R, U	A648.9-21	U, W, R, K
A416.12-14	W, R	A648.22-A649.9	R, W, U
A416.14-16	W, R	A649.9-20	R, W
A416.16-18	W, R	A649.21-24	W
A416.21-25	W, R, U	A649.24-A650.3	R, W
A416.26-A417.3	W, R, U	A650.4-9	U, R, W
A417.3-7	W, R, U	A650.10-16	R, W
A417.7-14	W, R, U	A650.16-21	R, W
A417.24		A650.22-A651.1	W, R
ftnt a 3-7	W, R	A651.1-10	R, W
A421.1-6	TR, I	A651.10-13	R, W, K, L
A421.15-20	TR, R	A651.13-20	R, W, U
A421.21-A422.3	R, I	A653.13-17	R, W
A422.3-9	R, I	A669.1-4	R, I
A422.10-12	R, I	A669.4-6	R, I
A422.12-13	R, U	A678.6-7	R
A422.13-15	R, W	A680.4	R
A425.16-18	R, TR	A682.12-19	R, W, U
A462.6-10	W, R	A683.2-7	R, W
A463.9-11	W, R	A694.23-25	R, W
A464.14-19	R	A694.25-A695.1	R
A464.19-21	R	A695.1-2	R, W
A464.21-24	TR	A695.2-3	R, W
A474.8-12	R, W, K	A695.12-15	R, W
A475.1-4	R, W	A701.21-A702.3	R, W, U
A476.7-12	W, K	A702.14-19	R, W, U
A476.14-A477.1	W, K	A703.17-20	TR
A477.15-18	W. L	A707.1-3	R, K, W
A477.18-21	W, K	A707.25-A708.2	TR, R, W
A480.5-8	TR	A710.8-11	R, TR, L, I
A515.14-A516.2	R, W, K	A711.6-14	R, TR, L, I
A530.20-A531.1+		A711.15-24	R, TR, L, I
A531.1-5	R, W, U	A727.5-6	R, TR, L, K
A551.14-16	R, W	A737.13-17	K, L
A572.3-8	W	A738.1-4	R, W
A573.15-16	R	A738.11-12	R, TR
A573.17-18	R, U, W	A751.9-14	R, TR, I
A473.19-A574.2	W, L, R	A751.17-22	R, TR, W
A574.2-3	W, L, R	A758.9-13	R, TR, L
A576.16-17	L, R	A758.13-15	R, TR, L
A577.23-A578.5	R, W, L	A758.19-21	R, L, TR, W
A614.11-15	R, W	A761.5-10	R, L, TR, W, K
A617.9-11	W	A761.10-16	R, L, TR, W, K
A620.6-8	R, L	A762.1-7	R, W, K, L
A642.10-12	R, L	A763.7-11	R
A642.16-19	R, I	A768.16-20	R, TR, W, L, K
A645.13-15+		A777.18-20	R, I
A645.15-18	R, W, K	A777.25-A778.1	R, I
A645.18-21	W, K, U	A795.17-A796.4	R, K
A647.16-18	R, W, U	A796.10-12	W, K

Section III

Object

12. Object Texts: Digest

Abbreviations

=	Is the same as (e.g., O = E)
−	Not (e.g., − O of E = T)
A	Appearance
E	Experience
I	Intuition
K	Knowledge
L	Limit
O	Object
refl	reflexive
R	Representation
T	Thing in itself
transc	transcendental

Note

Capital letters have sometimes been used to indicate a useful distinction of philosophical sense rather than the usual grammatical division.

Axvi.16-20	Essential purpose of the *Critique*: to refer to Os of pure understanding; to establish objective validity of *a priori* concepts.
Bix.7-12	Logic abstracts from all Os of K.
Bix.12-14	Reason deals with itself and O.
Bix.21-Bx.1	Two ways K relates to Os.
Bx.2-6	Reason determines its O *a priori*.
Bx.11-15	Math and physics determine their Os.
Bxvi.12-14	O conforms to K.
Bxvi.14-17	*A priori* K of O.
Bxvii.7-15	Since Is, if they were to be known, must relate as Rs to something as O which they determine, I must assume either that the concepts involved in this determination

conform to the O or that the Os (or what is the same thing, the E in which alone the Os as given can be known) conform to the concepts.

Bxvii.17-21
E is a kind of K which involves understanding. Understanding has rules which are prior to Os being given and so *a priori*.

Bxvii.21-Bxviii.2
O must conform to *a priori* concepts.

Bxviii.2-9
O of reason cannot be given in E.

Bxviii.9
ftnt a 3-6
O of reason cannot be tested in E.

6-12
A priori concepts and principles are used for viewing Os from two different points of view: as Os of the senses and understanding; as Os of mere thought for the isolated reason.

Bxix.1-6
A priori laws of nature as sum of Os.

Bxx.11-24
O as A conforms to mode of R.

Bxxiii.1-7
Reason measures itself by the way it chooses Os.

Bxxiii.7-9
All *a priori* K of O derives from the subject.

Bxxiii.16-Bxxiv.1
Metaphysics deals with Os.

Bxxv.19-Bxxvi.5
O as sensibly intuited vs. O as in itself.

Bxxvi.7-12
O as in itself can be thought.

Bxxvi.11 ftnt a 1-3
To know O, must be able to prove its possibility.

Bxxvii.2-12
Thing as O of E and as in itself.

Bxxvii.14-Bxxviii.4
O in twofold sense: A/T

Bxl.1 ftnt a 14-67
Os affecting our senses produce Rs.

A2.11-20
O appears to senses.

A2.21-A3.4
Certain modes of K leave the field of all posssible E and have the A of extending the scope of our judgments beyond the limits of E.

A11.17-A12.2
Transcendental K is occupied with the mode of our K of Os insofar as it is *a priori*.

A15.22-23
O given thru sense.

A15.23-24
O is thought.

A15.24-A16.1
O is given thru sense.

A16.1-4
O is given thru sense.

A19.1-10
K relates to O immediately thru I. Intuit O only when given. O is given only insofar as mind is affected; sensibility = receptivity of R thru mind affected by O.

A19.11-14
I is only way O can be given.

A19.15-16
Sensation = effect of O on faculty of R.

A20.1-3
I relates to O thru sensation.

A20.3-4
A = undetermined O of empirical I.

A22.12-14
Thru outer sense, O is represented as outside us.

B41.15-20
I = O affects subject.

A26.2-5
Receptivity = capacity to be affected by O.

A26.22-25
Subjective condition of outer intuition is the liability to be affected by Os.

A27.2-6
Os can by intuited as outside us.

A27.15-23
T viewed as O of sensible I.

A27.23-A28.5	Reality of space in regard to whatever can be presented to us outwardly as O.
A30.2-9	Outer O = R.
A34.17-A35.3	A = O; – O as A = O as T.
A35.17-19	Objective validity of time.
A37.18-22	Time is not in O; only in subject.
A38.14-21	A has two sides: (1) O in itself; (2) form of I is taken into account.
A39.5-9	O viewed as A vs. O as T.
A43.8-11	Os in themselves cannot be known.
A44.4-8	R of body in I contains nothing of O as T.
A44.18-25	R of O = O plus mode of being affected.
A45.13-16	O = A.
A46.10-11	Transcendental O is unknown.
A48.5-6	O is given *a priori*.
A48.7-15	Without a power of *a priori* I whose form is the universal *a priori* condition of the possibility of the O of outer I, and if the O (the triangle) is something in itself apart from any relation to the S, it could not be said that the necessary subjective conditions for the construction of a triangle necessarily belong to the triange itself.
A48.15-19	If the O is given antecedently to K, and not by means of it, the new element of figure could not be added to the concept of three lines as something that must necessarily be met in the O.
B66.20-B67.6	All Os of sense = A.
B67.6011	R contains only relation of O to subject.
B69.6-12	Outer and inner Is represent Os in A, the O plus its properties are viewed as given.
B69.12-15	In relation of O to subject, properties are modes of I. O as A vs. O as T.
B72.6-8	Mode of I depends on existence of O therefore, possible only if faculty of R is affected.
A50.5-6	O is given.
A50.12-13	Sensation involves the actual presence of O.
A51.9-11	I contains only the mode of being affected by O.
A51.11-13	Understanding is the faculty which enables us to think the O of sensible I.
A51.15-16	Without sensibility, O cannot be given, and without understanding it cannot be thought.
A51.17-21	It is just as necessary to make our concepts sensible by adding an O to them in I as it is to make out I intelligible by bringing them under concepts.
A55.19-21	Transc logic studies origin of modes of knowing, which cannot be attributed to O.
A56.19-22	Transc logic studies *a priori* Rs which relate to Os.
A57.1-3	"Transcendental" pertains only to critique.

A58.8-16	Reason and understanding think O *a priori*. Trans logic concerns the *a priori* relation of laws of reason and understanding to Os.
A58.15-19	Truth = agree with O.
A62.15-19	Transc analytic deals with elements necessary to think Os.
A68.13-15	No R except I is in immediate relation to O.
A77.4-9	Mind receives Rs of O.
A78.24-A79.1	The requirement for *a priori* knowledge of all Os is that the manifold of pure I be given first.
A79.21-26	Concepts apply *a priori* to Os of I in general.
A80.7-9	It is only by means of the original concepts of synthesis which the understanding contains within itself *a priori* that it can understand anything in the manifold of I, that it, think of O of I.
A85.8-11	The problem to which the deduction is responding is how concepts marked out for pure *a priori* employment in complete independence of all E can relate to Os which are not obtained from E.
A85.11-13	Concepts relate *a priori* to O.
A85.18-22	Both the concepts of space and time as forms of sensibility and the categories as concepts of the understanding relate to Os completely *a priori*.
A85.22-A86.3	They relate to Os without borrowing from E anything that can serve in the R of these Os.
A87.25-A88.1	Os (in regard to form) are given thru their being known, *a priori* in I.
A88.5-8	The pure concepts of understanding relate to Os universally apart from all conditions of sensibility through predicates of pure *a priori* throught.
A88.8-11	K, O, L
A89.10-11	Os appear only thru space and time.
A89.16-18	The categories of understanding do not represent the conditions under which Os are given in I.
A89.18-20	It is not necessary that Os be related to the function of understanding in order to appear to us.
A89.20-21	It is not necessary that understanding contain the *a priori* conditions of Os in order for them to appear.
A89.21-A90.1	The difficulty: how can the subjective conditions of thought have objective validity, that is, how can they be the conditions for the possibility of all K of Os.
A90.1-3	A can certainly be given independently of functions of understanding.
A90.9-12	It is *a priori* doubtful whether a concept such as cause may not be altogether empty and without Os anywhere in A.
A90.12-15	Os of sensible I must conform to the formal conditions of sensibility which lie *a priori* in the mind in order to be Os for us.

A90.15-18	It is not obvious that Os must likewise conform to the conditions which the understanding requires for the synthetic unity of thought.
A90.18-20	As might be so constituted that the understanding should not find them to be in accordance with the conditions of its unity.
A90.25-A91.2	I stands in no need whatsoever of the functions of thought.
A92.5-8	There are only two possible ways in which synthetic Rs and their Os can establish a necessary relation to one another.
A92.8-10	Either the O alone must make the R possible or the R alone must make the O possible.
A92.10-13	Thru sensation, O makes R possible.
A92.13-16	R in itself does not produce the existence of its O.
A92.16-18	The R is *a priori* determinant of the O if it is the case that only through the R is it possible to know anything as an O.
A92.19-A93.2	There are only two conditions of the possibility of the K of an O. The first is I thru which the O is given as A; the second is concept thru which an O is thought corresponding to this I.
A93.2-5	It is evident that the first condition, namely, that under which alone Os can be intuited, actually lies *a priori* in the mind as the formal ground of the Os.
A93.7-10	The question: do *a priori* concepts serve as antecedent conditions under which alone anything can be thought as an O in general.
A93.10-13	If so, then all empirical K of Os would necessarily conform to such concepts because it is only by presupposing them that anything becomes a possible O of E.
A93.13-16	All E contains, in addition to the I of the senses thru which something is given, a concept of an O as being given or as appearing.
A93.16-18	Concepts of Os in general underlie all empirical K as its *a priori* conditions.
A93.18-21	The objective validity of the categories as *a priori* concepts rests on the fact that, as far as form of thought is concerned, they alone make E possible.
A93.21-23	The categories relate necessarily and *a priori* to Os of E because it is only by their means that any O of E can be thought.
A94.5-7	Concepts which provide the objective ground of the possibility of E are for that reason necessary.
A94.10-13	The relation of the categories to any one O is due to their original relation to the possibility of E in which all Os of K are found.
B127.9-20	Hume saw that only concepts with an *a priori* origin could provide knowledge which transcends the limit of E. He was, however, unable to explain how it might be

possible for the understanding to think concepts which are not themselves connected in the understanding as being necessarily connected in the O. It had not occurred to him that the understanding itself thru these concepts might be the author of the E in which its Os are found.

B128.17-20   The categories are concepts of an O in general by means of which the O is regarded as determined in respect of one of the logical functions of judgment.

A98.8-10   Is in general, thru which Os can be given to us, constitute the whole field and O of possible E.

A96.19-21   The elements of all modes of *a priori* K must always contain the pure *a priori* conditions of a possible E and of an empirical O if something is to be thought thru them.

A96.21-A97.3   The concepts which contain *a priori* the pure thought involved in every experience, we find in the categories. By these means alone an O can be thought.

A97.3-10   The understanding as the faculty of thought is a faculty of K that is meant to relate to Os.

A104.6-7   The expression 'an O of R' requires clarification.

A104.7-11   As are only sensible Rs which, as such and in themselves, are not Os capable of existing outside the power of representation.

A104.11-16   The O corresponding to and distinct from K is thought only as "something in general = x".

A104.17-A105.2   The thought "relation of K to its O" contains an element of necessity. O is viewed as determining K. Unity constitutes the concept of O.

A105.3-9   The x (O) which corresponds to R is nothing to us.
x must be distinct from R.
The unity which O makes necessary is the formal unity of consciousness in the synthesis of Rs.

A105.20-22   R of "O = x" is the concept of this unity.

A106.13-19   Must be a transc ground of necessary unity of O without which it would be impossible to think O.

A106.19-21   O = x, the concept of which expresses necessity of synthesis.

A107.12-17   The R of Os is possible only by relation to transc apperception which is that unity of consciousness that precedes all data of Is and which makes possible all modes of K and the unification of modes of K with one another.

A108.7-14   Rules of synthesis make As necessarily reproducible and thereby determine an O for them, i.e., the concept of x in which they are necessarily interconnected.

A108.22-23   All Rs have their O; R can be O of R.

A108.23-A109.1   As are sole Os which can be immediately given.

A109.1-3   I is that in A which relates immediately to O.

A109.3-7	A = R, and R has O which cannot be intuited. This O = "object = x" (transc).
A109.8-11	Concept of transc "object = x", which is one and the same in all our K, gives all empirical concepts in general relation to O.
A109.12-15	This concept cannot contain a determinate I, therefore it refers only to the unity of a manifold in relation to O.
A109.15-18	This relation is only the necessary unity of consciousness and of the synthesis of a manifold into one R.
A109.18-A110.6	This unity must be *a priori* necessary or K would be without O. The objective reality of empirical K = relation to transc "object = x". This relation rests on the transc law that all As as giving O are subject to rules of synthesis.
A111.507	All relation of K to Os involves connection in accordance with universal and necessary laws.
A111.16-18	Categories are the fundamental concepts by which we think Os in general for As and have therefore *a priori* objective validity.
A112.13-13	Without the universal and necessary unity of consciousness, perceptions would not belong to any E and so would be without an O.
A114.19-24	Synthetic propositions asserting the universal unity of nature cannot be derived from the Os of nature themselves since this could take place only empirically and none but a merely accidental unity could be obtained.
A118.17-20	All Os of possible E must be represented *a priori* since the transcendental unity of the synthesis of imagination is the pure form of all possible K and is ultimately grounded in the unity of apperception which underlies the possibility of all K.
A121.18-23	If this unity of association did not have an objective ground which makes it impossible for As to be apprehended by the imagination in any way other than under the condition of a possible synthetic unity of apprehension, it would be merely accidental that As fit into a connected whole of human K.
A122.9-16	There must be an objective ground (one that can be comprehended *a priori* antecedently to all the laws of the imagination) upon which rests the possibility and necessity of a law that extends to all As. This ground constrains us to regard all As as data of the senses that must be associable in themselves and subject to a thorough-going connection in their reproduction.
A122.17-25	This objective ground of all association of As is their *affinity*. It is found in the principle of the unity of apperception in regard to all K that is to belong to me. According to this principle, all As must so enter

the mind or be apprehended that they conform to the unity of apperception. Such synthetic unity is objectively necessary because without it synthetic unity in thier connection would be impossible.

A123.1-6   The objective unity of all empirical consciousness is one consciousness (original apperception) is the necessary condition of all possible perception and the affinity of all As is a necessary consequence of a synthesis in imagination which is grounded *a priori* on rules.

A123.11-19   The affinity of As, and with it their association, and through this their reproduction according to laws, and so E itself is possible only by means of the transcendental funciton of imagination. Without tis transcendental function no concepts of Os would make up a unitary E.

A125.19-A126.2   Subjective conditions in nature of our mind are objectively valid conditions for K of O in E.

A126.21-A127.5   Nature is O of E grounded in unity of apperception.

A127.16-20   O = E.

A128.16-18   – O of E = T

A129.7-10   *A priori* concepts prior to K of O.

A129.11-18   Since a mere modification of our sensibility can never be met with outside ourselves, the Os as As constitute an O which is merely in us. This means that there must be a complete unity of As and all Os as As in one apperception.

A129.18-21   Unity of consciousness = form of K of O. Through it, manifold is thought as one O.

A129.21-A130.1   Mode of manifold in consciousness prior to K of O.
    I.e., categories = formal *a priori* K of O.

B134.13-16   Combination does not lie in Os and cannot be gotten from them.

B137.7-10   K = given Rs in determinate relation to O. O = that in whose concepts manifold of I is united.

B137.11-15   Unity of consciousness = relation of R to O.

B138.4-5   Thru unity of consciousness O is first known.

B138.6-7   Sunthetic unity of consciousness is objective condition of K.

B138.7-10   Synthetic unity of consciousness is a condition under which every I must stand in order to become an O for me.

B139.12-14   Transc unity of apperception unifies manifold in concept of O.

B142.22-26   To say 'The body is heavy' is not merely to state that the two Rs have always been joined in my perception, however often that perception be repeated; rather it is to assert that they are combined in the O, no matter what the state of the subject may be.

B144.4 ftnt a 1-5	O is given thru represented unity of intuition which includes systhesis, and therefore relation of manifold to apperception.
B146.14-B147.1	K = thought of O in general as related to Os of sense.
B147.19-B148.2	Categories given K only as related to Os of possible E.
B148.3-7	The preceding limits categories to Os.
A145.7-8	Schema of magnitude = generation (synthesis) of time itself in the successive apprehension of O.
A145.13-15	Schema of modality = is time itself as the correlate of the determination whether and how an O belongs to time.
A146.1-5	Schemata are the sole conditions under which concepts obtain relation to Os.
A146.18-20	Schema = phenomenon or sensible concept of O in agreement with the category.
A147.7-13	Pure concepts have no O and no meaning other than logical.
A148.17-A149.4	Principles lie at the foundation of all K of O.
A150.6-11	Self-contradiction nullifies a judgment even without reference to O.
A150.11-16	Concepts can be connected in a way not substantiated by O.
A155.20-23	If K is to relate to O, O must be given.
A156.1-5	"O is given" (i.e., immediate presentation) = R thru which O is thought relates to E actual or possible.
A156.5-6	Meaning of space and time depends on their relation to O.
B148.7-12	Space and time are the sole conditions for Os being given.
B148.15-B149.2	No K of O beyond sense is possible.
B149.11-16	K of possibility of O beyond sense is impossible.
B150.1-4	Categories relate to Os of I in general.
B150.10-20	Understanding can determine inner sense thru the manifold of given Rs in accord with the synthetic unity of apperception. And thereby think synthetic unity of apperception in the manifold of *a priori* sensible I, Which is the condition under which all Os of human I must stand necessarily.
B151.1-3	O = As (of which alone we have I).
B151.18-19	Imagination = faculty of representing in I an O that is *not itself present*.
B156.14-20	We know O only as we are affected.
B158.9-15	K of O distinct from me involves thought of O in general plus intuition.
B156.10-12	R of space and time mere schema of reproductive imagination that assembles Os of E.
B156.12-14	Apart from Os of E, Rs of space and time are meaningless.
A156.16-23	E rests on synthesis according to O of A in general.

A157.4-7   Synthetic *a priori* principles are impossible without O
                     in which synthetic unity can exhibit the objective real-
                     ity of its concepts.
A157.19-A158.1   Truth = agreement with O.
                     Truth = E contains only what is necessary to the syn-
                     thetic unity of E in general.
A158.2-5   Highest principle of all synthetic judgments = all Os
                     are subject to the necessary conditions of the synthetic
                     unity of manifold in a possible E.
A158.10-13   The conditions of the possibility of E in general =
                     conditions of the possibility of Os of E.
A158.14-A159.2   Every O that can be given must conform to the laws of
                     understanding.
B203.2-10   R of O first becomes possible thru the consciousness
                     of the synthetic unity of the homogeneous manifold
                     in I in general which is the concept of a magnitude
                     (*quantum*).
A165.24-A166.3   All K of O depends on synthesis of spaces and times.
A166.3-6   Whatever pure math establishes as valid in regard to
                     synthesis of the form of apprehension is necessarily
                     valid for the Os apprehended.
B207.10-11   The real = O of sensation.
B207.13-16   As = Os of perception.
B207.16-B208.1   Real of sensation as related to O in general = matter
                     for some O in general whereby something existing in
                     space and time is represented.
B208.14-18   Intensity of sensation = degree of influence by O.
B218.15-16   E = empirical K which determines O thru perception.
B218.9-B219.2   Synthetic unity = essential in K of O, i.e., in E as dis-
                     tinct from mere I or sensation.
B219.9-12   E = K of O thru perception. Therefore, the relation
                     involved in the existence of the manifold must be rep-
                     resented not as it is constructed in time, but as it is in
                     time objectively.
B219.12-16   Determination of the E of Os in time is possible only
                     thru their relation to time in general.
A175.23-A176.2   The real = synthesis in empirical consciousness in gen-
                     eral.
A180.8-9   O = A.
B225.4-6   O = A.
                     O of perception must contain the substrate which rep-
                     resents time in general.
A182.4-7   Thru mere apprehension, cannot tell whether the
                     manifold, as O of E, is coexisted or in sequence.
A183.22-23   In all As, the permanent = O itself = substance as phe-
                     nomenon.
B234.14-19   O = A.
B189.15-17   Every R can be an O.

A189.17-A190.3	What does "O" mean in respect to As when they are viewed not as Os (Rs), but as standing for (bezeichnen) O?
A190.3-7	As, as Os of consciousness (Rs) = their apprehension.
A190.9-12	If As were Ts, we could not determine from the succession of Rs how the manifold is connected in the O.
A190.24-A191.2	Transc meaning of concepts of O = the house is A, R, whose transc O is unknown.
A191.5-8	Content of successive apprehension is viewed as R. A which is given (although merely the sum of Rs) is viewed as O.
A191.8-10	Concept derived from Rs of apprehension must agree with this O.
A191.10-17	A (as distinct from Rs of apprehension) can be represented as an O distinct from them only if it (A) stands under a rule which distinguishes it from every other apprehension and necessitates one particular mode of connecting the manifold.
A191.17-19	O = that in a which contains the condition of this necessary rule of apprehension.
A193.13-17	Objective succession = order of manifold of A according to a rule such that the apprehension of what happens follows upon the apprehension of what precedes.
A194.13-22	Without this rule, Rs would not relate to Os.
A194.22-A195.3	Without this rule, sequence is not objectively necessary.
A195.3-5	Without this rule, sequence is not K of O.
A195.8-12	Without this rule, cannot say that O follows (something that precedes).
A195.12-17	The rule renders the subjective synthesis of apprehension objective.
A196.18-A197.1	Without the necessitating rule, we cannot ascribe succession (i.e., the happening of an event which previously did not exist) to O.
A197.1-2	The rule makes possible R of succession in O.
A197.3-10	Rs are always mere determinations of our mind in time, so why do we posit an O for them?
A197.10-16	Objective meaning cannot consist in the relation of R to R.
A197.16-20	"Relation to O" = subjecting R to necessary ordering rule.
A197.20-23	Objective meaning requires Rs stand in a necessary time-order.
A198.1-4	No O is represented thru the mere succession of Rs in the synthesis of apprehension.
A198.4-8	Thru perception or assumption of rule-controlled succession, O is represented.
A198.8-11	I.e., I apprehend an O to which I give a necessary position in time.

A198.11-16	R of an even tcontains the consciousness that something preceded the event otherwise the event could not have a time-relation.
A197.17-20	Understanding is required for the possibility of R of O.
A200.2-4	Absolute time is not an O of perception.
A200.16-20	E as actual = I regard the A as determined in its time-position, i.e., as an O rule-connected to perception.
A200.20-A201.1	The rule determining the time-position of an event is found in what precedes the event.
A201.1-4	The principle of sufficient reason is the ground of objective K of As in respect of their time-order.
A201.13-16	But in the synthesis of apprehension, the order is determined in the O, i.e., is an order of successive synthesis which determines O.
A202.2-9	The relation according to which the existence of an event is necessarily determined by something preceding in time is the condition of the objective validity of empirical judgments.
A202.10-13	Causal relation in the sequence of As is valid for all Os as under the conditions of succession being itself the ground of the possibility of such E.
A210.22-A211.7	Just as time contains the sensible *a priori* conditions of the possibility of a continuous advance of the existing to what follows, The understanding thru the unity of apperception and thru the series of causes and effects is the *a priori* condition of the possibility of a continuous determination of all positions for the As in this time. And thereby renders empirical K of the time-relations valid universally for all time, and therefore objectively valid.
B257.6-7	Coexistent = perceptions of an O can follow each other reciprocally.
B257.12-15	Synthesis of imagination in apprehension cannot reveal Os as coexistent.
B257.18-23	To say that reciprocal sequence of perceptions is objective (i.e., grounded in O), we need the pure concept of the reciprocal sequence of their determinations.
A212.1-7	Interaction is the condition for coexistence as possible O of E.
A213.2-4	In regard to O, everything is necessary without which the E of O is not possible.
A213.12-14	Only continuous influences in all parts of space can lead our senses from O to O.
A213.23-A214.5	Without community, there could be no unity of perception of As in space, no connection of the chain of empirical Rs, and no unity of Rs in time.

A214.11-16	If Os are to be represented as coexisting in mutual connection, they must mutually determine their position in one time.
A214.16-23	If the subjective community is to rest on an objective ground, the perceptions of As must make one another mutually possible. And the succession found in the perceptions as apprehensions must not be ascribed to the Os.
A215.17-20	Absolute time is not an O of perception.
A217.8-12	All Os of experience must be capable of being given.
A219.1-3	Categories of modality, in determing O, do not enlarge the concepts to which they are attached as predicates.
A219.8-12	The question: how is O plus its predicates related to understanding.
A220.5-11	A concept which contains a synthesis, but does not belong to E, is without relation to O.
A220.13-16	Possibility of O (which is thought thru synthetic *a priori* concepts) derives from the synthesis which constitutes the form of the empirical K of O.
A220.18-20	It is necessary logical condition that a concept of the possible not contain a contradiction. But this is not sufficient to determine the objective reality of the concept.
A221.1-3	The conditions of space and its determination contain *a priori* the form of E in general, and so have objective reality, i.e., apply to possible things.
A221.22-A222.5	The objective reality of concepts = they express *a priori* the relations of perceptions in every E in relation to the form of an E in general and to the synthetic unity in which alone Os can be empirically known. this is transc truth.
A223.19-23	We can give the concept of a triangle an O thru construction *a priori*.
A223.23-A224.2	But this would be the mere form of an O whose possibility would remain doubtful.
A224.12-16	The possibility of the concepts of both continuous magnitudes and magnitudes in general is clear only when they are viewed as formal conditions of the determination of O in E in general.
A224.16-19	Os given only thru E.
A224.19-23	We can know *a priori* the possibility of things by reference to the formal conditions under which anything in E is determined as O.
A225.1-4	The postulate in regard to *Actuality* does not require an immediate perception of O whose existence is to be known.
A225.4-8	But the O must be connected with some actual perception in accordance with the analogies of E in general.

B275.11-13	The empirically determined consciousness of my existence proves the existence of Os is space outside me. (See Topic 34.)
B277.11-12	Outer O necessary to determine the subject.
B278.20-23	Perceptions are possible only thru the reality of outer Os.
A226.23-A227.1	The existence of the Os of sense cannot be known completely *a priori*.
A233.19-23	The principles of modality do not enlarge the concept of R of Os (i.e., they are nto objectively synthetic).
A234.4-6	An O is possible if it stands in connection with the formal conditions of E.
A234.6-9	An O is actual if it stands in connection with perception.
A234.9-10	An O is necessary if it is determined thru the connection of perceptions according to concepts.
A234.13-17	"Postulate" in math = synthesis thru which we give ourselves an O.
A288.1-4	The possibility of a pure concept of understanding requires an I to exhibit its objective reality.
B288.15-18	Without I, we do not know whether categories have an O suited to them.
B289.16-20	The principle of causality can be proven only in regard to Os of possible E.
B289.20-23	The principle of causality is a principle only of the K of an O given in empirical I.
B291.7-11	To demonstrate the *objective reality* of the categories we need *outer Is*.
B292.17-21	The objective reality of the category of *community* is determined only thru outer I in space.
B293.18-22	The objective reality of *quanity* is exhibited only in outer I.
A237.7-15	The rules of understanding contain in themselves the ground of the possibility of E viewed as the sum of all K in which Os can be given to us.
A238.21-A239.1	As = Os of possible E.
A239.3-6	In every concept we require both the logical form of a concept in general and the possibility of giving it an O to which it can be applied.
A239.6-9	Without a given O, concepts have no meaning.
A239.9-11	Os can be given only in I.
A239.11-14	Pure I can precede the O *a priori*, and even this I can acquire its O (and so objective validity) only thru the empirical I of which it is the mere form.
A239.14-19	All concepts and principles have objective validity thru relation to empirical I.
A239.23-A240.3	All principles and Rs of Os have their meaning thru relation to empirical I.
A239.23-A240.3	All principles and Rs of Os have their meaning thru As, i.e., empirical Os.

A240.3-7	Concepts have sense, meaning, only thru presentation of an O in I.
A240.15-18	Even concepts in math derive their objective validity from E.
A240.19-A241.	Categories and principles cannot be defined in a real way, i.e., make the possibility of their O understandable, except thru reference to the conditions of sensibility, and so to the form of As, which are their only Os.
A241.1-5	Without this condition, there is no meaning, i.e., relation to O.
A241.19 ftnt a 1-5	Real definition = the clear property by which the defined O can always be known.
A241.19 ftnt a 5-8	Real explanation = the clarification of both the concept and its objective reality. Math presents Os in I.
A241.19-A242.9	Without the conditions of sensibility, concepts have no determinate O, and so no significance.
A243.7-15	The concept of cause without the sensible condition of time (in which something follows upon something else according to a rule) leaves in the pure category a mere something from which we conclude to the existence of something else. In which case we could not distinguish cause and effect nor could we even know how to apply the concept of any O.
A244.4-7	I can remove in thought every existing substance without contradiction, but this is not equivalent to the objective possibility of their non-existence.
A244.7-12	The pure categories of substance, cause, and community yield no explanation that determines the O.
A244.22-A245.1	The categories have a determinant meaning and relation to O only thru the conditions of sensibility.
A245.4-7	Sensible conditions are the only ways Os come under concepts.
A245.10-15	Without schemata, i.e., conditions of sensibility in general, the categories are not concepts thru which Os are known. They are mere modes for thinking Os for possible I in conformity with some function of understanding.
A246.6-10	Categories, apart from the conditions of sensibility, have no relation to Os, cannot define any O, and have no objective validity.
A246.11-17	Categories and principles apply only to Os of sense under the universal conditions of possible E.
A246.21-A247.1	Only As can be an O of E.
A247.7-8	Thought is the act which relates a given I to an O.
A247.8-11	Without the mode of I given , the O is transcendental.
A247.11-14	No O is determined thru a pure category.
A247.14-15	The pure category expresses the mere thought of O in general.

A247.16-19	The employment of a concept involves a function of judgment whereby an O is subsumed under the concept, and so involves at least the formal condition under which something can be given in I.
A248.14-18	Without sensibility, categories cannot be applied to an O.
A248.18-22	Categories are the pure form of the employment of understanding in regard to Os in general. Thru them alone, no Os can be determined.
A248.23-A249.1	Phenomena = As thought as Os according to unity of the categories.
A249.1-6	Noumenon = Os which ccan be given only thry intellectual I.
A249.7-19	The concept of As (as limited by the Transcendental Aesthetic) of itself establishes the objective reality of noumena, and justifies the division of Os into phenomena and noumena and of the world into that of the senses and that of understanding. And this distinciton refers not only to the differences between the ways the two worlds can be given but also to the way in which they are generally different from one another.
A279.19-22	If the senses represent something merely as it appears, this something miust also be a T, and an O of non-sensible I.
A249.22-24	A kind of K must be possible in which there is no sensibility and which alone has reality that is absolutely objective.
A249.24-A250.1	Thru this K, Os will be represented as they are.
A250.15-16	All Rs are referred by understanding to some O.
A250.16-18	Appearances = Rs, and understanding refers them to an x as their O.
A250.18-22	This x = transc O = "something = x" of which we can know nothing.
A250.22-24	This x is a correlate of the unity of apperception and serves only for the unity of the manifold of sensible I.
A250.24-25	By this unity, the understanding combines the manifold into the concept of an O.
A250.25-A251.1	This transc O cannot be separated from the sensible data since nothing would be left thru which it could be thought.
A251.1-5	So, it is not itself an O of K, but merely the R of As under the concept of O in general (aa concept which is determined thru the manifold of these As).
A251.6-11	Therefore, the categories do not represent an O given to understanding alone, but serve only to determine the transc O (which is the concept of something in general) thru that which is given in sensibility, in order to know As empirically under concepts of O.

A252.12-15	In order for noumenon to signify a true O, distinguishable form all phenomena, it is not enough that I free my thought from the conditions of sensible I.
A252.15-17	I must also have ground for assuming a kind of non-sensible I in which an O can be given.
A252.18-A253.3	Cannot prove or disprove the possibility of non-sensible I (but only that it is so for us).
	It is therefore an open question whether the notion of a noumenon be not a mere form of a concept and whether when abstraction is made from all sensibility any O whatever is left.
A253.4-6	The O to which appearance in general is related = transc O = completely undeterminate thought of *something* in general.
A253.6-7	The transc O cannot be entitled the *noumenon*.
A253.7-10	The transc O cannot be known in itself. It is conceived of merely as the O of sensible I in general and therefore is one and the same for all As.
A253.10-12	It cannot be thought thru any category since the category is valid only for bringing empirical I under the concept of O in general.
A253.14-16	The pure use of the category has no objective validity. It is valid only when applied to an I to give it the unity of an O.
B305.18-22	Illusion: Since the categories do not originate in sensibility, they seem to allow of application beyond sensible Os.
B306.3-7	An O is given thru the forms of sensibility.
B306.7-11	If Os are called "As", we distinguish the way we intuit them from their nature as in themselves.
B306.22-B307.2	When the understanding entitles an O in a certain relation mere phenomenon, it forms apart from that relation an R of an O in itself, and represents itself as also being able to form concepts of such Os.
B307.2-5	Since understanding has no concepts in addition to the categories, it supposes that the O in itself can be thought thru the categories.
B307.11-14	"Noumenon" in the negative sense = a T so far as it is not an O of sensible I.
B307.14-18	"Noumenon" in the positive sense = a T so far as it is an O of non-sensible I.
B308.16-20	To apply the categories to Os not viewed as appearances requires that we postulate a non-sensible I.
B308.20-24	The categories can be applied only to Os of E.
A253.19-20	If all thought (through categories) is removed from empirical K, no K of O remains.
A253.21-23	The affection of sensibility of R to O.
A253.23-A254.3	Apart from I, the form of thought remains, i.e., the mode of determining an O for the manifold of a possible I.

A254.3-6	The categories extend further than sensible I since they think Os in general without regard to the special mode in which they are given.
A254.7-10	The assumption that these Os can be given involves the assumption of the possibility of another kind of I (which we cannot validly make).
A254.15-18	The concept of a noumenon. i.e., of a thing which is not to be thought as an O of the senses but as a T, solely thru pure understanding, is not in any way contradictory.
A254.19-22	The concept of a *noumenon* is necessary to keep sensible I from being extended to T, and so to limit the objective validity of sensible knowledge.
A255.6-12	We have no concept of a possible I thru which Os outside the field of sensibility could be given.
A255.18-20	The division of Os into phenomena and noumena, and the world into a world of the senses and a world of the understanding, is inadmissible in the positive sense.
A255.22-24	No Os can be determined for intellectual concepts and so they are not objectively valid.
A255.24-A256.5	The categories require the unity of thought plus a possible I for their relation to O.
A256.8-11	Noumenon (in the negative sense) is not a special O, i.e., an intelligible O.
A256.11-14	We cannot represent the possibility of an understanding which could know its O in a non-sensible I (rather than discursively thru categories).
A257.15-22	The question: do understanding and reason have a special employment in regard to noumena, i.e., is the O which is thought as intelligible given to the understanding alone.
A257.22-27	Or: does the understanding have a transc employment which has noumena for its O. The answer is no.
A258.1-9	"Sense represents Os as they apppear and understanding as they are = O must be represented as an O of E" i.e. as appearance in complete intercconnection, and not as apart from a relation to possible E (as an O of pure understanding).
A.258.9-11	Os of pure understanding cannot be known by us.
A258.15-16	Only understanding in conjunction with sensibility can determine Os.
A258.16-19	Concepts and I in separation provide Rs which cannot be applied to determinate Os.
A259.21-23	The concept of pure intelligible Os lacks the principles for the possiblity of its application.
A259.23-25	We cannot think how an intelligible O could be given.
A259.25-A260.3	The problematic thought (noumenon) which leaves open a placce for them serves only, like an empty space, for the limiting of empirical principle, without

itself containing or revealing any other O of K beyond the sphere of those principles.

A260.4-5	*Reflection* is not concerned with Os themselves with a view to deriving concepts from them direactly.
A262.28-A263.1	Trans reflection concerns the Os themselves, and therefore contains the ground of the possibility of the objective comparison of Rs with each other.
A263.12-A264.3	The difference of spatial positions is sufficient ground for the numerical difference of Os of the senses.
A265.15-19	We are acquainted with substance in space only thru active forces attracting or repelling Os.
A265.21-A266.3	Substance, as O of pure understanding must have inner determinations and powers which pertain to its inner reality (which must be either thinking or like it).
A267.17-20	In sensible I, all Os are determined merely as As.
A269.6-10	Concepts of comparison (unlike categories) do not present the O acccording to what constitutes its concept (quantity, reality), But only serve to describe in its manifoldness the comparison of the Rs which is prior to the concept of things.
A269.19-23	To advance to Os thru concepts, we must use transc reflection to determine for which cognitive faculty they are to be Os.
A277.13-17	Matter is not among the Os of pure understanding. The transc O which may be the ground of matter as A = a mere x which we cannot understand.
A278.14-22	Sensibility can never be used to investigate the relation of sensibility to O.
A278.26-A279.6	Appearances are not included as Ts among Os of pure understanding. As = only Os of K.
A279.13-18	The general application of concepts to an O in general (in the transc sense) without determining whether it is an O of the senses or of intellectual Is reveals limitations in the notion of the O which forbid a non-empirical employment of the concepts.
A279.18-21	The R of an O as a thing in general, when taken without sensible determination and independently of any empirical condition, is self-contradictory.
A279.21-24	Therefore, we either abstract from O (as in logic) or we must think it under the conditions of sensible I.
A280.1-2	As cannot be Os in themselves.
A285.3-7	We are given a determinate O thru the self-subsistent permanent relations in matter.
A285.8-11	If I abstract from these relations there is nothing more left for me to think. This fact, however, does not rule out the concept of a thing as A nor the concept of an O in *abstracto*.

A289.14-24	This error is due to the fact that apperception, and with it thought, precedes all possible determinate ordering of representations.
	Consequently, we think something in general, And we both determine it in sensible fashion and distinguish from this mode of I it the universal O represented *in abstracto*.
	We then try to determine this O by thought alone,
	Which is a mere logical form without content, But which seems to be a mode in which the O exists in itself (noumenon) without regard to our senses.
A290.15-18	To the concepts of all, many, and one there is opposed the concept which cancels everything, i.e., *none*.
	So, the O of a concept to which no assignable I corresponds is nothing.
A290.18-21	I.e., it is a concept without an O (*ens rationis*), like noumena, which cannot be counted among the possibilities nor declared to be impossible.
A297.6-10	The fundamental rules and maxims of reason have the look of objectivity.
A298.1-4	Reason suffers from a natural illusion which presents its subjective principles as objective.
A302.16-21	Reason is not directly applied to Os.
A307.23-A308.4	The logical maxim (to find the unconditioned whereby the conditioned K obtained thru understanding can be brought to completion) can only become a principle of pure reason thru the assumption that if the conditioned is given, the whole series of conditions, subordinated to one another (a series which is therefore itself unconditioned) is likewise given, i.e., is contained in the O and its connection.
A338.12-15	There is no concept for the O of the transcendental ideas, even though such ideas are a necessary product of reason according to its own original laws.
A338.15-A339.3	In respect of any O that would be adequate to the demands of reason, it is impossible to form a concept of the understanding that allows of being exhibited and intuited in a possible E.
A339.3-7	Only problematic concepts of such Os are possible.
A339.8-14	Due to an inevitable illusion, we ascribe objective reality to the ideas of reason.
A341.17-A342.3	The 'I think', thru the nature of our faculty of Rs, enables us to distinguish two kinds of Os.
A342.3-4	'I', as thinking, am an O of inner sense (and am called 'soul').
A342.4-5	The O of outer sense is called 'body'.
A346.10-14	Consciousness is not an R distinguishing a particular O, But a form of R in general, i.e., of R insofar as it is K.

A347.5-6	Thinking beings as Os are nothing more than the transference of my consciousness to other things.
A348.18-A349	By themselves, the categories have no objective meaning.
A350.4-6	The 'I' is in all thoughts, but in this R there is no I by which it is distinguished from other Os of I.
A353.23-A354.1	In order to represent a thinking being, I must substitute my own subject for this O.
A354.17-19	We may not transform the 'I think' into a condition of the possibility of K of Os, i.e., into a concept of thinking of being in general.
A357.13-17	Since the thinking subject is represented as an O of inner sense, it cannot (as thinking) be an O of outer sense, i.e., an A in space.
A358.4-7	Thoughts, feelings, desires, and resolutions can never be Os of outer sense.
A358.7-12	The something which underlies As and affects our sense so that it obtain Rs of space, matter, shape, etc., may yet, when viewed as noumenon (or better, as transc O), be at the same time the subject of our thoughts.
A358.15-19	Extension and impenetrability concern only sensibility and its I insofar as we are affected by unknown Os.
A360.24-A361.4	Soul = transc O of inner sense.
A361.18-A362.4	K thru E of the numerical identity of an external O requires that one attend to that permanent element in the A to which as subject everything else is related as determination, and note its identity throughout the times in which the determinations change.
A362.4-5	I am an O of inner sense.
A362.18-21	If I view myself from the standpoint of another person (as an O of his outer I), it is this outer observer who first represents me in time,
	For in the apperception, time is represented as in me.
A362.21-A363.3	Though the 'I' accompanies with complete identity all Rs at all times, I may not conclude to the objective permanence of myself.
A366.6-9	T = transc O, and is represented as something external, and its permanence as appearance can be observed.
A370.8-10	Matter = is a species of Rs (I), which are called external, not as standing in relation to Os in themselves external, but because they relate perceptions to the space in which all things are external to one another, while space itself is in us.
A370.22-24	External Os = appearances = Rs.
A370.24-25	The Os of these Rs exists only thru their Rs.
A371.6-9	We do not need inference to establish the reality of either outer Os or the O of inner sense (i.e., my thoughts).

A371.9-12	In both cases the Os = Rs.
A372.8-13	If outer appearances as Rs are produced in us by their Os, and if these Os = Ts, then the existence of their Os can be known only thru inference.
A372.15-19	That x outside us (in the transc sense) which is the cause of outer Is, = O which we think in the R of matter.
A372.22-A373.1	The transc O is not known.
A373.1-4	The empirical O, if represented in space = external O. The empirical O, if represented only in time-relation = inner O.
A373.9-15	Empirically external Os = things which are in space.
A373.16-19	Space and time are *a priori* Rs which are forms of sensible I prior to any real O which by determining our sense thru sensation enables us to represent the O under those sensible relations.
A374.3-5	Perception = a given sensation as referred to an O in general, although not as determining that O.
A374.5-7	We can picture in imagination many Os which have no empirical place in space to time outside the imagination..
A374.8-11	Perception is that whereby the material needed to enable us to think Os of sensible I must first be given.
A375.10-12	The real = the material of all Os of outer Is is given in space independently of imaginative invention.
A375.15-A376.6	No O outside us (in the transc sense) corresponds to perception. Such as could not be intuited and represented as outside us since such R and I presuppose space, and reality in space = reality of R = the perception itself.
A376.19-A377.4	Space = mere form of Rs, and has objective reality in relation to outer A, which are themselves merely Rs.
A378.8-13	Outer Os of perception are not Ts. They are merely Rs of which we can become immediately conscious.
A378.16-19	Outer Os as Ts could not be known as real since we depend on Rs which are in us.
A379.19-22	The 'I' as represented thru inner sense in time and Os in space outside me are specifically distinct A. But they are not necessarily different things.
A379.23-A380.5	The transc O which underlies outer As = matter. The transc O which underlies inner I = thinking being. In both cases, the transc O = the unknown ground of As.
A381.13-17	Time, which has nothing abiding, yields K only of change of determinations, not of any O that can be determined.
A381.19-20	R of 'I' has no manifold.
A381.20-A382.2	Therefore it seems to represent to denote a simple O.
A382.6-8	'I' is not a concept of O.

A382.8-12	'I' = mere form of consciousness which can accompany the two kinds of R and which can make them into K of something is given in I which can be used as material for R of O.
A393.10-13	We treat As as Os in themselves and we are not concerned with their transc ground.
A393.13-15	Such a concern would require the concept of a transc O.
A394.10-12	It may be possible that unknown Os may be known after death, although not as bodies.
A396.14-15	Illusion = treating the subjective conditions of thinking as K of O.
A397.13-18	In thinking in general, we abstract from all relation of the thought to any O (whether of the senses or of pure understanding), the synthesis of a thought in general, it is not objective, but merely the synthesis of the thought with the subject, which is mistaken for a synthetic R of O.
A398.3-6	'I' = logical unity of thought in which one abstracts from all Os.
A398.8-9	But it is represented as an O which I think, i.e., I myself and its unconditioned unity.
A400.4-8	If I know something as simple in concept only and not in the field of A, I have no K of O,
	But only of the concept which I make for myself of a something in general that cannot be intuited.
A400.12-17	The apperception 'I' is in concept substance, simple, etc.
	But these predicates are not supported by I and, therefore, have no consequences that are valid for Os of E.
A402.6-8	We cannot know as O that which is required in order to know any O.
A402.8-11	The determining self (the thought) is distinguished from the determined self (the thinking subject) in the same way K is distinguished from its O.
B406.26-29	I think = I know an O.
	I know an O only in so far as I determine a given I with respect to the unity of consciousness in which all thought consists.
B406.32-B407.1	Modes of self-consciousness in thought = concepts of Os (categories).
B407.2-4	But are mere functions which do not give thought an O to be known.
	And so do not give even myself as O.
B407.4-8	The O is not the consciousness of the determining self, but only that of the determinable self, i.e., of my inner I so far as its manifold can be combined according to the universal condition of the unity of apperception in thought.

B407.10-15	The 'I' that thinks must be regarded as subject and cannot belong to thought as a mere predicate,
	But this does not mean that I as O am a self-subsistent being or substance.
B408.16-18	The identity of the subject (logical unity of meaning and function of R 'I'—see: B407.20-24) of which I am conscious in all my Rs does not concern an I of the subject given as O.
B409.12-14	Analysis of consciousness of myself in thought in general gives no K of me as O.
B409.14-16	Logical exposition of thought in general has been mistaken for a metaphysical determination of the O.
B411.11 ftnt a 1-4	'Thought' can be taken in two senses: (1) as relating to O in general, and so to an O as it may be given in I; (2) as it consists in relation to self-consciousness.
B411.11 ftnt a 4-5	In (2), no O is being thought.
B411.11 ftnt a 8-11	In (2), we mean 'thought' (abstracting from all Os) in which 'I' serves as the subject of consciousness.
B415.2-4	The permanence of the soul as the O of inner sense, cannot be demonstrated.
B415.4-6	Its permanence during life is per se evident since the thinking being (as man) is also an O of outer sense.
B421.21-B422.1	The unity of consciousness, which underlies the categories, can be mistaken for an I of the subject as O, and the category of substance is then applied to it.
B422.1-2	But this unity is only the unity in thought by which no O is given.
B422.5-7	The subject of the categories merely by thinking the categories cannot have a concept of itself as an O of the categories.
B422.14 ftnt a 11-13	The 'I think' precedes the E which is required to determine the O of perception thru the category in respect of time.
B422.14 ftnt a 14-15	The category of existence does not apply to an indeterminately given O.
B428.10-14	The proposition 'I think' or 'I exist thinking' is an empirical proposition that is conditioned by empirical I,
	And so is conditioned by the O (the self which is thought).
B429.5-6	I think myself as I do any O in general from whose mode of intuition I abstract.
B430.4-9	If the thinking self is to go beyond merely distinguishing itself as O in itself thru the 'I' and also determine the mode of its existence, i.e., know itself noumenon,
	It would need an empirical I of itself as the condition of the employment of its logical functions as categories of substance, cause, etc.
B430.9-13	But this is impossible since inner empirical I is sensible and yields only data of A,

	Which furnish nothing to the O of pure consciousness for the K of its separate existence, but can serve only for E.
A414.8-15	"Substantial" = concept of O in general.
A 437.34-37	An absolutely simple O can never be given in any possible experience.
A468.20-24	Os must be represented in I.
A468.24-A469.3	Os of Reason = mere thought-entities.
A478.6-9	Os of Reason = mere thought-entities.
A479.1 ftnt a 6-11	The transc subject of all inner A is not itself A and so is not given as O.
A480.21-23	Natural As are Os which are given to us independently of our concepts and the key to them lies not in us and our pure thinking, but outside us.
A481.22-25	Os of Reason = mere thought-entities.
A482.2-4	Os of Reason = mere thought-entities.
A482.5-7	Os of Reason = mere thought-entities.
A484.8-13	Os of Reason = mere thought-entities.
A489.15-18	Os of Reason = mere thought-entities.
A489.18-21	Os of Reason = mere thought-entities.
A490.16-A491.3	All Os of E = As = Rs
A491.19-21	Transc idealism admits the reality of the Os of outer I (as intuited in space) and of all changes in time (as represented by inner sense).
A491.21-A492.3	Without Os in space there would be no empirical Rs whatsoever.
A492.3-6	As = Ts.
	As = Rs.
A492.6-11	The inner sensible I of our mind (as O of consciousness) which is represented as being determined by the succession of different states in time is not the proper self as it exists in itself, i.e., is not the transc subject.
A492.19-20	The Os of E are never given in themselves, but only in E, and have no existence outside it.
A494.8-10	Os = Rs connected in space and time according to the laws of the unity of experience.
A494.10-12	The non-sensible cause of these Rs cannot be known and so cannot be intuited as O.
A494.12-15	Such as O would have to be represented as in neither space nor time.
A494.15-17	Transc O = the purely intelligible cause of As in general.
A494.19-20	To this transc O, we can ascribe the whole extent of possible perceptions.
A494.20-21	We can say that its is given in itself prior to all E.
A494.21-23	As conform to it, but are not given in themselves.
	They are given only in E since they are mere Rs.
A494.23-A495.3	Which as perceptions mark out a real O only in so far as the perception (the representation) connects with all others according to the rules of the unity of E.

A495.3-4	Real things in past time are given in the transc O of E.
A495.4-12	But they are Os for me and real in past time only in so far as I represent to myself that a regressive series of possible perceptions in accord with empirical laws, i.e., the course of the world, leads us to a past time-series as the condition of present time,
	A series which, however, can be represented as actual not in itself but only in the connection of a possible E.
A495.21-A496.1	Os = Rs, and are given only in a possible E.
A496.8-11	Os = As.
A496.17-21	As = Os only in so far as they (the As) belong to the series of the empirical regress.
A500.9-14	It is natural to view As as Ts and as Os given to pure understanding and to abstract from the conditions under which Os can be given.
A508.13-17	As = empirical Rs (and not Os in themselves).
A514.1-3	The series of conditions in the regress cannot be regarded as being given as infinite in the O.
A538.1-2	'Intelligible' = whatever in an O of the senses is not A.
A538.2-6	If a thing in the sensible world which must be regarded as A has in itself a faculty which is not an O of sensible I, but thru which it can be the cause of As,
	Its causality can be regarded from two points of view.
A538.12-15	This twofold manner of conceiving the faculty possessed by an O of the senses does not contradict any of the concepts which we have to form of As and of a possible E.
A538.15-17	Since As are not Ts, they must rest on a transc O which determines them as mere Rs.
A538.17-A539.4	This transc, O has both the quality in terms of which it appears and a causality which is not A, but whose effects are As.
A540.7-12	The intelligible character of the subject of this causality can never be immediately known.
	It would have to be thought in accordance with the empirical character
	Just as we are constrained to think a transc O as underlying As.
	Though we cannot know what it is in itself.
A546.23-A547.2	Man is to himself both phenomenon and, in regard to certain faculties whose acts cannot belong to sense, a purely intelligible O.
A547.2-8	Reason views its Os exclusively in the light of ideas (and thereby is distinguishable from all empirical conditioned powers) And in accordance with them determines the understanding which then makes empirical use of its own pure concepts.
A557.9-11	The transc O of outer sensible I gives I in space only.
A563.9-10	Ts are never Os to us.
A565.18-23	The transc ideas have a purely intelligible O.

A582.11-14	Due to a natural illusion we regard this principle, which applies only to those things which are given as Os of our senses, as being valid for things in general.
A583.4 ftnt a 1-4	The ideal of the *ens realissinum*, although it is a mere R, is first realized, i.e., made into an A, then hypostatised, and finally, by the natural progress of reason towards the completion of unity, is personified.
A589.7-12	Concepts which although objectively insufficient, if connected with valid obligations, should be accepted.
A592.1-4	The objective reality of the idea of an absolutely necessary being is not proved from the fact that reason needs it.
A592.4-7	This idea instructs us about an unattainable completeness and so serves to limit the understanding and does not extend it to new Os.
A613.21-A614.1	The trans O lying at the basis of As (and with it the reason why our sensibility is subject to certain supreme conditions rather than others) is for us inscrutable.
A614.2-3	The thing itself is given, but we can have no insight into its nature.
A614.7-9	The ideal of pure reason is not given as a thinkable O.
A615.22-A616.1	While I may be obliged to assume something necessary as a condition of the existent in general, I cannot think any particular thing as in itself necessary.
A616.1-3	I cannot complete the regress to the conditions of existence except by assuming a necessary being, Yet I am never able to begin with such a being.
A616.4-8	If I am constrained to think something necessary as a condition of existing things, but am unable to think any particular thing as in itself necessary, It follows that necessity and contingency do not concern the things themselves, Otherwise there would be a contradiction.
A616.8-9	Consequently, neither of these two principles is objective.
A619.10-13	We cannot avoid the trans subreption by which the formal principle (of a systematic and necessary unity based on the ideal of the supreme being) is represented as constitutive and by which this unity is hypostatised.
A619.13-18	It is the same in the case of space. Space is only a principle of our sensibility, But since it is the primary source and condition of all shapes (which are only limitations on itself) It is taken as something absolutely necessary, existing in its own right, and as an O given *a priori* in itself.
A619.21-A620.2	It is natural that the idea of an *ens realissimum* as the supreme case should be reprensented in its character of supreme condition as an actual O.

A620.2-9	We are unable to conceive what can be meant by the absolute necessity of the supreme being as a thing in and by itself
	Since the concept of necessity is only to be found in our reason, as a formal condition of thought,
	And it does not allow of being hypostatised as a material condition of existence.
A621.23-A622.2	All synthesis and extension of our K refer only to possibile E, and therefore only to Os of the sensible world.
A639.19-21	K of the existence of the O consists in the fact that the O is posited in itself beyond the mere thought of it.
A643.16-18	Reason is never in immediate relation to O.
A643.19-22	Reason does not create concepts of O but merely orders them.
A644.1-2	Reason has understanding and its effective application as its only O.
A644.2-7	As understanding unifies the manifold in the O thru concepts, reason unifies the manifold of concepts thru ideas.
A644.21-23	There is an illusion that the lines of concepts to an idea end in a real O outside the field of empirically possible K.
A645.21-24	Ideas are not concepts of Os.
A648.9-21	To say that the constitution of Os or the nature of the understanding which knows them as such is in itself determined to systematic unity
	And that we can postulate this unity *a priori* without reference to any special interest of reason,
	And that we are therefore in a position to maintain that K of the understanding in all of its possible modes (including empirical K) has the unity required by reason and stands under common principles from which its various modes can be deduced—
	That would be to assert a trans principle of reason
	And would make the systematic unity necessary not only subjectively and logically, as method, but also objectively.
A650.22-A651.1	The logical principle by which reason prescribes the unity of rules presupposes a trans principle according to which such a systematic unity is *a priori* assumed to be necessarily inherent in the O.
A663.16-23	These principles (of systematic unity) seem to be transc
	And although they contain mere ideas for the guidance of reason in its empirical employment (ideas which reason follows only asymptotically)
	they yet possess, as synthetic *a priori* propositions, objective but indeterminate validity, and serve as rules for possible E.

A664.9-12	Principles of pure reason can never be constitutive since they can never have an O *in concreto.*
A664.17-18	Understanding is an O for reason just as sensibility is an O for understanding.
A665.12-18	The idea of reason is an analogn of a schema of sensibility.
	But the application of the concepts of the understanding to the schema does not yeald K of the O in itself (as in the case of the application of the categories to their sensible schemata),
	But only a rule or principle for the systematic unity of all employment of the understanding.
A665.18-A666.2	Every principle which prescribes *a priori* to the understanding thoroughgoing unity in its employment holds indirectly of the O of E.
	So the principles of pure reason have objective reality in regard to that O. Not in order to determine anything in it, but only to indicate the procedure whereby the empirical and determinate employment of the understanding can be brought into complete harmony with itself.
A666.6-9	All subjective principles which are derived not from the constitution of an O but from the interest of reason in regard to a possible perfect of the K of th O are called maxims or reason.
A666.9-12	There are maxims of speculative reason, which rest completely in its speculative interest, although they seem to be objective principles.
A666.13-15	When merely regulative principles are treated as constitutive and employed as objective, they may conflict with one another.
A669.20-A670.3	If the ideas of reason are to have even the least objective validity (no matter how indeterminate) and are not to be mere empty thought-entities.
	A deduction of them must be possible, however great its difference from that given of the categories.
A670.5-7	There is a difference between something being given to reason as an O *absolutely* and merely as an O *in the idea.*
A670.7-8	In the first case, concepts are used to determine the O.
A670.8-10	In the second case, there is only a schema for which no O (even hypothetical one) is directly given.
A670.10-12	The second enables us to represent other Os in an indirect manner, i.e., in their systematic unity thru their relation to this idea.
A670.12-16	The concept of a highest intelligence is a mere idea, i.e., its objective reality does not consist in its referring directly to an O.

A670.16-20   This concept is only a schema constructed in accor-
                  dance with the conditions of the greates possible unity
                  of reason,
                  The schema of the concept of a thing in general
                  Which serves only to secure the greatest possible sys-
                  tematic unity in the empirical employment of reason.

A670.20-23   We then, as it were, derive the O of E from the sup-
                  posed O of this idea,
                  Viewed as the ground or cause of the O of E.

A671.3-6   The idea of pure reason does ot show us how an O is
                  constituted, but how we should seek the constitution
                  and connections of Os.

A671.6-11   The three transc ideas do not directly relate to, or
                  determine, any O corresponding to them.
                  Nevertheless, as rules of the empirical employemnt of
                  reason, they lead us to systematic unity, under the pre-
                  supposition of such an O *in the idea.*

A671.11-15   And since they thus contribute to the extension of
                  empirical K, without being able to run counter to it,
                  We may conclude that it is a necessary maxim of rea-
                  son to proceed always in accordance with such ideas.

A671.15-24   This is the transc deduction of all ideas of speculative
                  reason, not as constitutive principles of the extension
                  of K to more Os that E can give,
                  But as regulative principles of the systematic unity of
                  the manifold of empirical K in general.

A672.23-A673.4   The greatest possible extension of reason is secured by
                  viewing all Os *as if* they derived their origin from a self-
                  subsistent, original, creative reason (the archetype).

A673.13-16   Except for the cosmological ideas, we may assume they
                  are objective without the assumption resulting in an
                  autonomy.

A673.23-A674.1   We are not justified in introducing thought-entities
                  which transcend all our concepts (though without con-
                  tradicting them) as being real and determinate Os
                  merely on the authority of an interest of speculative
                  reason.

A674.4-5   They should be regarded only as analoga of real
                  things, not as in themselves real things.

A674.5-9   We remove from the O of the idea the conditions
                  which limit the concept provided by understanding,
                  But which alone make it possible to have a determi-
                  nate concept of anything.

A674.14-16   If we assume such ideal beings, we do not extend our
                  K beyond the Os of possible E.

A674.16-19   We extend only the empirical unity of such E thru the
                  systematic unity for which the schema is provided by
                  the idea.
                  The idea is, therefore, merely a regulative principle
                  (not a constitutive principle).

A674.19-23	To posit a real being corresponding to the idea is not to extend our K by transc concepts.
A674.23-24	This being is posited only in the idea and not in itself.
A674.24-A675.2	And therefore only as expressing the systematic unity which is to serve for the empirical employment of reason.
A675.2-4	It decides nothing in regard to the ghround of this unity or the inner character of the being on which this unity depends.
A675.7-10	Speculative reason does not determine the objective validity of the God-concept, But yields only the idea of something which is the ground of the highest and necessary unity of all empirical reality.
A675.10-13	We must think this something on the analogy of a real substance that, in conformity with the laws of reason, is the cause of all things.
A675.13-14	This is how we must think it if we think it as a special O.
A675.14-18	And do not remain satisfied with the mere idea of the regulative principle of reason and, Leave aside the completion of all conditions of thought as too much for human understanding.
A675.18-21	But this would be inconsistent with the pursuit of that complete systematic unity in K to which reason sets no limits.
A676.22-A677.2	When I think a being that corresponds to a transc idea, I may not assume any such thing as existing in itself Since no concepts thru which I am able to think any O as determined are adequate for such a purpose. The conditions which are required for the objective validity of my concepts are excluded by the idea itself.
A677.3-7	The concepts of reality, substance, causality, and even that of necessity in existence have no meaning that could be used for the determination of any O apart from their use in making possible the empirical K of an O.
A677.7-9	Concepts can be used to explain the possibility of things in the world of sense, but not explain the possibility of the universe itself.
A677.9-11	Such a ground of explanation would have to be outside the world, and could not therefore be an O of possible E.
A677.11-14	Though I cannot assume the existence of such an inconceivable being in itself, I may assume it as the O of a mere idea, relative to the world of sense.
A677.21-22	We are constrained to realize the idea of systematically complete unity, i.e., posit for it a real O.
A677.22-24	This O must be posited, but not as known in itself.

A678.3-6   By analogy with realities in the world, i.e., with sub-
                stances, causality, and necessity, I think a being which
                possesses all this in the highest perfection.

A678.6-7   Since the idea depends only on my reason, I can thing
                this being as *self-subsistent reason.*

A678.8-9   Which thru ideas of the greatest harmony and unity is
                the cause of the universe.

A678.9-13   I thus omit all conditions which might limit the idea,
                Merely in order to make possible systematic unity of
                the manifold in the universe and so the greatest possi-
                ble empirical employment of reason.

A678.13-15   I do this by representing all connections as if they
                were ordinances of a supreme reason,
                Of shich our reason is only a faint copy.

A678.22-24   I cannot know the O os such an idea as to what it is in
                itself.

A679.11-15   We cannot presuppose the reality in itself (in terms of
                the concepts of reality, substance, causality, etc.) of the
                transc O of our idea.

A680.5-10   Pure reason is occupied with nothing but itself.
                What is given to it is not Os that have been brought ot
                the unity of the empirical concept,
                But those modes of K supplied by the understanding.

A680.10-14   The unity of reason is the unity of system. This sys-
                tematic unity does not serve objectively as a principle
                that extends the application of reason to Os,
                But subjectively as maxim that extends its application
                to all possible empirical K of Os.

A680.14-19   Since the systematic connection which reason can give
                to the empirical employment of the understanding not
                only furthers its extension, but also guarantees its cor-
                rectness,
                The principle of such systematic unity is to that extent
                objective,
                But only in an indeterminate way.

A680.19-21   This is not a constitutive principle that enables us to
                determine anything in regard to its direct O.

A680.21-23   But merely a regulative principle and maxim to further
                and strengthen *in infinitum* (indeterminately) the
                empirical employment of reason.

A681.1-2   Reason cannot think this systematic unity except by
                giving to the idea of this unity an O.

A6814.2-5   And since E cannot give an example of complete sys-
                tematic unity,
                The O which we assign to the idea can never be sup-
                plied by E.

A681.5-8   This O is a mere idea (*ens rationis ratiocinatae*).
                It is not assumed to be somehting that is real abso-
                lutely and in itself.

A681.8-12	It is postulated only problematically so that we may view all connection of the htings of the world of sense as if they had their ground in such a being.
A682.5-6	The first O os such an idea (i.e., the idea of systematic unity) is the 'I' itself, viewed as thinking nature or soul.
A684.6-10	In the use of the psychological idea (which signifies merely the schema of a regulative concept) I abstract from nature in general, i.e., from all predicates of any possible experience And therefore from all conditions for thinking an O for such a concept.
A684.10-11	It is only in relation to an O that the concept can have a meaning.
A684.12-15	When reason is itself regarded as the determining cause, as in the case of freedom, i.e., in the case of practical principles, we must proceed as if we had before us an O of the pure understanding (not of the senses).
A685.27-A686.2	We have no ground to assume in an absolute manner (i.e., to suppose in itself) the O of the God-idea.
A686.20-21	The highest formal unity, which rest only on the concepts of reason, is the purposive unity of things.
A686.21-24	The speculative interest of reason makes it necessary to view all order in the owrld as if it had originated in the purpose of a supreme reason.
A686.24-A687.4	Such a principle, as applied in the field of experience, makes available to reason new views as to how the world may be connected according to teleological laws, and thereby make possible their greatest systematic unity.
A693.4-9	The most complete purposiveness must be presupposed *a priori* in nature, i.e., as belonging to its essence, Since we could not otherwise be required to search for it And so through all its gradations to approximate to the supreme perfection of an Author of all things, A perfection that, as absolutely necessary, must be knowable *a priori*.
A693.9-13	The regulative principle prescribes that systematic unity as a *unity in nature*, Which is not known merely empirically But is presupposed *a priori* (in an indeterminate manner) Be presupposed absolutely, and consequently as following from the essence of things.
A696.13-17	If I begin with a supreme purposive being as the ground of all things, the unity of nature is surrendered as being foreign and accidental to the nature of things

And as not capable of being known from its own universal laws.

A694.2-9   The investigation of nature keeps to the claim of natural causes in conformity with their natural laws.

It proceeds in accordance with the idea of an Author of the universe,

But not in order to deduce from it the purposiveness for which it is looking

But in order to obtain K of the existence of such an Author from the purposiveness.

A694.9-12   By looking for this purposiveness in the essence of the things of nature and, as far as possible, in the essence of things in general,

It seeks to know the existence of the supreme being as absolutely necessary.

A694.16-17   Complete purposive unity constitutes what is, in the absolute sense, perfection.

A694.17-23   If this unity is not found in the essence of the things which constitute the whole O of experience, i.e., of all objective K,

And therefore is not found in the universal and necessary laws of nature,

How can we infer directly from this unity the idea of a supreme and absolutely necessary perfection of an original being as the source of all causality?

A694.23-25   The greatest possible systematic unity (and, therefore, purposive unity)

Is the training school for the use of reason.

A694.25-A695.1   And is the foundation of the possibility of its greatest possible employment.

A695.1-2   The idea of such unity is, therefore, connected to the very nature of reason.

A695.2-3   Consequently this idea is legislative for us.

A695.3-6   It is natural, therefore, to assume a legislative reason (*intellectus archetypus*) as the O of our reason from which all systematic unity of nature is to be derived.

A695.20-A696.4   If we ask whether there is anything distinct from the world which contains the ground of its order and of its connection according to universal laws,

The answer is undoubtedly yes.

A696.4-7   Since the world is a sum of As, and therefore there must be a ground which is thinkable by pure understanding.

A696.7-9   If we ask whether this being is a substance, of the greatest reality, necessary, etc., the question is without meaning.

A696.9-11   For all the categories thru which we might attempt to form a concept of such an O have only an empirical employment.

A696.11-13	The categories have no meaning when not applied to Os of possible experience.
A696.16-A697.1	We can think this transc being by analogy with the Os of E, but only as O in the idea and not in reality.
A697.1-4	I.e., only as being a substratum (to us unknown) of the systematic unity, order, and purposiveness of the arrangement of the world.
A697.4-5	An idea which reason must form as the regulative principle for its investigation of nature.
A697.8-10	It is merely an idea which does not relate directly to a being distinct from the world.
A697.10-11	But to the regulative principle of the world's systemataic unity.
A697.11-14	It relates to this unity only thru the schema of a supreme intelligence which, in its originating the world, acts according to wise purposes.
A697.14-18	We have not thereby decided what this primordial ground of the unity of the world may be in itself. We have decided only how to use the idea of it in relation to the systematic employment of reason in regard to things of the world.
A697.19-21	We *must* assume a wise and omnipotent Author of the world, and on these grounds.
A697.23-A.698.2	But in this case, all we have done is to presuppose a mere transc O of which, as it is in itself, we have no concept, i.e., we have not extended our K beyond the field of possible E.
A698.2-6	It is only in relation to the systematic and purposive ordering of the world which we are constrained to presuppose in order of study nature, That we think this unknown being by analogy with an intelligence (an empirical concept).
A698.6-10	I.e., in regard to the ends and perfections which are to be grounded upon it, We have endowed it with just those properties which, in conformity with the conditions of our reason, Can be regarded as containing the ground of such systematic unity.
A698.11-12	This idea is valid only in regard to the employment of our reason in reference to the world.
A698.12-14	We are thinking a being in idea only, and consequently we cannot attribute to it a validity that is absolute and objective.
A698.22-A699.4	We may regard seemingly purposive arrangements as purposes, And so derive them from the divine will mediately thru special natural means which have been established for the furtherance of that will.

And yet, as the construction of a concept (a universal R) it must in its R express universal validity

For all possible Is which fall under the same concept.

A713.19-24 So I construct a triangle by representing the O which corresponds to this concept either by imagination in pure I or, in accordance with it, on paper in empirical I.

In both cases the pattern is represented completely *a priori*.

A714.10-14 Just as this single O is determined by certain universal conditions of construction So the O of the concept to which the single O corresponds as its schema must likewise be thought as universally determined.

A719.7-11 In mathematical problems there is no question of existence,

But only of properties of Os in themselves, i.e., only in so far as these properties are connected with the concepts of the Os.

A719.20-21 All K relates to possible I since it is only thru them that an O is given.

A720.13-14 The only concept which represents *a priori* the empirical content of As is the concept of a *thing* in general.

720.15-17 And the *a priori* synthetic K of this thing in general can give only the mere rule of the synthesis of that which perception gives *a posteriori*.

A720.17-19 It can never give an *a priori* I of the real O, since this must be empirical.

A720.20-22 Synthetic propositions in regard to things in general, the intuition of which cannot be given *a priori*, are transcendental.

A723.4-8 In the field of As, in terms of which all Os are given, there is the form of I and the matter.

A723.8-10 The latter signifies something which is met in space and time which therefore contains an existence corresponding to sensation.

A723.11-15 In regard to the material element, which can be given in a determinate way only empirically,

We have nothing *a priori* except indeterminate concepts of the synthesis of possible sensations

To the extent that they belong to the unity of apperception in a possible experience.

A723.15-19 In regard to the formal element, we can determine our concepts in *a priori* I

By creating in space and time thru a homogeneous synthesis the Os themselves

These Os being viewed as mere *quanta*.

A728.18-21 I can never be certain that the clear R of a given concept (which as given may still be confused) has been completely effected unless I know that it is adequate to its O.

A808.15-18	The idea of a moral world has objective reality,
	Not as referring to an O of intelligible I (we are unable to think such an O).
A808.18-20	But as referring to the sensible world as an O of pure reason in its practical employment.
A813.2-5	Without a God and a moral world the ideas of morality are Os of approval but not sources of purpose and action.
A814.19-24	Moral theology leads to the concept of a sole, all-perfect, and rational primordial being
	Speculative theology has no objective ground on which it might even point the way to this being or yield conviction in regard to its existence.
A816.21-A817.4	Without the unity of nature we would have no reason since there would be no fertilisation thru Os which afford material for necessary concepts.
A820.1-4	Truth assertions require both objective grounds and subjective causes in the mind of the one who makes the judgment.
A820.4-7	If the judgment is valid for everyone possessed of reason, its ground is objectively sufficient.
A820.9-11	Persuasion is mere illusion because the ground of the judgment which is subjective is regarded as objective.
A820.13-16	Truth depends upon agreement with the O.
A822.9-11	Believing is a judgment that is subjectively sufficient by objectively insufficient.
A840.17-21	The legislation of reason (i.e., philosophy) has two Os: nature and freedom.

13. Object: Special Terms

Abbreviations

=	Is the same as
K	Knowledge
O	Object
R	Representation
transc	Transcendental

Contents

13.1 Object = x

13.2 Transcendental Object

the correlate of the unity of apperception (the unity of the manifold): something = x.

A250.25-A251.1 Transc O cannot be thought without sense data, i.e., a referent cannot be thought without something to refer.

A251.1-5 Transc O is not an O of K.

A251.6-11 Transc O = concept of something in general which is determined by categories.

A253.4-6 Transc O = thought of something in general.

A253.6-7 "Transc O" is not the same as "Noumenon".

A253.7-10 Transc O is conceived of as O of sensible intuition in general.

A253.10-12 Transc O cannot be thought through the categories. (cf. A251.6-11 above)

A277.13-17 Transc O is the ground of matter as appearance.

A288.10-23 Thought of "O in itself" = "Transc O" which is the cause of appearance, and is not itself an appearance, and cannot be thought through the categories; it may be called "noumenon".

A358.7-12 Transc O = noumenon = underlying cause of appearances.

A360.24-A361.4 "Soul" = Transc O of inner sense.

A366.6-9 Thing in itself = Transc O.

A372.15-19 and The cause of outer intuition is not the O we

A372.22-A373.1 think in the R of matter but is the transc O.

A379.23-A380.5 Transc O which underlies both outer appearances and inner intuition is in itself neither matter nor thinking being, but the unknown ground of those appearances which are the source of empirical concepts.

A479.1 ftnt a 1-4 Transc O not given.

A492.6-11 Transc subject = the self proper as its exits in itself and is unknown.

A494.10-18 Transc O = nonsensible cause of Rs, cannot be intuited as O, intelligible cause of appearances in general, something corresponding to sensibility viewed as receptivity.

A494.19-23 To this transc O we can ascribe the whole extent and connection of our possible perception, and say that it is given in itself prior to all experience. Appearances conform to it.

A495.3-4 Real things in past time given in transc O of experience.

A538.15-17 Appearances must rest upon a transc O which determines them as representations.

A538.17-A539.4 May ascribe to transc O both the quality in terms of which it appears and a causality which is not appearance (though the effect is appearance).

A565.18-23 Transcendent ideas have a purely intelligible O = transc O.

13.3 Object in General

A254.3-6	The categories think O in general without regard to the mode or sensibility in which they are given, and so extend beyond sensible intuition. (Compare this to: A251.1-5, A251.6-11, A253.4-6, A279.18-21.)
A279.13-18	The notion of O in general contains limits which prohibit the nonempirical use of concepts.
A279.18-21	The R of O as thing in general, when taken without sensible determination and independent of any empirical condition, is self-contradictory.
A274.3-5	Perception is sensation that has been referred to O in general, but not as determining that O.
A290.7-10	
A290.10-14	
A400.4-8	To know something as simple in concept only is merely to form the concept of something in general that cannot be intuited.
B411.11 ftnt a 1-4	O in general is the O as it may be given in intuition.
B429.5-6	O in general as abstracting from the mode of its intuition.
A414.8-15	"Substantial" = concept of O in general.
A416.1-5	The idea of absolute totality does not refer to the pure concept of a totality of things in general.
A582.11-14	O of senses is not the same as things in general.
A720.15-19	The *a priori* synthetic knowledge of the thing in general gives only the mere rule of the synthesis of what perception may give a *posteriori*.
A845.10-18	Metaphysics treats of the understanding and reason in a system of concepts and principles which relate to O in general.

13.4 Intelligible Object

B306.11-17	Intelligible entities = noumena
A256.8-11	Noumenon in the problematic sense is not an intelligible O.
A257.15-22	O thought as given merely to the understanding is the intelligible O, i.e., noumenon.
A257.22-27	The understanding does not have a nonempirical use in regard to noumena, i.e., intelligible Os.
A259.21-23	The concept of pure intelligible Os lacks principles for the possibility of its application.
A259.23-25	We cannot think how an intelligible O could be given.
A285.11-12 and	(Together these texts seem to equate
A286.3-5	"noumenon" and "intelligible O".)
A286.3-5	Intelligible Os as something thought through pure categories without any schema or sensibility are impossible.
A287.4-9	We cannot assume Os of pure thought, i.e., noumena.
A546.23-A547.2	Man is to himself an intelligible O.

A565.18-23	The transcendent ideas of reason have a purely intelligible O, i.e., transc O, which cannot be known or determined in terms of distinctive inner predicates.
A565.23-A566.3	We cannot establish the possibility of such an O, and may not assume it. It is a mere thought-entity.
A566.4-8	Contingency of appearances forces us to look for a grounding in an intelligible O.
A566.8-12	If we assume a self-subsistent reality outside the field of sensibility, appearances can only be viewed as contingent modes whereby things that are themselves intelligences represent intelligible Os.
A639.26-A640.6	Reason can show the consistency of the knowledge of God with every point of view from which intelligible objects can be regarded.

13.5 Universal Object

A289.16-24	The universal O represented *in abstracto* seems to be a mode in which the O exists in itself (*noumenon*), whereas it is merely a logical form without content.

13.6 Objects in Themselves

A42.11-13	We do not know what Os may be in themselves.
A43.1-4	We do not know the constitution of Os in themselves.
A43.8-11	We cannot know what Os are in themselves.
B306.22-B307	R of Os in themselves formed by the understanding as the correlate of O as phenomenon.
B307.2-5	Understanding supposes that Os in themselves can be thought through the categories.
A280.1-2	Appearances cannot be Os in themselves.
A288.10-15	O in itself = transc O = cause of appearances.
A301.26-A302.4	Os in themselves not determined according to concepts and principals.
A370.8-10	Rs do not stand in relation to Os in themselves.
A380.6-11	"Objects of our senses as they are in themselves."
A393.10-13	In experience, we treat appearances as Os in themselves, and do not concern ourselves about their ground.
A393.13-15	Investigation of the ground of appearances would require the concept of the transc O.
B430.4-9	For the 'I' to distinguish itself as O in itself is not the same as for it to know itself as noumenon.
A468.20-24	Every O, both in itself and in its relations ought to be represented in intuition.
A508.13-17	Appearances are empirical Rs, and not Os in themselves.

13.7 Object in the Idea

A350.22-A351.4	The proposition 'The Soul is substance' signifies a substance only in idea, not in reality.
A482.2-4	The absolutely unconditioned totality of synthesis of appearances can be met with nowhere outside our idea.
A670.5-12	'O in the idea' is only a schema for which no O, even hypothetical, can be directly given. It enables other Os to be represented indirectly as in systematic unity through relation to the idea.
A671.6-11	The three transc ideas do not directly relate to or determine any O which corresponds to them. They merely lead to systematic unity under the presupposition of *O in the idea*.
A674.23-24	Creative reason (See A672.23-A673.4) is posited only in the idea.
A679.18-20	(Same as for A674.23-24.)
A681.8-12	An O is given to the idea of unity by reason in order that we may view the connections in the world of sense *as if* it had its ground in such a being.
A696.16-A697.1	We think this being by analogy with the Os of experience, but only in the idea.
A698.12-14	(Same as for A696.16-A697.1.)
A771.15-19	(Same as for A671.6-11.)

13.8 Object *in abstracto*

A285.8-12	O *in abstracto* in not noumenon.
A289.16-24	The universal O represented in abstracto is not noumenon but a merely logical form without content.

14. Object: Topics

Contents

14.1 Appearance and Object

Bxx.11-24
Bxxvii.14-Bxxviii.4
A20.3-4
A34.17-A35.3
A36.13-16
A38.14-21
A45.13-16
B66.20-B67.6
A89.10-11
A89.18-20
A90.1-3
A90.6-9
A90.9-12
A91.12-15
A92.11-13
A92.19-A93.2
A93.5-7
A93.13-16
A95.8-10
A104.7-11
A104.17-A105.2
A108.7-14
A109.1-3
A109.3-7
A109.18-A110.6
A130.6-10

B151.1-3
A143.11-14
A156.16-23
B203.2-10
B207.13-16
A180.8-9
B225.4-6
A183.22-23
B234.14.19
A189.13-A190.3
A190.3-7
A190.9-12
A190.24-A191.2
A191.5-8
A191.10-17
A191.17-19
A193.13-17
A198.1-4
A200.16-20
A201.1-4
A202.10-13
A210.22-A211.7
A213.23-A214.5
A214.16-23
A238.21-A239.1
A239.23-A240.3

A240.19-A241.1
A246.21-A247.1
A248.23-A249.1
A249.7-19
A249.19-22
A250.16-18
A251.1-5
A251.6-11
A253.4-6
A253.7-10
B306.7-11
B308.16-20
A258.1-9
A267.17-20
A277.13-17
A278.26-A279.6
A280.1-2
A285.8-11
A288.10-15
A289.4-7
A297.6-10
A357.13-17
A358.7-12
A361.18-A362.4
A362.18-21
A366.6-9
A370.22-24
A372.8-13

A376.19-A377.4
A379.19-22
A379.23-A380.5
A393.10-13
A400.1-4
A430.9-13
A479.1 ftnt a 6-11
A480.21-23
A490.16-A491.3
A492.3-6
A494.15-17
A494.21-23
A496.8-11
A496.17-21
A500.9-14
A508.13-17
A538.1-2
A538.2-6
A538.17-A539.4
A540.7-12
A566.4-8
A566.8-12
A581.13-19
A581.19-23
A613.21-A614.1
A638.2-6
A696.9-11
A723.4-8

14.2 Categories, Concepts, Ideas, and Object

Axvi.16-20
Bxvii.21-Bxviii.2
A79.21-26
A80.7-9
A85.8-11
A85.11-13
A85.18-22
A85.22-A86.3
A88.5-8
A88.8-11
A89.16-18
A8918-20
A89.20-21
A89.21-A90.1
A90.12-15
A90.15-18
A90.25-A91.2

A92.19-A93.2
A93.7-10
A93.18-21
A93.21-23
A94.5-7
A94.10-13
B127.9-20
B128.17-20
A96.14-19
A96.21-A97.3
A104.17-A105.2
A105.20-22
A108.7-14
A109.8-11
A111.5-7
A111.16-18
A114.19-24

A400.12-17
B406.32-B407.1
B421.21-B422.1
B422.5-7
B422.14 ftnt a 11-13
B422.14 ftnt a 14-15
B428.10-14
A414.8-15
A480.21-23
A547.2-8
A566.19-21
A579.2-4
A580.12-15
A583.4 ftnt a 1-4
A589.7-12
A592.1-4
A592.4-7
A614.7-9
A619.21-A620.2
A642.14-16
A643.19-22
A644.2-7
A644.21-23
A645.21-24
A663.16-23
A665.13-18
A669.20-A670.3
A670.5-7
A670.8-10
A670.10-12
A670.12-16
A670.20-23
A671.3-6
A671.6-11

A671.15-24
A672.23-A673.4
A673.13-16
A674.5-9
A674.14-16
A675.7-10
A675.10-14
A676.22-A677.3
A677.3-7
A677.9-11
A677.11-14
A677.21-22
A678.22-24
A679.11-15
A680.5-10
A681.1-2
A681.2-5
A681.5-8
A682.5-6
A684.6-10
A684.10-11
A685.27-A686.2
A696.9-11
A696.11-13
A697.23-A698.2
A759.15-A760.1
A771.2-7
AA7718-9
A788.3-10
A801.7 ftnt a 1-3
A808.15-18
A813.2-5
A814.19-24
A816.21-A817.4

14.3 Existence and Object

B72.6-8
A92.13-16
A145.1-2
B207.16-B208.1
B219.9-12
B219.12-16
A186.14-16
A186.17-21
A186.21-A187.1
A187.2-4
A202.2-9

B257.6-7
B257.12-15
A212.1-7
A214.11-16
A225.1-4
B275.11-13
A226.23-A227.1
A234.6-9
A244.4-7
A288.10-23
A289.16-24

A370.24-25
A372.8-13
B422.14 ftnt a 14-15
B428.10-14
B430.9-13
A492.19-20
A569.21-A570.3
A579.2-4
A592.14-17
A592.17-A593.1
A593.1-3
A593.3-6
A593.6-12
A593.13-22
A593.23-24
A593.24-26
A593.26-A594.1
A594.1-17
A594.18-22
A594.22-A595.8
A595.8-14
A595.15-18
A595.18-23
A595.24-A596.2
A596.2-3
A596.4-11
A596.12-14
A596.14 ftnt a 1-10
A596.14-A597.6
A597.7-18
A597.18-A598.1
A598.1-7
A598.8-13
A598.13-15
A598.15-18

A598.19-21
A598.21-23
A598.23-25
A598.25-A599.1
A599.1-6
A599.6-10
A599.10-11
A599.11-19
A599.19-21
A599.22-24
A600.1-4
A600.4-7
A600.7-12
A600.12-18
A600.18-A601.2
A601.2-6
A601.6-8
A601.9-11
A601.11-13
A601.13-16
A601.16-23
A601.24-A602.1
A602.1-3
A602.3-5
A602.6-12
A602.12-15
A602.16-21
A603.1-3
A612.3-9
A619.21-A620.2
A639.17-19
A639.19-21
A676.22-A677.3
A677.11-14
A724.4-17

14.4 Experience and Object

Bxxvii.2-12
A2.21-A3.4
A86.11-16
A91.2-9
A93.10-13
A93.13-16
A93.18-21
A93.21-23
A94.10-13
A126.21-A127.5

A127.16-20
A128.16-18
B147.19-B148.2
B161.11-14
B165.13-16
B156.1-4
A156.10-12
A156.12-14
A156.16-23
A157.19-A158.1

A158.2-5
A158.10-13
B218.15-16
B218.19-B219.2
B219.9-12
A182.4-7
A200.16-20
A217.8-12
A220.5-11
A221.1-3
A221.22-A222.5
A224.12-16
A224.16-19
A224.19-23
A225.4-8
A234.4-6
B289.16-20
A237.7-15
A238.21-A239.1
A240.15-18
A243.7-15
A246.11-17
A246.21-A247.1
B308.20-24
A258.1-9

A361.18-A362.4
A380.6-11
B410.10-18
B422.14 ftnt a 11-13
A490.16-A491.3
A492.19-20
A494.8-10
A494.20-21
A495.3-4
A495.21-A496.1
A582.7-9
A636.1-6
A637.21-A638.1
A638.2-6
A665.18-A666.2
A670.20-23
A671.15-24
A674.14-16
A677.9-11
A681.2-5
A696.11-13
A696.16-A697.1
A771.2-7
A771.8-9

14.5 Intelligible and Object

B306.11-17
A256.8-11
A257.15-27
A259.21-25
A286.3-5

A494.15-17
A538.1-6
A540.7-12
A546.23-A547.2
(A670.12-16)

14.6 Intuition and Object

Bxxv.19-Bxxvi.5
A19.1-10
A19.11-14
A20.1-3
A20.3-4
A27.2-6
A27.15-23
A38.14-21
A48.7-15
B69.6-12
B69.12-15
B72.6-8
A51.9-11

A68.13-15
A78.24-A79.1
A79.21-26
A87.25-A88.1
A90.12-15
A90.25-A91.2
A92.19-A93.2
A93.2-5
A93.13-16
B128.17-20
A95.8-10
A109.1-3
A109.3-7

14.7 Knowledge and Object

Bxvi.14-17
Bxxiii.7-9
Bxxvi.11 ftnt a 1-3
A19.1-10
A43.8-11
A87.25-A88.1
A93.10-13
A104.11-16
A104.17-A105.2
A109.8-A110.6
A125.19-A126.2
A129.7-10
A129.11-18
A129.18-21
A129.21-A130.1
B137.7-10
B138.4-5
B138.6-7
B142.22-26
B146.14-B147.1
B147.19-B148.2
B148.15-B149.2
B149.11-16
B156.14-20
B158.9-15
B165.13-16
B166.3 ftnt a 5-6
A148.17-A149.4
A150.6-11
A155.20-23
A165.24-A166.3
B218.15-16
B218.19-B219.2
B219.9-12
A195.3-5
A201.1-4
A210.22-A211.7
A220.13-16
A224.19-23
A225.1-8
A226.23-A227.1
B228.15-18
B289.20-23
A237.7-15

A245.10-15
A250.16-A251.11
A253.19-20
A254.19-22
A256.11-14
A258.9-11
A259.23-25
A278.26-A279.6
A288.10-21
A346.10-14
A354.17-19
A358.15-19
A361.18-A362.4
A372.8-13
A372.22-A373.1
A378.16-19
A379.23-A380.5
A381.13-17
A382.8-12
A394.10-12
A396.14-15
A400.4-8
A402.6-8
B406.26-29
B407.2-4
B409.12-14
B430.4-9
B430.9-13
B404.10-12
A566.19-21
A613.21-A614.1
A639.19-21
A644.21-23
A665.13-18
A666.6-9
A671.15-24
A674.14-16
A677.3-7
A677.22-24
A678.22-24
A719.20-21
A720.15-19
A759.15-A760.1

14.8 Meaning, Sense, and Object

A139.16-19
A147.7-13

A197.10-23
A239.6-9

A239.23-A240.3
A240.19-A241.5
A243.2-7
A244.22-A245.1

A248.18-22
A684.10-11
A696.11-13

14.9 Metaphysics and Object

(See Topic 11, M; See Appendix 1, 2, 3.)

Axx.1-7
Axx.7-9
Axx.9-12
Axxi.1-2
Bxiv.9-11
Bxiv.11-13
Bxvi.12-14
Bxvi.14-17
Bxxi.1 ftnt a 3-10
Bxxi.1-9
Bxxii.4-8
Bxxii.9-11
Bxxiii.1-7
Bxxiii.9-16
Bxxiii.16-Bxxiv.1
Bxxiv.1-5
Bxxiv.5-7
B7.6-7
B7.7-9
Bxxxi.13-15
B21.16-B22.5
B22.6-12
B22.12-19
B22.19-21
B22.22-23
A23.13-17
B159.10-12
A841.1-7

A841.8-14
A841.15-22
A841.24-A842.6
A842.18-A843.8
A843.8-12
A844.7-17
A845.5-9
A845.10-18
A845.18-A846.1
A846.1-8
A846.9-16
A846.16-21
A846.22-A847.2
A847.2 ftnt a 3-13
A847.12-A848.7
A848.7-11
A848.21-A849.9
A849.10
A849.10-14
A849.14-23
A849.23-A850.7
A850.8-12
A850.12-15
A850.18-21
A850.22-23
A850.23-A851.5
A851.5-12
A853.1-7

14.10 Necessity, Rules, and Object

A94.5-7
A104.17-A105.2
A105.3-9
A105.20-22
A106.13-19
A106.19-21
A108.7-14

A109.15-18
A109.18-A110.6
B150.10-20
B168.3-11
A145.3-4
A158.2-5
A166.3-6

A191.10-17
A191.17-19
A193.13-17
A194.13-22
A194.22-A195.3
A195.3-5
A195.8-12
A195.12-17
A196.18-A197.1
A197.1-2
A197.16-20
A197.20-23
A198.4-8
A198.8-11
A200.16-20
A200.20-A201.1
A202.2-9
A213.2-4
B277.11-12
A234.9-10
A254.19-22
A402.6-8
A592.1-4

A616.8-9
A619.13-18
A619.21-A620.2
A648.9-21
A664.9-12
A665.13-18
A665.18-A666.2
A666.6-9
A666.9-12
A666.13-15
A669.20-A670.3
A671.15-24
A680.10-14
A680.19-21
A684.12-15
A685.11-15
A695.3-6
A724.4-17
A788.3-10
A792.18-24
A802.17-22
A808.1-3
A816.21-A817.4

14.11 Noumenon and Object

A249.1-6
A249.7-19
(A249.19-22)
(A249.22-A250.1)
A252.12-15
A252.15-17
A252.18-A253.3
A253.6-7
B306.11-17
(B306.22-B307.2)
(B307.2-5)
B307.11-14
B307.14-18
(B308.16-20)
A254.15-18

A254.19-22
A256.8-11
A257.15-22
A257.22-27
(A258.1-9)
(A258.9-11)
A285.11-12
A287.17-20
A287.20-A288.1
A288.10-23
A290.18-21
A358.7-12
(A378.8-13)
B430.4-13

14.12 Object as affecting sense

B1.1-8
A19.1-10
A19.15-16
B41.15-20
A26.12-15

A26.22-25
A44.18-25
B72.6-8
A50.12-13
A51.9-11

14.13 Object as given

14.14 Possibility and Object

(See Topic 8)

A199.17-20
A212.1-7
A213.2-4
A214.16-23
A220.13-16
A223.23-A224.2
A224.12-16
A224.19-23
B278.20-23
A234.4-6
B288.1-4
B289.16-20
A238.21-A239.1
A239.3-6
A240.19-A241.1
A244.4-7
A246.11-17
A249.22-24
A252.18-A253.3
B306.11-17
A253.23-A254.3
A254.7-10
A255.6-12
A255.24-A256.5
A256.11-14
A258.1-9
A259.21-23
A262.28-A263.1
A285.11-12
A286.5-9
A354.17-19
A394.10-12
B410.11-19
B430.9-13
A494.10-12
A494.19-20
A495.4-12
A495.21-A496.1
A565.23-A566.1
A581.13-19
A581.19-23
A582.2-4
A582.4-7
A582.7-9
A582.9-11

A596.4-11
A596.12-14
A596.14 ftnt a 1-10
A596.14-A597.6
A597.7-18
A597.18-A598.1
A598.1-7
A598.8-13
A598.13-15
A599.6-10
A599.10-11
A599.11-19
A599.19-21
A599.22-24
A600.1-4
A600.4-7
A600.7-12
A600.12-18
A600.18-A601.2
A601.2-6
A601.6-8
A601.9-11
A601.11-13
A601.13-16
A601.16-23
A601.24-A602.1
A602.1-3
A602.3-5
A602.6-12
A602.12-15
A602.16-21
A603.1-3
A629.23-A630.16
A644.21-23
A674.14-16
A677.9-11
A696.11-13
A719.20-21
A724.4-17
A759.15-A760.1
A769.20-A770.9
A770.10-16
A770.16-771.7
A788.3-10

14.15 Reality and Object

A145.1-2   A157.4-7

14.16 Reason and Object

A675.7-10
A680.5-10
A680.10-14
A680.14-19
A681.1-2
A684.12-15
A685.11-15
A695.3-6
A723.15-16

A771.8-9
A796.4-5
A798.5-8
A802.17-22
A808.1-3
A808.15-18
A816.21-A817.4
A820.4-7
A840.17-21

14.17 Representation and Object

Bxx.11-24
B1.1-8
A19.1-10
A19.15-16
A22.12-14
A30.2-9
A44.4-8
A44.18-25
B67.6-11
B69.6-12
B72.6-8
A56.19-22
A68.13-15
A77.4-9
A92.5-8
A92.8-10
A92.10-13
A92.16-18
A104.6-7
A104.7-11
A105.3-9
A105.20-22
A107.12-17
A108.22-23
A109.3-7
A109.15-18
A118.20-21
B137.7-10
B137.11-15
B144.4 ftnt a 1-5
B150.10-20
B151.18-19
B160.19 ftnt a 1-6
A156.1-4
A156.10-12
A156.12-14

B203.2-10
B207.16-B208.1
B208.8-11
B225.4-6
A189.13-15
A189.15-17
A189.17-A190.3
A190.3-7
A190.9-12
A190.24-A191.2
A191.5-8
A191.8-10
A191.10-17
A197.1-2
A197.3-10
A197.10-16
A197.16-20
A197.20-23
A198.1-4
A198.11-16
A199.17-20
A213.23-A214.5
A214.11-16
A233.19-23
A239.23-A240.3
A249.19-22
A249.24-A250.1
A250.15-16
A250.16-18
A251.1-5
A251.6-11
A252.1-7
B306.22-B207.2
A253.21-23
A256.11-14
A258.1-9

14.18 Sensibility, Intuition, and Object

A140.3-9
A143.11-14
B203.2-10
B207.10-11
B207.16-B208.1
B208.8-11
B218.19-B219.2
A213.12-14
A214.16-23
A215.17-20
A225.1-4
A225.4-8
B278.20-23
A226.23-A227.1
A234.6-9
A234.9-10
B288.1-4
B288.15-18
B289.20-23
B291.7-11
B292.17-21
B293.18-22
A239.9-11
A239.11-14
A239.14-19
A240.3-7
A240.19-A241.1
A241.19-A242.9
A243.2-7
A243.7-15
A244.22-A245.1
A245.4-7
A245.10-15
A246.6-10
A246.11-17
A247.7-8
A247.8-11
A247.16-19
A248.14-18
A249.19-22
A249.22-24
A250.22-24
A250.23-A251.1
A251.6-11
A252.12-15
A252.22-A253.3
A253.7-10
B305.18-22
B206.3-7
B306.11-17

B307.11-14
B308.16-20
A253.21-23
A254.3-6
A254.19-22
A255.18-20
A256.11-14
A258.1-9
A263.12-17
A267.17-20
A278.14-22
A279.13-18
A279.18-21
A279.21-24
A285.16-17
A286.5-9
A286.12-17
A286.17-22
A287.4-9
A287.9-13
A287.15-17
A287.20-A288.1
A288.15-18
A288.19-21
A299.21-23
A289.16-24
A342.3-4
A357.13-17
A358.4-7
A358.15-19
A366.6-9
A373.16-19
A374.3-5
A374.8-11
A375.15-A376.6
A378.8-13
A379.19-22
A380.6-11
B415.2-4
B415.4-6
B422.14 ftnt a 11-13
A430.9-13
A491.19-21
A492.6-11
A494.15-20
A494.23-A495.3
A538.1-2
A538.2-6
A538.12-15
A546.23-A547.2

14.19 Space and Object

14.20 Subject and Object

A362.21-A363.3
A379.19-22
A381.19-22
A381.20-A382.2
A382.6-8
A382.8-12
A398.3-6
A400.12-17
A402.8-11
B406.32-B407.1
B407.4-8
B407.10-15
B408.16-18

B409.12-14
B411.11 ftnt a 1-11
B421.21-B422.1
B422.5-7
B428.10-14
B429.5-6
B430.4-9
B430.9-13
A479.1 ftnt a 6-11
A492.6-11
A540.7-12
A682.5-6

14.21 Synthesis and Object

A48.5-6
A48.7-15
A48.15-19
A90.15-18
B127.9-20
A108.7-14
A109.15-18
A109.18-A110.6
A121.18-23
A122.9-16
A122.17-25
B134.13-16
B138.6-7
B139.12-14
B142.22-26
B144.4 ftnt a 1-5
B150.10-20
B160.19 ftnt a 1-6
A145.7-8
A156.16-23
A157.4-7
A157.15-18
A157.19-A158.1

A158.2-5
B203.2-10
A165.24-A166.3
A166.3-5
B218.19-B219.2
A190.9-12
A191.10-17
A193.11-13
A198.1-4
A201.13-16
B257.12-15
A220.5-11
A220.13-16
A221.22-A222.5
A234.13-17
A250.24-25
A397.13-18
B407.4-8
A494.8-10
A621.23-A622.2
A644.2-7
A720.15-19
A723.15-26

14.22 Thing in itself and Object

Bxxvi.7-12
Bxxvii.2-12
Bxxvii.14-Bxxviii.4
A27.15-23
A34.17-A35.3

A38.14-21
A39.5-9
A44.4-8
B69.12-15
A104.7-11

A128.16-18
A143.11-14
A190.9-12
A239.19-22
B306.22-B307.2
B307.2-5
B307.14-18
A252.1-7
A254.15-18
A254.19-22
A278.25-A279.6
A280.1-2

A286.17-22
A287.4-9
A366.6-9
A372.8-13
A378.8-13
A378.16-19
A492.3-6
A500.9-14
A538.15-17
A563.9-10
A566.17-19
A566.19-21

14.23 Time and Object

A35.17-19
A37.18-22
B67.6-12
A89.10-11
A90.12-15
B148.7-12
A143.11-14
A143.28-31
A143.31-34
A143.34-36
A145.7-8
A145.13-15
A156.5-6
A156.10-12
A156.12-14
A165.24-A166.3
B207.16-B208.1
B219.9-12
B219.12-16
B225.4-6
A197.3-10
A197.20-23
A198.8-11
A109.11-16
A200.2-4
A200.16-20
A200.20-A201.1
A201.1-4
A201.13-16

A202.2-9
A210.22-A211.7
A213.23-A214.5
A214.11-16
A215.17-20
A243.7-15
A362.4-5
A362.18-21
A362.21-A363.3
A371.6-9
A373.1-4
A373.16-19
A374.5-7
A379.19-22
A379.23-A380.5
A381.13-17
B407.4-8
B415.2-6
B422.14 ftnt a 11-13
B430.9-13
A479.1 ftnt a 6-11
A491.19-21
A492.6-11
A494.8-10
A494.12-15
A495.4-12
A724.4-17
A788.3-10

14.24 Transcendental Apperception and Object

A107.12-17

A123.1-6

A126.21-A127.5
A129.18-21
B137.11-15
B138.4-5
B139.12-14
B144.4 ftnt a 1-5
B150.10-20
A210.22-A211.7
A250.22-24
A350.4-6
A353.23-A354.1
A362.21-A363.3
A379.19-22
A381.19-20
A381.20-A382.2
A382.6-8
A382.8-12

A398.3-6
A398.8-9
A400.12-17
B406.32-B407.1
B407.2-4
B407.4-8
B407.10-15
B409.16-18
B411.11 ftnt a 1-11
B421.21-B422.1
B422.1-2
B422.14 ftnt a 11-13
B428.10-14
B430.4-13
A479.1 ftnt a 6-11
A682.5-6

14.25 Transcendental Logic and Object

A55.19-21
A56.19-22
A57.1-3

A57.8-16
A62.15-19

14.26 Transcendental Reflection and Object

A260.4-5
A262.28-A263.1

A269.19-23

14.27 Understanding, Thought, and Object

Axvi.16-20
Bxvii.17-21
Bxix.1-6
Bxxvi.7-12
A57.8-16
A97.3-10
A125.19-A126.2
B150.10-20
A158.14-A159.2
A199.17-20
A210.22-A211.7
A219.8-12
B288.1-4
A240.19-A241.1

A245.10-15
A247.7-8
A248.18-22
A248.23-A249.1
A250.15-16
A250.16-18
A250.24-25
A250.25-A251.1
A251.6-11
A252.12-15
B306.11-17
B306.22-B307.2
B307.2-5
A253.19-20

14.28 Viewpoints and Object

Bxxvii.2-12
A39.5-9
A44.4-8
B69.12-15
A104.7-11
A143.11-14
B219.9-12
A189.13-A190.3
A190.9-12
A191.5-8
A191.10-17
A219.7-19
A249.19-22
B306.7-11
B306.11-17
B308.16-20
A255.18-20

A38.14-21
A258.1-9
A287.4-9
A341.17-A342.3
A358.7-12
A379.19-22
B407.4-8
B411.11 ftnt a 1-4
A500.9-14
A538.2-6
A538.12-15
A546.23-A547.2
A566.8-12
A672.23-A673.4
A823.21-23
A823.23-26

15. Noumenon

Abbreviations

E!	Exists, is independently real
=	Is the same as (e.g., T=N)
−	Not (e.g., −KN)
/	Existential distinction (e.g., P/N)
#	Distinction by abstraction or construction (e.g., T #A)
A	Appearance
C	Concept
I	Intelligible
K	Can know
L	Limit, only
N	Noumenon
P	Phenomenon
T	Thing in itself

A3.5-7	KAL
A206.17-24	I=T
A249.1-6	T=N
A249.7-19	E!N, I=N, T=N
A251.12-17	T=N
A252.1-8	T=M, T#A
A252.8-10	−KN
A252.10-12	T=N, A/T
A252.22-A253.3	−KN

16. Phenomenon

Abbreviations

=	Is the same as (e.g., A=P)
/	Existential distinction (e.g., P/N)
A	Appearance
I	Intelligible
N	Noumenon
P	Phenomenon
T	Thing in itself

B155.11-B156.1	A=P
A146.18-20	Schema=P
A183.22-23	A=P
A205.1-4	A=P
A206.17-24	A=P
A248.23-A249.1	A=P, Definition of P
A249.7-19	A=P, I=N
A251.12-17	A=P
A252.12-15	P/N
B306.7-8	A=P, Definition of P
B306.22-B307.2	A=P, A/T
A255.18-20	A=P
A257.15-22	A=P
A265.13-15	A=P
A277.5-8	A=P
A545.11-18	A=P
A546.23-A547.2	A=P, P/N
A563.16-21	A=P, A/T
A798.16-22	A=P

17. Thing in Itself

Abbreviations

E!	Exists, is independently real
=	Is the same as (e.g., T=N)
−	Not (e.g., −KN)
/	Existential distinction (e.g., A/T)
+	Distinction of aspects (e.g., A+T)
A	Appearance
C	Concept
I	Intelligible
K	Can know

L	Limit, only
N	Noumenon
P	Phenomenon
r	represents
S	Subjects
T	Thing in itself

Bxx.1-6	–KT, E!T
Bxx.7-11	E!
Bxx.11-24	–KT, A/T
Bxxv.19-Bxxvi.5	–KT
Bxxvi.7-12	–KT, E!T
Bxxvii.2-12	E!T, A+T
Bxxvii.14-Bxxviii.4	A+T
A30.2-9	–KT, A/T
A30.9-12	–KT, A/T
A34.17-A35.3	–KT, A/T
A36.3-4	–KT
A42.3-A43.5	–KT, A/T
A42.11-13	–KT
A43.1-4	–KT
A44.1-4	E!T
A44.4-8	E!T, A/T
A44.18-25	A/T, –KT
A45.13-16	–KT
A46.6-11	A/T, –KT
A49.6-9	–KT
B66.20-B67.6	A/T, –KT
B67.19-B68.3	A+T
B68.4-9	A+T
B68.18-22	A+T
B68.22-B69.5	A+T
B69.12-15	A+T
B72.6-8	A/T, E!T
A101.11-14	A/T
A105.3-9	A/T, E!T
A109.3-7	A/TA128.16-18–KT
B155.11-B156.1	P+N
B156.14-20	A+T
B157.1-5	A+T
B158.3-5	A+T
B164.9-11	A/T
A190.12-15	E!T, –KT
A190.15-22	A/T
A190.24-A191.2	–KT
A191.2-4	A/T
A206.17-24	–KT
A238.21-A239.1	–KT
A249.1-6	I=N

A249.19-22	A+T, E!T
A250.16-18	A/T
A251.1-5	E!T
A251.12-17	A=P, T=N
A251.17-21	E!T
A252.1-7	E!T, A/T
B306.22-B307.2	A=P, T=N
B307.5-10	I=T, A/T
B307.11-14	N=LC
B307.19-23	N=LC, T=N
B308.16-20	T=N
A254.15-18	T=N
A276.14-17	−KT, − Art
A276.20-21	A/T
A277.1-3	−KT
A278.26-A279.6	−KT
A284.25-A285.3	A/T
A287.9-13	−KT
A288.10-15	A/T
A358.7-12	E!T, T=N
A358.15-19	E!T, −KN
A359.12-15	E!T
A239.15-18	E!T
A359.22-A360.4	A+T
A360.13-17	I=T
A360.24-A361.4	−KT
A366.6-9	−KT
A369.6-11	A/T
A372.15-17	A/T, E!T
A372.22-A373.1	−KT
A373.6-9	A/T
A375.15-A376.6	A/T
A378.8-13	A/T
A378.16-19	A/T
A379.23-A380.5	−KT
A391.4-11	−KT
A391.22-23	E!T, A/T
A392.3-10	−KT
A394.3-10	−KT
B410.10-18	−KT, Thing in general
B422.14 ftnt a 19-20	T=N
B427.23-B428.3	A/T
A492.3-6	A/T
A492.6-11	−KT, A+T(s)
A492.12-14	A/T(s)
A493.4-9	A/T
A493.17-20	A/T, E!T
A493.20-22	A/T
A493.22-A494.3	A/T
A496.4-8	−KT, A/T

A496.17-21	–KT
A498.22-A499.3	A/T
A506.3-5	A/T
A536.16-21	A/T
A537.1-5	E!T, A/T
A538.2-6	A+T(s)
A538.6-7	A+T(s), E!T, I=T
A538.12-15	A+T(s)
A538.15-17	E!T, A/T
A538.17-A539.4	A+T
A539.4-17	A+T
A539.17-19	A+T
A539.20-22	A+T
A540.7-9	–KT
A540.10-12	–KT
A540.13-A541.4	A+T
A552.12-18	A+T
A555.16-17	A+T
A556.20-21	A/T
A561.8-11	A+T
A563.9-10	–KT
A566.12-16	–KT
A575.14-A576.6	C of T as Ideal
A584.4-6	–KT
A613.21-A614.1	–KT
A614.2-3	–KT, E!T
A677.22-24	–KT
A679.18-22	–KT
A719.2-7	Thing in general
A720.13-14	Thing in general
A720.15-17	Thing in general
A720.20-22	Thing in general
A740.7-27	A/T

18. Appearances

Abbreviations

E!	Events, is independently real
=	Is the same as (e.g., A=R)
–	Not (e.g., –KN)
/	Existential distinction (e.g., A/T)
A	Appearance
Apperc	Apperception
C	Concept
I	Intelligible
K	Can Know
L	Limit, only

N	Noumenon
O	Object
P	Phenomenon
R	Representation
r	Represents
S	Subject
T	Thing in Itself

Bxx.1-6	KAL
Bxx.11-24	ArT
Bxx1.1 ftnt a 3-10	KA
Bxxv.19-Bxxvi.5	KA
Bxxvi.7-12	
Bxxvii.14-Bxxviii.4	A+T
A20.3-4	Definition of A
A20.5-6	Intuition
A20.6-8	−ArT
A20.15-18	A/T
A30.2-9	A=R
A34.17-A35.3	A=O, A=R
A38.14-21	A+T
A42.3-9	−ArT
A42.10-11	A/T
A44.1-4	E!T
A44.4-8	A=R
A45.13-16	A=O, KA
A45.22-A46.6	−ArT
A46.6-11	−KT, A=O
A48.25-A49.6	A/T
A49.6-9	KA
B66.2-B67.6	A=O
B68.4-9	A=R
B69.6-12	A=O
B69.12-15	A=O
A93.5-7	KA
A101.11-14	A=R
A104.7-11	A=R
A105.3-9	A=R, A/T
A108.23-A109.1	A=O
A109.3-7	A/T, A=R
A110.6-9	A subject to apperc
A113.10-12	A=R, Apperc and unity of A
A114.4-13	A=R
A119.13-15	KA
A120.2-5	KA
A125.14-19	Apperc and unity of A
A127.24-A128.5	Apperc and unity of A
A128.7-9	Apperc and unity of A
A129.2-7	KA

A196.14-17	Apperc and unity of A, Time
A198.1-4	Apperc and unity of A, Time
A198.11-16	Time
A199.9-15	Time
A199.15-16	Time
A199.22-24	Time
A200.2-4	Time
A200.4-6	Time
A200.9-14	Time
A20016-20	Time
A201.13-16	Apperc and unity of A, Time
A201.22-23	Time
A202.2-9	Time
A202.14-18	Time
A204.16-20	Action
A204.21-23	Action
A205.13-17	Action
A205.23-A206.4	Action
A205.13-17	Creation
A206.17-24	A=P
A206.25-A207.7	Action
A208.6-11	Time
A209.2-6	Time
A209.6-8	Time
A210.4-7	Time
A210.22-A211.7	Apperc and unity of A, Time
A212.1-7	Action
A207.24-A228.4	Causality
A228.12-17	Apperc and unity of A
A230.15-19	Apperc and unity of A
B293.11-14	A=O
A237.5-7	Apperc and unity of A
A238.21-A239.1	A/T
A239.23-A240.3	A=O
A246.21-A247.1	A=O
A248.23-A249.1	A=P, A=O
A249.7-19	A=P
A249.19-22	A+A
A249.24-A250.1	A+A
A250.16-18	A=R, A/T
A251.6-11	Apperc and unity of A
A251.12-17	A=P, A/T
A251.17-21	A!T
A251.21-A252.1	A/T
A252.1-7	E!T. Art, A/T
A253.4-6	(Transcendental O relates to A in general)
A253.7-10	−K O (transcendental)
B306.7-17	A=P, I=T
B307.19-23	A=N
A256.17-19	T=N, N=LC

B429.23-B430.1	A+T
B430.9-13	S=A
A479.1 ftnt a 6-11	−T(S)=A
A480.21-23	A=O
A490.16-A491.3	A=R, A=O, KA, A/T
A491.4 ftnt a 1-4	A/T
A491.13-18	A/T
A492.6-11	Art, S=A
A492.12-14	S(=A)/T
A493.11-14	A/T, A=R
A493.14-17	A/T
A493.20-22	A/T
A493.22-A494.3	A/T, A=R
A494.15-17	I=T
A494.21-23	Art< A/T, A=R
A498.33-A499.3	A=R, A/T
A499.6-9	A/T
A500.19-25	No whole of A
A505.5-7	A/T
A505.19-22	A/T
A506.6-12	No whole of A, A=R
A506.12-A507.1	A/T
A507.1-4	A/T, A=R
A507.4-8	A/T
A508.13-14	A/T
A514.3-5	A/T
A521.2-8	A/T
A522.12-16	KA
A525.19-21	A/T
A525.22-A526.6	A/T
A530.20-A531.1	
+A531.1-5	A/T
A531.5-9	A/T
A531.16 ftnt a 2-8	A/T
A535.11-14	A/T
A536.16-21	A/T
A537.1-5	A=R, A/T
A537.5-7	Art
A537.10-13	Freedom and Necessity
A538.1-2	−D=A
A538.2-6	A+T
A538.12-15	A+T
A538.15-17	A/T
A539.4-10)	
A539.10-17)	
A539.17-19)	A+T, I=T, Multiple Causality
A539.20-22	Time, A+T
A540.7-9	− KT
A540.10-12	Must think transcendental O, -KT
A540.13-15	A+T

A798.16-22
A803.10-145
A811.4-5

A=P
Multiple causality
Two orders

19. Intelligible

Bxxviii.12-16
Bxl.1 ftnt a 38-42
B68.4-9
B68.13-15
B72.16-21B115.13-15
B115.11-B156.1
B158.1 ftnt a 14-15
B158.15-B159.1
B159.6-9
B162.11 ftnt a 1-4
A138.16-20
A249.1-6
A249.7-19
B306.11-17
B307.14-18
B308.20-24
A255.21-22
A257.15-22
A259.21-23
A286.3-5
A289.4-7
B430.22-B431.3
B431.5-8
A433.13-34
A433.51-61
A466.4-7
A466.7-10
A494.15-18
A530.20-A531.1
A531.5-9
A531.16 ftnt a 2-8
A537.8-10A537.10-13
A538.1-2
A538.9-12
A539.10-17
A539.20-22
A540.3-6
A540.7-12
A541.1-4
A541.12-18
A541.18-22
A544.8-14

A544.14-19
A545.4-8
A545.11-18
A545.18-23
A545.23-A546.1
A546.1-5
A546.5-10
A546.23-A547.2
A552.12-16
A547.2-8
A551.5-6
A551.14-16
A551.16-A552.1
A552.12-16
A553.13-14
A553.15-17
A555.16-17
A556.12-14
A557.1-3
A557.5-9
A560.18-22
A560.22-A561.2
A561.10-11
A561.11-14
A561.26-A562.3
A562.4-7
A562.11-16
A562.16-21
A563.21-A564.1
A564.6-9
A564.12-17
A564.17-20
A564.21-23
A565.18-23
A566.4-8
A566.8-12
A566.12-16
A566.21-A567.5
A583.4 ftnt a 7-10
A672.12-14
A672.16-23
A672.23-A673.4

20. Idealism

Abbreviations

=	is the same as (e.g., A=R)
−	Not (e.g., F−I)
A	Appearances
F	Feeling
I	Intuition
O	Object
R	Representation
S	Space
T	Time
Uc	Understanding and/or imagination as cause of necessary order according to rules.

A30.2-9	S
A32.18-21	T
A32.21-A33.1	T, I
A33.1-4	T
A33.4-6	T, I
A33.6-8	T, I, O
A33.9-10	T, I
A34.4-6	R, T, O
A34.17-A35.3	T, I, O=A
A35.3-6	T, I
A35.22-A36.2	T, I
A36.4-9	T, I, O=A
A36.9-13	S, T, A, O
A36.13-16	T, O, A
A37.6-7	T, I
A37.7-9	T, R
A37.9-11	T, R, O
A37.11-16	T, I, R
A37.16-17	T
A37.19-22	T, I
A38.14-21	S, T, I, R=A
A39.5-9	O=A
A39.11-15	S, T, A
A42.13-14	S, T, I
A42.22-24	S, T, I
A44.4-8	R=A, I
A44.18-25	O=R, I
A45.13-16	O=A
A46.6-11	A=R, I, S
A48.19-25	S, O, A
A48.25-A49	I, O, S, T, A
A49.6-9	A
B66.20-B67.6	O=A, I
A80.7-9	A
A87.25-A88.1	O=R, I
A89.10-11	S, T, A
A90.12-15	I, S, T, O
A92.8-10	A
A92.16-18	A
A93.5-7	A
A93.7-10	A
A93.10-13	A
A93.16-18	A
A93.18-21	A
A94.1-5	A
A94.5-7	A
A94.10-13	A, O
A100.9-13	A, Uc
A101.15-20	I, Uc
A104.7-11	A=R

A109.3-7	A=R, O
A115.9-13	I
A120.1-7	A, O
A123.11-19	Uc
A125.14-19	Uc
A126.21-A127.5	Uc, A, O
A127.11-15	A, Uc, I
A127.16-20	Uc
A127.24-A128.33	Uc, A
A128.7-9	Uc
A128.16-18	O=A
A129.2-7	O, R
A129.11-18	O=A
A129.21-A130.1	I=R, Uc
B129.11-B130.1	Uc
A130.6-10	A
A130.10-12	A
A137.11-15	Uc, R, O
B137.24-B138.1	Uc
B138.1-2	Uc
B138.4-5	O
B154.6-13	I, Uc
B163.16-18	A, Uc
B136.18-24	Uc
B164.1-5	A, Uc, I
B164.11-13	A=R
B164.13-15	A=R
B165.2-5	Uc
B166.4-5	O
B167.4-8	Uc
A141.21-33	Uc
A141.23-A142.4	Uc
A143.11-14	T, I, O=A
A158.10-13	Uc, O
A158.14-A159.2	Uc, O
A165.15-18	I, S, T
A165.24-A166.3	Uc
A166.3-6	Uc, O
A175.23-A76.2	Uc, O
A186.8-11	A
A186.14-16	Uc
A234.14-19	Uc, A=O
A190.3-7	Uc, A=O=R
A190.9-12	A=C=R
A190.24-A191.2	A=R
A191.2-4	A
A191.5-8	A=O=R
A191.10-17	Uc, A, O, R
A193.3-6	Uc
A193.13-17	Uc, O, A

A193.20-21	Uc
A196.9-14	Uc
A196.14-17	Uc, A
A216.3-5	Uc
B274.17-21	S
B275.11-B278.20	
A230.15-19	Uc
A250.16-18	A=R, O
A251.21-A252.1	A=R
B308.3-6	S, T, Uc
A369.6-11	A=R, S, T, I
A369.11-14	S, T
A370.1-4	S
A370.4-5	R
A370.7-10	A=R, S, O
A370.12	S
A370.15-19	S
A370.22-23	S
A370.23-24	O=A=R
A370.24-25	O=R
A370.25-A371.1	=R
A371.9-12	O=R
A371.24-A372.3	S, A=R
A372.8-13	A=R
A372.19-20	O=A=R
A372.20-22	O=A=R
A373.4-5	S, T
A374.17	S=R
A374.19 ftnt a 1-2	S=R
A374.19 ftnt a 3-4	S=R
A374.19 ftnt a 4-5	S=R
A374.19 ftnt a 5-9	A=R
A375.5-6	S=R, A=R
A375.9-10	S=R
A375.12-14	S
A375.14-15	S
A375.15-A376.6	I, O, S=R
A376.19-A377.4	S=R=A
A378.16-19	O, S
A379.4-8	Ego=A
A383.5-12	A=R
A384.14-21	A
1384.21-A385.4	A
A392.3-10	A=R
A392.15-20	S=R
B410.10-18	Uc
A429.14 ftnt b 1-2	S, I, O
A429.14 ftnt b 2-7	S, A
A429.14 ftnt b 7-11	S, A, I
A429.14 ftnt b 11-17	S, A, I

B431.23-24	S, I
A431.25-26	S, I
A431.26-29	S, A
A431.30-35	S, O
A431.35-41	S, A
A431.47-A433.3	S, A
A433.34-41	S, A, I
A433.51-61	S, I
A443.12 ftnt a 1-2	T
A454.20-21	T, A
A490.16-A491.3	O, A, S, T, A=R
A491.4 ftnt a 1-4	O
A491.4-7	R
A491.13-18	A, T, O
A491.19-21	O, I, S, T, R
A491.19-21	I, S, O=R
A492.3-6	S=R, T=R, A=R
A492.6-11	Ago=A
A493.12-14	Ego=A
A492.19-20	O=R
A493.10-11	Uc, O=R
A493.11-14	A=R
A493.14-17	A=R
A494.6-7	S, T
A494.12-15	S, T
A494.21-23	A=R
A495.21-A496.1	O=R
A498.22-A499.3	A=R
A499.6-9	S, T, A=R
A504.20-A505.3	O
A505.3-5	R
A505.5-7	A
A505.19-22	A
A506.3-5	A=R
A506.6-13	A=R
A506.12-A507.1	A=R
A507.1-4	A=R
A507.4-8	A
A507.8-12	I, O
A508.1-5	S, T, A
A508.5-11	A
A508.11-13	A
A508.13-17	A=R, I, S, T
A510.10-12	A
A514.3-5	A
A514.5-9	A
A525.22-A526.2	R, I, A
A537.16-20	A
A553.7-9	A=R
A619.13-18	S

21. Aspects Distinction vs. Existence Distinction

Aspects Distinction	E! Distinction
Bxviii.9 ftnt a 6-12	A36.4-9
Bxx.11-24	A37.18-22
Bxxvii.14-Bxxviii.4	A39.5-9
Bxxviii.12-16	A42.2-3
Bxxix.11-15	A42.3-9
A27.15-23	A42.10-11
A35.7-16	A44.18-25
A38.14-21	A45.13-16
B155.8-11	A46.6-11
B155.11-B156.1	B67.19-B68.3
B156.14-20	B68.18-21
A138.13-20	B68.22-B69.5
B191.5-8	B69.6-12
A191.10-17	B69.12-15
A193.7-11	B72.6-8
A206.17-24	A50.5-6
A249.7-19	A50.12-13
A249.19-22	A51.5-9
A249.24-A250.1	A51.9-11
A250.10-14	A55.19-21
B307.11-14	A105.3-9
B307.19-23	A109.3-7
B307.23-B308.2	A114.4-13
A254.15-18	A125.14-19
A255.18-20	A126-A127.5
A359.18-21	A127.11-14
A359.22-A360.4	A127.16-20
A366.5-9	A127.24-A128.33
B430.4-8	A128.7-9
A443.38-46	A128.16-18
A461.7-11	A129.11-18
A461.11-19	B154.2-3
A461.19-29	B155.8-11
A461.29	B155.11-B156.1
A536.7-9	B156.14-20
A536.16-21	B158.1 ftnt a 13-14
A537.1-5	B164.5-9
A537.10-13	A249.7-9
A537.13-15	B306.8-11
A537.16-20	B306.11-17
A538.2-6	B308.24-B309.1
A538.6-7	B427.23-B428.3
A538.7-9	A492.12-14
A538.9-12	A492.19-20
A538.12-15	A493.11-14

Section IV

Representation

22. Representation Texts: Digest

Abbreviations

=	Is the same as (e.g., A = R)
–	Not (e.g., –R of things as given = R of T)
A	Appearance
I	Intuition
O	Object
R	Representation
T	Thing in itself

Note
Capital letters have sometimes been used to indicate a useful distinction of philosophical sense rather than the usual grammatical division.

Bxvii.7-15	Intuition as R must be related to O.
Bxx.11-24	–R of things as given = R of T.
Bxxvii.12-14	R of freedom not self-constradictory.
Bxl.1 ftnt a 14-19	Rs as determinations of me require a permanent distinct from them.
Bxl.1 ftnt a 24-33	Consciousness of my existence is more than consciousness of R.
Bxl.1 ftnt a 38-42	There is my intellectual consciousness of my existence in the R 'I am'.
Bxl.1 ftnt a 60-67	–R of something permanent = permanent R. R refers to an external permanent something that is distinct from all Rs.
B1.1-8	Rs are produced by Os acting on senses.
A19.1-10	Receptivity for Rs is sensibility.
A19.15-16	Sensation is the effedt of an O on the faculty of R.
A20.13-14	Pure R is without sensation.
A22.12-14	By outer sense, we prepresent O as outside us.
A23.19-25	R 'outside of' presupposes R of space.

B68.4-9	All sense Rs = appearance.
B68.18-B69.5	If the faculty of coming to consciousness of oneself
	Is to seek out (to apprehend) that which lies in the mind, it must affect the mind. Only in this way can it intuit itself. The form of this self-intuition (which form exists antecedently in the mind)
	Determines the R of time the mode in which the manifold is together in the mind. Since it intuits itself not as it would represent itself if immediately self-active, But as it is affected by itself, i.e., as it appears, not as it is.
B69.6-12	The I of outer Os and the self-tuition of the mind.
	Represent the Os and the mind in space and time as they affect our senses, i.e., as they appear and are actually given.
B72.6-8	Our mode of I is dependent upon the existence of the O.
	It is possible, therefore, only if the faculty of R is affected.
A50.1-3	Knowledge derives from two fundamental sources of the mind.
	The first is the capacity for receiving Rs, i.e., receptivity for impressions.
A50.3-5	The second is the power of knowing an O thru these Rs, i.e., spontaneity
A51.5-9	Sensibility (receptivity) = power of mind to receive Rs when it is affected.
A56.6-9	General logic deals only with that form which understanding gives Rs whatever their origin.
A56.12-17	Transcendental logic studies the possibility of *a priori* Rs.
A56.19-22	Transcendental logic studies *a priori* Rs that relate to Os.
A68.13-15	No R except I is in immediate relation to an O.
A68.17-21	Judgment is the mediate knowledge of an O, I.e., is the R of a R of it,
A69.4-8	Judgments are functions of unity among Rs.
A77.4-9	Mind receives Rs of Os.
A78.22-24	Transcendental logic teaches how the pure synthesis of Rs is brought to concepts.
A79.3-6	Concepts which give unity to synthesis are Rs of necessary synthetic unity.
A79.8-10	The function which gives unity to the Rs in a judgment also gives unity to the synthesis of Rs in an I.
A92.5-8	There are only two possible ways in which synthetic Rs and Os obtain necessary relation to one another.
A92.8-10	Either the O makes the R possible or the R makes the O possible.
A92.10-13	In regard to sensation, the O makes the R possible. In this case, the R is never *a priori*.

A121.12-17	The preferential connection of R with R is due to the rule in imagination called "association of Rs".
A123.20-22	'I' is the correlate of all Rs.
A129.21-A130.1	I = sensible Rs.
B129.7-11	The manifold of R can be given in an I that is mere receptivity.
	The form of this lies *a priori* in the faculty of R.
	It is merely the mode in which the subject is affected.
B129.11-B130.6	Combination = act of spontaneity of the faculty of R.
B130.6-11	'Combination' is the only R that can't be given.
B130.22-B131.5	Combination of the R of the synthetic unity of the manifold.
	R of this unity can't arise out of combination.
	R of this unity plus R of manifold give the concept of combination.
B131.1 ftnt a 1-7	Regardless of content, consciousness of Rs must be distinguished when the manifold is considered.
B131.2-5	R of unity plus R of manifold make possible the concept of combination.
B131.15-B132.4	'I think' accompanies all Rs.
B132.4-15	R 'I think' = act of spontaneity.
	R 'I think' = pure apperception.
	R 'I think' = self-consciousness which generates the R 'I think'.
	R 'I think' can't be accompanied by any further R.
B132.17-B133.2	R as *mine* = Rs belong to one self-consciousness
	And so conform to the condition of one universal self-consciousness.
B133.4-7	Identity of apperception is possible only thru the consciousness of the synthesis of Rs.
B133.7-13	Empirical consciousness which accompanies Rs is without relation to the identity of the subject.
	That relation comes from my joining R with R and being conscious of this synthesis.
B133.12-18	R of the identity of consciousness is possible only thru the synthesis of Rs in one consciousness.
B134.1-6	The thought 'Rs given in intuition belong to me' = the thought 'I unite them in one self-consciousness'
	But is not itself consciousness of the synthesis of Rs.
B134.16-B135.3	Combination belongs only to understanding which is the faculty of bringing Rs to the unity of apperception.
B135.10-14	Thru R of 'I', nothing is given.
B135.17-21	I am conscious of the self as identical in regard to the manifold of Rs in intuition because I call them all mine
	Thereby constituting one intuition.
B135.21-B136.1	The above = I am conscious *a priori* of the necessary synthesis of Rs which = the original synthetic unity of apperception and under which all given Rs stand.

B164.11-13	A = R of T as unknown in itself.
B164.13-15	As = R of T as unknown in itself.
B164.13-15	As as R are subject only to the laws of synthesis.
A140.22-24	Schema = R of a universal procedure of imagination for providing an image for a concept.
A142.11-16	Schema = transcendental product of imagination which concerns the determination of inner sense in general in respect of its form (time).
	In respect of all Rs that are to be connected *a priori* in conformity with the unity of apperception.
A145.5-6	The schema of each category makes possible the R of time determination.
A145.8-10	The schema of quality = synthesis of sensation with the R of time.
A156.1-5	'O is given' (i.e., immediate presentation) = R thru which is is thought relates to experience (actual or possible).
A156.10-12	R of space and time is a mere schema of reproductive imagination that assembles Os of experience.
B202.12-B203.2	Rs of space and time are generated.
B203.2-10	R of O first becomes possible thru consciousness of the synthetic unity of the manifold and homogeneous in intuition in general as the concept of a *quantum*.
A162.21-A163.3	A line can't be represented without its being drawn.
B207.16-B208.1	The real of sensation as related to O in general = matter for some O in general
	Whereby something is represented as existing in space and time.
B208.8-11	Sensation is not an objective R.
A167.19-24	Sensation does not involve synthesis from parts to the whole R.
B219.5-8	Apprehension contains no R of any necessity which determines the appearancaes to have connected existence in space and time.
B219.9-12	Experience = knowledge of O thru perception.
	Therefore the relation involved in the existence of the manifold must be represented not as it is constructed in time,
	But as it exists objectively in time.
B219.16-18	Experience = R of necessary connection perception.
A177.15-18	Inner sense = sum of all Rs.
A183.1-3	The permanent = substratum of the empirical R of time.
A186.14-16	Permanence = mode in which we represent the existence of O in the field of appearances.
A189.11-13	Every R may be entitled to O.
A189.13-15	Every R can be an O.
A190.3-7	As as Os of consciousness = their apprehension.
A190.9-12	Mind deals only with Rs.
A190.12-15	Ts affect us thru Rs.

A213.23-A214.5	Without community, there would be no unity of perception of an appearance in space, no connection of the chain of empirical Rs, no unity of Rs in time.
A214.11-16	In order to represent Os as coexisting in mutual connection they must mutually determine their position in one time and thereby stand in the community of apperception and constitute a whole.
B275.19-21	Perception of the permanent is possible only thru a thing outside me And not thru the mere R of a thing outside me.
B277.3-5	R 'I am' expresses the consciousness which can accompany all thought.
B278.7-10	Consciousness of myself in the R 'I' is not intuition. It is the mere intellectual R of the spontaneity of the thinking subject.
B278.15-20	From the fact that the existence of outer things is required for the possibility of a determinate consciousness of the self, It does not follow that every intuitive R of outer things involves their existence, For their R could be a product merely of imagination.
B278.20-23	Such Rs are reproductions of previous perceptions.
A233.19-23	The principles of modality do not enlarge the R of O.
A242.15-A243.2	Permanence subtracted from substance = mere logical R of subject.
A245.20-23	Pure categories are mere Rs of things in general. So far as the manifold of their I would have to be thought thru a logical function.
A249.19-22	Senses represent something as it appears,
A249.24-A250.1	Thru intellectual I, Os are represented as they are.
A250.15-16	All Rs are referred by the understanding to Os.
A250.16-18	Appearances = Rs.
A251.1-5	The transcendental O is not itself an O of knowledge. it is merely the R of A under the concept of O in general, A concept which is determined thru the manifold of these As.
A251.6-11	Categories do not represent an O given to the understanding alone.
A251.21-A252.1	As = R.
A252.1-7	The word 'appear' indicates a relation to T, i.e., to an O independent of sensibility Whose immediate R is sensible.
B306.22-B307.2	When understanding calls an O a phenomenon, it forms an independent R of an O in itself And represents itself as able to have concepts of such an O.
A253.21-23	Affection of sensibility by itself = relation of R to O.
A258.1-9	The statement "sense represents Os as they appear and understanding represents them as they are" = O must be represented as O of experience,

A347.5-7	R of a thinking being is possible only thru the transference of my consciousness to other things.
A350.4-6	There is no I in the R 'I'.
A350.7-10	We perceive this R as present in all thought, But not that it is an abiding I.
A350.16-18	Consciousness is alone what makes Rs = thoughts.
A252.15-18	The *nervus probandi* of the argument of transcendental psychology is: If the multiplicity of Rs is to form a single R, they must be contained in the absolute unity of the thinking subject.
A353.3-8	Unity of thought = many Rs as collective.
A353.23-A354.1	In order to represent a thing being, I must substitute my subject for the O.
A354.2-4	We demand the absolute unity of the subject of a thought only because otherwise we could not say ' I think' (the manifold in one R).
A354.19-22	We can represent a thinking being only by putting ourselves and the formula of our consciousness in the place of the other.
A355.4-7	'I am simple' = R 'I' contains no manifold and is an absolute logical unity.
A355.8-10	The psychological proof is founded on the indivisible unity of an R which governs only the verb in its relation to a person.
A355.14-17	The R of 'I' means a something in general (transcendental subject), the R of which must be simple because there is nothing determinate in it.
A355.17-19	Nothing can be represented that is more simple than that which is represented thru the conception of a mere something.
A355.19-21	The simplicity of R of subject is not eo ipso knowledge of the simplicity of the subject itself.
A357.13-17	Since the thinking subject is represented as an O of inner sense It can't, as thinking, be an O of outer sense, i.e., an A in space.
A358.7-12	The something which underlies A and affects our sense so that it obtain Rs of space, matter, shape, etc., May, viewed as noumenon (or transcendental O) be the subject of our thoughts.
A358.12-15	The mode in which outer sense is affected gives no intuition of Rs, will, etc.
A359.15-18	I may assume that the substance in relation to outer sense possesses thoughts which can be consciously represented in its own inner sense.
A362.20-21	In apperception, time is represented in me.
A362.21-A363.3	'I' accompanies all Rs at all times.
A363.18 ftnt a 4-15	(Kant postulates the possibility of substance communicating their Rs to other substances).

A364.11-16	R 'I' is the only permanent A which we encounter in the soul.
	But this also may be in flux.
A366.6-9	T = transcendental O, and is represented as something external
	And its permanence as A can be observed.
A366.10-13	To observe 'I' in the change of Rs I must use myself as the correlate together with the universal conditions of my consciousness.
A369.6-11	A = R.
A370.1-5	The transcendental idealist admits the existence of matter assuming only the certainty of his Rs, i.e., cogito ergo sum.
A370.8-9	Matter = external R.
A370.19-22	I am conscious of my Rs, therefore both I and the Rs exist.
A370.22-24	External Os = As = Rs.
A370.24-25	The Os of these Rs exist only thru these Rs.
A371.3-6	R of me as thinking subject belongs to inner sense.
	R of extended things belongs to outer sense.
A371.9-12	The Os of both inner and outer sense = Rs.
A371.24-A372.3	External things (i.e., matter) = Rs.
A372.8-13	If outer As as Rs are produced in us by their Os, and these Os = Ts, the existence of these Os can be known only thru inference.
A372.15-19	– That something outside us (in the transcendental sense), which is the cause of our outer I = O which we think in the R of matter.
A372.19-20	Appearances = R.
A373.16-19	Space and time are *a priori* Rs which are forms of sensible I prior to any real Os Which by determining our sense thry sensation enables us to represent os under sensible relations.
A374.11-13	Perception represents something real in space.
A374.13-15	Space = R of the possibility of coexistence
	Perception = R of reality.
A374.16-17	This reality is represented in space.
A374.17	Space = R.
A374.18-19	The real in space = the represented in space.
A374.19 ftnt a 1-2	The real space = the represented in space.
A374.19 ftnt a 3	Space = R.
A374.19 ftnt a 3-4	The real in space = the represented in space.
A374.19 ftnt a 4-5	The real in space = the represented in space.
A374.19 ftnt a 5-9	Things exist only in their Rs.
	A = R.
A374.19-A375.1	The given, i.e., that which is represented thru perception, is real.
A375.1-4	The real = that which is immediately given thru empirical I.

	Only the real can be pictured in imagination since the real in I can't be invented.
A375.9-10	A = R.
A375.15-A376.6	No O 'outside' us (in the transcendental sense) corresponds to perception. It can't be intuited and represented as outside us since these require space and the real in space = R = perception.
A376.19-A377.4	Space = form of Rs.
	It has objective reality in relation to outer As (i.e., Rs).
A378.13-15	Space = inner mode of R in which perceptions are connected.
A378.16-19	Outer Os as Ts could not be known as real since we depend on Rs which are in us.
A379.19-22	'I' as represented thru inner sense in time and Os in space outside me are specifically distinct As
	But not necessarily different things.
A381.19-20	R of 'I' has no manifold.
A381.20-A382.2	Therefore it seems to represent or denote a simple O.
A382.8-12	'I' = mere form of consciousness which can accompany the two kinds of Rs
	And which can make them into knowledge if something is given in intuition which can be used as material for the R of O.
A391.1-4	There is no knowledge of the transcendental cause of the Rs in outer sense.
A391.4-11	If matter is T, then it can't be the cause of Rs since it shows no causality other than movement.
A393.6-8	The transcendental O is the cause of outer As (Rs).
A398.8-9	The 'I' is represented as an O which I think.
A401.23-25	Categories represent the synthesis of the manifold of intuition in so far as the manifold has unity in apperception.
A401.25-27	Self-consciousness in general is the R of that which is the condition of all unity And is itself unconditioned.
A403.19-21	Reason represents subsistence, reality, and unity as the unconditioned conditions of the possibility of a thinking being.
A405.7-11	The R 'I am' expresses the pure formula
	all my experience in general
	And presents itself as valid for all thinking beings.
A408.16-18	The identity of the subject (the logical unity the meaning, and function of the R 'I'—cf. B407.20-24) of which I am conscious in all Rs, does not concern an I of the subject given as O.
B411.11 ftnt a 1-7	'Thought' as it consists in relation to self-consciousness represents merely the relation of self as subject (as form of thought).
B419.14-17	The absolute unity of apperception = the R 'I'.
B422.9-11	The subject in which the R of time has its ground can't thereby determine its existence in time.

B422.14 ftnt a 21-24	To call the 'I think' an exmpirical proposition does not mean that the 'I' is an empirical R.
B422.14 ftnt a	Without an empirical R to supply the material for thought The *actus* 'I think' would not occur.
B429.6-9	− If I represent myself as the subject or ground of thoughts, these modes of R = categories of substance or cause.
A452.12 ftnt a 2-4	Subjectively, in actual consciousness, the R of time, like all Rs, is given only in connection with perceptions.
A490.16-A491.3	All Os of experience = As = Rs.
A491.19-21	Transcendental idealism admits the reality of os in outer I and all change in time as represented in inner sense.
A492.6-11	− The inner sensible I of our mind as an O of consciousness whih is represented as determined by the succession of different states in time = the proper self as it exists in itself, i.e., = the transcendental subject.
A493.11-14	Appearances as Rs are real only in perception Which is nothing but the reality of an empirical R, i.e., A.
A493.22-A494.3	As = Rs.
A494.4-6	The faculty of sensible intuition = receptivity = capacity for being affected with Rs.
A494.6-7	The relations among which are mere forms of sensibility.
A494.8-10	And as connected in space and time according to the laws of the unity of experience = Os.
A494.10-12	The non-sensible cause of these Rs can't be known and so can't be intuited as O.
A494.12-15	Such an O would have to be represented as in neither space nor time.
A494.21-23	As = Rs.
A495.4-12	Things of past time are real only in so far as I represent a regressive series of possible perceptions in accord with the empirical laws, i.e., that the course of the world leads us to a past time-series. This series is represented as actual not in itself but in connection with possible experience.
A495.21-A496	Os = Rs.
A498.22-A499.3	As as Rs can be given only in so far as I know them.
A400.19-25	We man not assume the totality of the synthesis and the series thereby represented.
A506.3-5	Since the series is made up of subordinated Rs, they (the series) exist only in the dynamical regress.
A506.6-12	As, which exist only in Rs, can't be a total series Which is possible only for Ts.

A507.1-4	As = Rs.
A508.13-17	As = empirical Rs and not Os in themselves.
A537.1-5	As = Rs.
A538.15-17	Since As are not Ts, they must rest on a transcendental O which determines them as Rs.
A547.9-12	Imperatives indicate that either reason has causality or at least we so represent it.
A563.7-9	A = R.
A563.16-21	Phenomenon = R.
A566.8-12	As can be viewed as contingent modes whereby beings that are themselves intelligences represent intelligible Os.
A577.23-A578.5	Reason, by representing the necessary complete determination of things, does not presuppose the existence of a being corresponding to this idea.
A581.13-19	Reality in the field of A (that which corresonds to sensation) must be given, Otherwise it could not be thought nor its possibility represented.
A581.19-23	An O of the sense can be completely determined only if it is compared with all possible predicates int he field of A, and so represented positively or negatively.
A583.4 ftnt a 1-4	The ideal of the *ens realissimum* is a mere R.
A615.18-22	No existence can be represented as absolutely necessary since I can always think its non-existence.
A619.10-13	We can't avoid the transcendental subretion by which the formal principle of the regulative use of the ideal of the necessary original being is represented as constitutive and then hypostatised.
A619.21-A620.2	It is natural that the idea *ens realissimum* be represented as an actual O and as necessary.
A658.12-18	Things can be represented from the stand-point of a concept as the station of an observer determining an horizon.
A670.10-12	Ideas of pure reason enable us to represent other Os indirectly as in systematic unity thru their relation to the idea.
A674.9-13	In thinking the O of an idea, we think an x which we represent as standing to the sum of A analgous to the way As stand to one another.
A700.10-18	In thinking the cause of the world, we may represent it thru various unavoidable anthropomorphisms.
A701.1-7	We represent the regulative law of systematic unity (A700.18-22) as involving the idea of a supreme Author.
A720.10-13	The matter of As by which things are given in space and time, can only be represented in perception *a posteriori*.
A720.13-14	The only concept which represens *a priori* this empirical content of As is the concept of a thing in general.

A720.24-A721.1	Transcendental propositions contain only the rule according to which we seek empirically for the synthetic unity of that which is incapable of intuitive representation *a priori*, i.e., perception.
A801.7 ftnt a 3-5	Feeling is not a faculty by which things are represented.
A802.5-7	A will which can be determined independently of sensuous impulses, and so by motives represented only by reason = free will.
A802.12-15	We can control impressions on the faculty of sensuous desire thru Rs of the useful or injurious.
A811.3-4	We are forced by reason to represent ourselves as belonging to a moral world.
A815.26-A816.5	The world must be represented as having originated from an idea if it is to be in harmony with that use of reason which is founded entirely on the idea of a supreme good, i.e., the moral good.

23. Signs, Point (To the Nonempirical)

Bx1 ftnt a 60-67	refer
A19.11-14	character
A97.22-A98.2	point
B142.3-4	indicate
A136.2-5	mark
A143.5-7	points
A180.2-4	mark
A197.16-20	character
A198.11-16	refer
A198.24-A199.2	refer
A220.13-16	character
A225.9-15	mark
A225.15-17	mark
A252.1-7	indicate
A252.8-12	signify
A252.12-15	signify
A359.21-22	sign
A373.21-22	exhibit
A374.1-3	indicate
A381.17-A382	denote
A415.1-7	point
B422.14 ftnt a 17-21	denote
A539.4-6	character
A539.6-10	character
A539.13-17	character
A539.17-19	character

Section V

Deduction

24. Deduction: Preliminary Texts

25. Deduction in A: Linear Content

Abbreviations

A.	Actual Objects: Idealism/Realism
Ap.	*A priori*
Deduc.	Deduction
Descrip.	Descriptivism
Emp.	Empirical
E.	Entities/Apriorism
Fac. Dis.	Faculty Discourse
Ident. State.	Identity Statement
M.A.	Mind as Act
M.U.S.	Mind as Unitary Subject
M.K.S.	Mind as Knowing the Self
Nec.	Necessary
O.	Object
Perspec.	Perspectivism
Rep.	Representationalism
Trans.	Transcendental

Note

In its first occurence, each abbreviation will be given in parentheses after the term or terms for which it stands.

A85.4-8	Entities/A priorism (E.)
A85.8-11	Limit
A85.11-13	Deduction (Deduc.)
A85.13-16	Empirical (Emp.) Deduc.
A85.16-17	Emp. Deduc.
A85.18-22	E. Acutal Objects: Idealism/Realism (A.)
A85.22-A86.3	No Emp. Deduc., E.
A86.11-16	Mind as Act (M.A.)
A86.16-19	Descriptivism (Descrip.)
A86.20-22	No Emp. Deduc., E.
A86.23-A87.1	No Emp. Deduc.
A87.4-6	Transcendental (Trans.) Deduc.
A87.6-10	No Emp. Deduc., E.
A87.11-14	No Emp. Deduc., E.
A87.17-20	E.
A87.21-24	E., A.
A87.25-A88.1	A.
A88.2-5	Categories need Deduc.
A88.5-8	A.
A88.8-11	A.
A88.11-17	Trans. Deduc. Necessary (Nec.)
A89.1-5	Trans. Deduc. Nec.

A89.16-18	A.
A89.18-20	A.
A89.20-21	A.
A89.21-A90.1	A.
A90.1-3	A.
A90.3-6	Nec.
A90.6-9	A.
A90.9-12	A.
A90.12-15	A.
A90.15-18	M.A., A., E.
A90.18-20	A., M.A.
A90.21-24	A.
A90.24-25	A.
A90.25-A91.2	A.
A91.2-9	A.
A91.9-11	E.
A91.11-12	E.
A91.12-15	E.
A91.15-18	E.
A91.19-20	E.
A91.20-A92.1	E.
A92.1-4	E.
A92.5-8	A.
A92.8-10	Idealism vs., Realism
A92.10-11	Limit
A92.11-13	Sense
A92.13-16	Limit
A92.16-18	Idealism, M.A.
A92.19-A93.2	*A priori* (Ap.), Object (O.)
A93.2-5	Ap., O., Sense
A93.5-7	Ap., O., Sense, Nec.
A93.7-10	Ap., O.
A93.10-13	Idealism, O.
A93.13-16	Realism, O.
A93.16-18	Ap., E.
A93.18-21	Ap., E.
A93.21-23	Ap., E.
A94.1-5	Ap., E.
A94.5-7	Ap., E.
A94.7-10	Ap., Limit
A94.10-13	Ap., E.
A94.14-18	E., Limit, Faculty Discourse (Fac. Dis.)
A94.18-21	Fac. Dis., M.A.
A94.21-23	Fac. Dis., M.A., E.
A95.3-7	E., Limit
A95.7-8	Limit
A95.8-10	Limit
A95.10-13	Limit, E.
A95.14-15	Limit
A95.15-16	Limit, E.

A106.6-12	Nec.
A106.6-9	M.A.
A106.10-12	M.A.
A106.13-19	M.U.S., E.
A106.19-21	A.
A106.22-A107.1	A., M.U.S., Realism
A107.1-3	Mind as Knowing Self (M.K.S.)
A107.3-6	M.K.S.
A107.6-8	Nec., E.
A107.8-11	Nec., E.
A107.17-21	E., M.U.S.
A107.21-24	E., M.U.S.
A108.1-4	M.A.
A108.11-20	M.U.S.
A108.4-7	M.K.S.
A108.4-20	Realism
A108.7-20	E.
A108.7-14	Nec., Ident. State.
A108.12-14	A.
A108.14-20	M.A.
A108.14-A109.7	A.
A108.22-A109.7	Rep., Realism
A109.3-18	A.
A109.8-A110.10	E.
A109.12-15	Realism
A109.15-18	Ident. State., M.A.
A109.15-A110.10	Nec.
A109.18-20	Realism, Perspec.
A110.6-9	E., M.U.S.
A110.9-10	E., M.U.S.
A110.11-15	E., M.U.S.
A110.15-17	M.U.S.
A110.17-18	M.U.S.
A110.19-20	M.U.S.
A111.1-3	M.U.S.
A111.5-7	M.U.S.
A111.13-16	M.U.S.
A111.16-18	E., A.
A111.20-23	E., M.U.S.
A112.4-6	E., M.A.
A112.6-10	E., M.A., M.U.S.
A112.10-13	M.U.S.
A112.16-18	E.
A112.19-22	E.
A113.15-20	E., M.U.S.
A113.20-23	M.A.
A114.15-19	M.U.S.
A114.19-24	M.A.
A115.3-6	Descrip.
A115.6-9	E.

A125.5-7	M.A.
A125.7-11	M.A.
A125.11-13	M.A.
A125.14-19	M.A.
A125.17-A126.2	Nec., E.
A126.3-7	Fac. Dis.
A126.8	Fac. Dis.
A126.8-10	Fac. Dis.
A126.10-11	Fac. Dis.
A126.11-13	Fac. Dis.
A126.13-15	Realism
A126.15-18	Realism, E.
A126.18-21	Nec., E.
A126.18-A127.15	M.A.
A127.16-20	E.
A127.20-24	Belief
A127.20-A128.6	A.
A127.24-A128.9	E.
A128.10-13	M.A.
A128.13-15	M.A., E.
A129.2-7	Rep.
A130.2-4	M.A.
A130.4-6	E.
A130.6-10	Idealism
A130.10-12	Idealism
A130.12-14	M.A., M.U.S., E.

26. Deduction in A: Topical Content

Topics

1. Actual Object: Idealism/Realism
2. A priori
3. Belief
4. Categories need Deduction
5. Deduction
6. Deduction, Empirical
7. Deduction, Transcendental
8. Descriptivism
9. Entities/A priorism
10. Faculty Discourse
11. Idealism
12. Identity Statements
13. Limit
14. Mind as Act
15. Mind as Knowing Self
16. Mind as Unitary Subject
17. Necessity
18. Object

19. Perspectivism
A104.17-A105.2
A109.18-A110.6
A122.9-18

20. Realism
A92.8-10
A93.13-16
A98.16-A99.1
A106.22-A107.1
A108.4-20
A108.22-A109.7
A109.12-15
A109.18-A110.6
A120.1
A120.1-2
A120.2-5
A126.13-15
A126.15-18

21. Representationalism
A97.11-13
A97.13-14
A98.16-A99.1
A99.10-11
A104.6-7
A104.7-11
A108.23-A109.7
A115.9-13
A129.2-7

22. Sense
A93.2-5
A93.5-7
A97.14-15
A97.16
A99.7-9
A99.10-11

27. Deduction in B: Linear Content

Abbreviations

A	Actual Object
Ap.	A priori
Deduc.	Deduction
Descrip.	Descriptivism
Emp.	Empirical
E.	Entities/A priorism
Fac. Dis.	Faculty Discourse
Ident. State.	Indentity Statement
M.A.	Mind as Act
M.U.S.	Mind as Unitary Subject
M.K.S.	Mind as Knowing the Self
Nec.	Necessary
Perspec.	Perspectivism
Rep.	Representationalism
Trans.	Transcendental

B129.7-11	Belief
B139.7-B130.1	A.
B129.7-B130.6	Fac. Dis., Rep.
B130.1-22	M.A.
B130.6-13	Rep., E.
B130.16-22	Fac. Dis.
B130.20-B131.5	Rep.

B130.20-B131.14	E., Ident. State.
B131.1 ftnt a 1-7	Realism
B131.2-5	Rep.
B131.5-6	M.U.S.
B131.6-9	M.U.S., E.
B131.9-10	M.A.
B131.10-14	M.U.S., E.
B131.15-B132.4	Rep.
B132.3-8	Sense
B132.4-6	Nec.
B132.7	Realism, M.U.S., Ident. State.
B132.7-8	Perspec.
B132.7-15	A., M.A.
B132.7-B133.2	E.
B132.10-11	Ident. State.
B132.20-23	A. (cf., B131.1 ftnt a 1-7)
B133.4-16	M.A.
B133.4-18	Realism, Descrip.
B133.9-16	Rep.
B133.18 ftnt a 12-15	M.U.S., E.
B133.18 ftnt a 15-16	M.U.S., Ident. State., Fac. Dis., E.
B134.1-6	Rep., M.A.
B134.8-10	M.U.S., E.
B134.10-16	M.A.
B134.13-B135.3	Belief
B135.3-5	M.U.S.
B135.6-10	Nec., E.
B135.6-14	Rep.
B135.14-16	M.A., E.
B135.16-17	Fac. Dis.
B135.17-B136.1	M.U.S.
B135.21-B136.1	Nec.
B136.2-5	Sense
B136.2-8	Nec.
B136.5-8	M.U.S.
B136.8 ftnt a 1-8	Rep.
B136.8 ftnt a 1-10	Descrip.
B136.8-10	E.
B136.10-B137.1	M.A., M.U.S.
B137.1-5	M.U.S., M.A.
B137.2-4	Ident. State., Rep.
B137.6-7	Fac. Dis.
B137.7-16	A., M.U.S.
B137.11-16	Ident. State.
B137.15-16	Fac. Dis.
B137.17-21	M.U.S.
B137.17-B138.7	Sense
B137.21-24	M.A.
B137.24-B138.7	M.A., Ident. State.
B138.2-7	M.U.S.

B138.6-7	Realism
B138.7-10	M.U.S.
B138.10-12	M.U.S.
B138.13-20	Rep.
B138.16-17	A.
B138.19-21	Nec.
B138.21-B139.4	Rep.
B138.24-B139.4	M.U.S., M.A.
B139.12-14	M.U.S.
B139.14-18	M.U.S.
B139.20-B140.3	M.A.
B140.3-9	Nec.
B140.3-10	M.U.S.
B140.9-10	M.U.S.
B140.10-13	M.U.S.
B140.14-16	Nec.
B141.8-14	M.U.S., M.A., E.
B141.8-B142.26	A.
B141.14-B142.3	M.U.S., M.A., E.
B142.1-14	M.U.S.
B142.1-26	Rep.
B142.5-12	Nec.
B142.14-19	M.U.S.
B142.19-21	M.A.
B142.22-26	Realism
B143.1-3	Nec., Belief
B143.1-6	M.U.S.
B143.1-14	E.
B143.4-6	Ident. State.
B143.4-6 + B143.10-12	A. (cf., B93.5-7)
B143.4-10	M.A.
B143.7-10	M.A., M.U.S., E.
B143.10-12	Ident. State., M.A., E.
B143.12-14	Nec., M.A., E.
B144.1-3	Rep., Nec., M.A., M.U.S., Belief, Sense
B144.1-4	Descrip.
B144.4 ftnt a 1-2	A., Rep., Sense
B144.4 ftnt a 2-5	M.A., M.U.S.
B144.4-8	M.U.S., Sense, E.
B144.8-10	M.A., Sense
B144.10-16	Fac. Dis., Sense, Belief, M.U.S.
B144.20-B145.5	Sense
B145.3-5	M.A.
B145.6-9	Sense
B145.10-15	M.A.,Fac. Dis.
B145.15-22	Descrip., Fac. Dis., M.A., M.U.S., E., Sense
B145.19-22	A.
B145.22-B146.4	E., Limit, M.A., M.U.S., Sense
B146.5-6	Realism
B146.6-9	M.A., Sense, E.

B146.8-14	A.
B146.9-12	M.A., Sense
B146.12-14	M.A.
B146.14-16	Belief, Sense
B146.16-B147.1	A.
B147.1-B148.2	Sense
B147.4-6	M.A., E.
B147.8-11	E.
B147.12-14	Rep.
B147.14-19	E., M.A.
B147.24-B148.2	A.
B148.3-12	Sense
B148.3-B149.23	Limit
B148.7-8	E.
B148.10-15	E.
B148.12-15	A., Limit, E.
B148.16-18	A.
B148.20-22	M.U.S.
B148.20-B149.2	A.
B149.3-6	Sense, Limit
B149.3-16	A.
B149.6-9	Sense, Limit
B149.9-11	Sense, Limit
B149.16-23	E.
B149.20-23	Sense, Limit, M.A.
B150.1-6	A.
B150.4-6	E., Limit
B150.6-9	M.U.S.
B150.10-13	Fac. Dis.
B150.10-19	Sense, Rep., M.A., M.U.S.
B150.10-B152.17	Fac. Dis.
B150.12-13	A., Fac. Dis.
B150.16-19	Nec.
B150.19-B151.3	A.
B151.4-5	Nec.
B151.4-10	Rep.
B151.4-B152.14	M.A.
B151.13-18	M.U.S., Rep.
B151.13-B152.19	Sense
B151.18-19	Fac. Dis., Rep. A.
B151.19-23	Belief
B151.23-B152.9	A., M.A.
B152.9-12	M.A.
B152.12-17	M.A.
B152.20-B155.7	Sense
B153.2-B155.6	M.A.
B153.10-13	A.
B153.13-14	Fac. Dis., Belief
B153.17-21	Ident. State., A.
B153.24-B154.2	Fac. Dis.

B162.12-B163.15	Descrip
B162.14-B163.5	Nec.
B163.5-11	M.A., Ident. State.
B163.11-15	E.
B163.16-18	M.A., E.
B163.16-24	E., Belief, M.A.
B164.1-5	A.
B164.5-9	Belief
B164.9-11	Nec., Realism, Limit
B164.11-15	Rep.
B164.13-15	Belief
B164.15-16	M.A.
B164.16-19	Descrip.
B164.18-21	M.A.
B164.21-B165.2	A.
B165.2-5	Nec., M.A., E.
B165.5-9	M.A., Limit
B165.5-12	A.
B165.5-16	A. (See B164.13-15.)
B165.17	M.A., Limit, E.
B165.17-19	A., M.A., Limit, Sense
B165.19-20	Sense, Limit, Belief
B165.20-B166.1	A., Sense, Limit
B166.1	Sense, Ident. State.
B166.1-3	E., Limit
B166.4-5	E., Limit
B166.5-8	E.
B166.8-11	E., Limit, Nec.
B166.11-B167.4	E., Limit, Belief
B167.4-8	E., Limit
B167.21-B168.18	E., Nec., Limit, A.
B168.8-11	A.

28. Deduction in B: Topical Content

Topics

1. Actual Objects: Idealism/Realism
2. Belief
3. Descriptivism
4. Entities/A priorism
5. Faculty Discourse
6. Identity Statement
7. Limit
8. Mind as Act
9. Mind as Unitary Subject
10. Necessity
11. Perspectivism
12. Realism

13. Representationalism
14. Sense
15. Space as Determinative of Synthesis
16. Time as Determinative of Synthesis

4. *Entities/A priorism*
—continued
B141.8-14
B141.14-B142.3
B143.1-14
B143.7-10
B143.10-12
B143.12-14
B144.4-8
B145.15-22
B145.22-B146.4
B146.6-9
B147.4-6
B147.8-11
B147.14-19
B148.7-8
B148.10-15
B148.12-15
B150.4-6
B158.9-15
B159.10-12
B159.12-15
B159.15-B160.1
B160.1-6
B160.11-19
B160.15-19
B161.6-14
B163.11-15
B163.16-18
B163.16-24
B165.2-5
B165.17
B166.1-3
B166.4-5
B166.5-8
B166.8-11
B166.11-B167.4
B167.4-8
B167.21-B168.18

5. *Faculty Discourse*
B129.7-B130.6
B130.16-19
B134.16-B135.3
B135.16-17
B137.6-7
B137.15-16
B144.10-16
B145.10-15
B145.15-22

B150.10-13
B150.10-B152.17
B150.12-13
B151.18-19
B153.13-14
B153.24-B154.2

6. *Identity Statement*
B130.20-B131.14
B132.7
B132.10-11
B133.18 ftnt a 15-16
B137.2-4
B137.11-16
B137.24-B138.7
B143.4-6
B143.10-12
B153.17-21
B161.6-10
B163.5-11

7. *Limit*
B145.22-B146.4
B148.3-B149.23
B148.12-15
B149.3-6
B149.6-9
B149.9-11
B149.20-23
B150.4-6
B158.5-9
B159.1-9
B164.9-11
B165.5-9
B165.17
B165.17-19
B165.19-20
B165.20-B166.1
B166.1-3
B166.4-5
B166.8-11
B166.11-B167.4
B167.4-8
B167.21-B168.18

8. *Mind as Act*
B130.1-19
B131.9-10
B132.7-15
B133.4-16

Section VI

Mind's Self-Activity

29. Actionalism

Abbreviations

A	Affect, act on (Subject acts on itself)
G	Generate, product
I	Imagination
r	Relate
RC	Reason causes
SA	Self-activity
Sy	Synthesis
U	Understanding

Bxii.1-3	G, I	A101.20-22	Sy, I
Bxii.3-6	G, I	A101.22-A102.1	Sy
Bxii.6-9	U	A102.6-11	Sy
A1.1-3	U, Sy	A103.1-3	Sy
A20.8-10	S	A103.3-6	Sy
B67.19-B68.3	A	A103.6-8	Sy
B68.18-21	A	A103.8-12	Sy
B68.22-B69.5	A, SA	A103.15-18	Sy
A77.12-16	Sy	A103.18-A104.2	Sy, G
A79.1-2	Sy, I	A105.11-18	G
A79.12-17	Sy, U	A112.4-6	Sy, U
B111.7-11	U	A113.15-20	Sy
A86.11-16	Sy, U	A115.9-13	Sy, I
A92.8-10	G	A115.14-A116.3	Sy, I
A92.16-18	G	A116.4-9	Sy
A94.18-21	Sy	A116.16-18	Sy
A99.3-4	Sy, r	A116.21-A117.2	Sy
A99.11-14	Sy	A117.2	
A99.14-18	Sy	ftnt a 14-17	Sy
A99.19-21	Sy	A118.3-6	Sy, I
A99.21-A100.2	Sy	A118.6-7	Sy, I
A100.2-3	Sy	A118.8-11	Sy, I
A101.9-11	Sy	A118.12-14	Sy, I
A101.15-20	Sy, I	A118.17-20	Sy, I

B233.16-22	I, Sy
B234.3-7	Sy
B234.10-14	Sy
B234.14-19	Sy
A190.7-9	G
A193.20-21	Sy
A197.16-20	Sy
A201.5-9	Sy, I
A201.13-16	Sy
A205.8-9	A
A210.9-10	Sy
A210.11-17	G
A220.5-11	Sy
A220.13-16	Sy
A224.5-11	Sy, I
B277.1	
ftnt a 5-10	I
A231.4-5	U, Sy
A234.11-13	G
A234.13-17	Sy, G
A234.17-19	G
A237.1-5	U, I, Sy
A240.7-13	Sy
A247.7-8	r
A250.15-16	U, r
A250.24-25	Sy, U
A261.8-10	A
A261.10-15	r

A305.19-A306.2	Sy, U, RC
A317.19-23	RC
A238.19-20	RC
A397.13-18	Sy
B407.4-8	A
B418.11-17	A
B428.18-20	Sy
A534.7-9	SA
A539.20-22	RC
A546.15-16	SA
A546.23-A547.2	RC
A548.20-22	RC
A548.23-A549.1	RC
A550.11-17	RC
A551.1-5	RC
A551.5-6	RC
A553.17-20	RC
A555.16-17	RC
A556.5-6	RC
A556.8-9	RC
A556.9-12	RC
A583.4	
ftnt a 5-7	U, Sy
A807.16-18	RC
A808.1-3	RC
A808.11-15	RC
A808.18-20	RC
A835.4-9	SA

30. Affinity

A113.4-6	A659.22-A660.2
A113.20-A114.3	A660.3-12
A121.12-17	A660.13-18
A121.23-A122.2	A660.18-22
A122.2-6	A661.4-10
A122.9-16	A661.13-17
A122.17-25	A661.17-22
A123.1-6	A662.1-4
A123.11-19	A662.8-11
A572.11 ftnt a 1-9	A662.11-A663.15
A657-A658.3	A668.6-19
A656.3-10	A766.23-A767.3
A659.8-17	A833.21-A834.6
A659.17-22	A834.6-9

31. Synthesis/Receptivity

Contents

1. Formally Autonomous Receptivity
2. Formally Autonomous Imagination Determines
3. Understanding Determines Through Imagination
4. Understanding Determines Directly
5. Understanding Must Think Unity, Therefore Unity Must Be

*1. Formally Autonomous
  Receptivity*
Bxvii.3-7
Bxl.1 ftnt a 24-33
Bxl.1 ftnt a 50-53
A16.1-5
A19.1-10
A20.6-8
A20.15-18
A20.19-A21.6
A22.1-8
B67.19-B68.3
B68.15-18
B68.18-21
B68.225-B69.5
B69.12-15
B72.6-8
A50.1-6
A50.16-A51.2
A51.5-9
A51.9-11
A52.2-5
A68.6-11
A77.4-9
A85.18-22
A86.11-16
A87.25-A88.8
A89.18-21
A90.1-3
A90.6-12
A90.15-20
A90.21-24
A90.24-25
A90.25-A91.2
A99.3-4
A111.7-10
A124.4-7
A126.10-11

A127.5-15
A127.24-A128.6
B129.7-11
B131.15-B132.4
B136.2-8
B136.8-10
B139.18-B140.3
B145.6-9
B154.6-13
B157.10-B158.3
B158.15-B159.6
B160.11-15
B160.15-19
B160.19 ftnt a 10-14
B160.19-B161.5
B139.23-A140.9
A167.1-5
A170.2
A71.4-20
A171.21-A172.2
A176.6-13
B219.2-8
B219.9-16
A221.1-6
A224.5-11
A244.22-A245.1
A245.1-10
A247.11-15
A247.16-22
B305.18-B306.3
B307.23-B308.9
A253.19-23
A267.20-22 (Cf. A292.18-22)
A268.1-9
B422.14 ftnt a 26-29
B426.18-b427.2
A480.21-23

2. *Formally Autonomous*
   Imagination Determines
A78.4-11
A78.22-24
A78.24-A79.7
A79.8-12
A101.20-22
A120.7-14
A120.14-16
A123.1-6
A123.11-19
B151.18-23
A136.2-5
A136.8-11
A137.10-15
A138.13-20
A138.21-A139.7
A139.23-A140.9
A140.10
A140.22-24
A141.6-8
A141.23-A142.4
A141.11-16
A145.15-16
A145.20-24
A156.10-12
A201.5-13
B257.12-18
A224.5-11
A245.1-10
A246.16-22

3. *Understanding Determines*
   Through Imagination
A79.8-12
A79.12-17
A120.1-4
A109.15-18
A124.14-16
B151.4-10
B151.13-18
B151.23-B152.12
B153.24-B154.2
B154.6-13
B154.13-22
B156.2-8
B156.8-14
B156.14-20
B160.19 ftnt a 1-6
B162.1-11

B162.11 ftnt b 1-7
B164.15-18
A136.2-5
A136.8-11
A137.10-15
A138.13-20
A138.21-A139.7
A139.23-A140.9
A140.22-24
A142.7-11
A142.11-16
A145.20-24
B233.13-22
A237.1-7

4. *Understanding Determines Directly*
B67.11-B69.5
A105.11-18
A126.21-A127.15
A127.24-A128.6
B129.7-11
B129.11-B130.1
B130.1-6
B130.6-13
B132.17-B133.2
B133.7-13
B134.13-B135.3
B135.17-21
B136.2-8
B136.8-B137.1
B137.17-21
B137.24-B138.5
B138.7-10
B138.13-20
B139.4-11
B139.12-14
B140.3-9
B141.8-14
B143.4-7
B143.7-10
B143.10-14
B144.1-4
B144.4 ftnt a 1-5
B144.4-8
B144.10-16
B144.16-B145.3
B145.15-22
B150.1-4
B150.10-20
B151.4-10

5. *Understanding Must Think Unity,*
    Therefore Unity Must Be
    —continued
A210.22-A211.7
B257.18-23
B258.5-7
A213.2-7
A215.20-25

A216.8-13
A217.12-17
A237.1-7
A250.18-25
A251.6-11
B305.18-B306.3
B309.3-9

Section VII

Mind Relations

32. Equivalences

B68.11-13	Consciousness of the self (apperception) is the simple representation 'I'.
A106.22-A107.1	The original and transcendental condition of the unity of consciousness is transcendental apperception.
A107.12-17	The pure original and unchangeable consciousness, i.e., transcendental apperception, is the unity of consciousness which precedes all data of intuition and which makes representation of objects possible.
A108.7-14	The original and necessary consciousness of the identity of the slef is a consciouness of an equally necessary unity of the synthesis of all appearances according to concepts or rules which make them necessarily reproducible and so determine and object for their intuition in which they are necessarily interconnected.
A109.15-18	Relation to an object is the necessary unity of consciousness and of the synthesis of the manifold.
A111.11-13	The *a priori* conditions of a possible experience are the conditions of the possibility of the objects of experience.
A113.12-15	Self-consciousness or original apperception is a transcendental representation.
A117.2 ftnt a 17-24	The bare representation 'I' in relation to all other representations (the collective unity of which it makes possible) is transcendental consciousness. The possibility of the logical form of all knowledge is necessarily conditioned by relation tot his apperception as a faculty.
A199.1-4	The unity of apperception in relation tot he synthesis of imagination is the understanding. This same unity, with reference to the transcendental synthesis of imagination is the pure understanding.
A123.20-22	The abiding and unchanging 'I' is pure apperception, And as the correlate of all representations makes it possible for us to be conscious of them.

A129.18-21	The unity of possible consciousness constitutes the form of all knowledge of objects. Thru it the manifold is thought as belonging to a single object.
B132.4-15	The representaiton 'I think' is an act of spontaneity. It is pure original apperception. It is that self-consciousness which generate the representation 'I think' which in all consciousness is one and the same.
B133.18 ftnt a 15-16	The faculty of apperception is the understanding itself.
B134.1-6	The thought that the representations given in intuition belong to me is equivalent to the thought that I unite them in one self-consciousness.
B135.17-B136.1	I am conscious of the self as identical in regard to the manifold of representations given to me in intuition because I call them all mine and so apprehend them as one intuition. This is the same as saying that I am conscious to myself *a priori* of a necessary synthesis of representations, i.e., the original synthetic unity of apperception.
B137.1-5	Without combination in one consciousness nothing can be thought or known since the given representations would not have in common the act of the apperception 'I think' and so could not be apprehended together in one self-consciousness.
B137.11-15	The unity of consciousness constitutes the relation of representations to an object.
B138.21-24	Pure apperception is the representation 'I am'.
B143.4-7	The act of understanding by which the manifold of given representations is brought under one apperception is the logical function of judgment.
B166.1-3	Empirical knowledge is experience.
B207.12-13	Perception is consciousness with sensation.
A362.14-16	"Whole is in me, as individual unity," is the same as "I am numerically identical in all this time".
A419.14-17	The absolute unity of apperception is the simple 'I' in the representation to which all combination or separation that constitutes thought relates.
A576.5-6	The concept of that which possesses all reality is the concept of the thing in itself as completely determined.

33. Priority Language

Contents

p	means "is prior to"
1.	Apperception p. Categories

2.   Apperception p. Synthesis
3.   Categories p. Synthesis
4.   Synthesis p. Categories
5.   Categories p. Apperception
6.   Synthesis p. Apperception
7.   Affinity p. Synthesis
8.   Reciprocal Priority between Apperception and both Categories and Synthesis.

1. Apperception p. Categories
A79.12-17
A106.13-A107.1
A107.6-11
A107.12-17
A107.21-24
A111.20-A112.4
A116.12-16
A116.19-21
A124.7-11
A127.5-11
B144.10-16
A343.2-5
A401.21-22

2. Apperception p. Synthesis
A97.16-22
A106.13-A107.1
A107.6-11
A107.12-17
A108.1-4
A108.14-20
A113.10-20
A115.14-A116.3
A116.4-9
A116.12-16
A116.19-21
A116.21-A117.2
A117.2 ftnt a 6-8
A117.2 ftnt a 8-10
A118.3-6
A119.1-4
A112.8-25
A127.5-11
A129.18-A130.1
B133.7-13
B133.18 ftnt a 12-16
B134.16-B135.3
B137.1-5
B137.10-16

B139.12-14
B140.3-9
B142.3-14
B143.4-7
B145.15-22
B150.6-9
B153.10-13
B154.2-6
B157.6-9
A289.14-16
A354.14
B422.14 ftnt a 11-14

3. Categories p. Synthesis
A78.18-19
A78.22-24
A79.3-6
A79.8-12
A79.12-17
A103.15-A104.2
A105.3-9
A106.6-9
A109.12-18
A109.18-A110.6
A119.4-8
A123.1-6
B144.1-4
B151.4-10
B161.6-11
A289.14-16

4. Synthesis p. Categories
A78.12-15
A105.11-18
B131.9-10

5. Categories p. Apperception
A105.3-9
A105.18-22
A108.7-14

Section VIII

Subject

34. Subject Texts: Digest

Note

Capital letters have sometimes been used to indicate a useful distinction of philosophical sense rather than the usual grammatical division.

Bx1.1 ftnt a 14-19

The permanent cannot be an intuition in me for all grounds of determination of my existence which are to me met within me are representations—

And as representations require a permanent distinct from them in relation to which their change, and so my existence in the time wherein they change, may be determined.

Bx1.1 ftnt a 24-33

Through inner experience I am conscious of my existence in time (consequently of its determinability in time).

This is more than to be conscious of my representation;

It is identical with the empirical consciousness of my existence which is determinable only through relation to something which, while bound up with my existence, is outside me.

This consciousness of my existence in time is bound up by way of identity with the consciousness of a relation to something outside me.

It is therefore experience and sense, not invention or imagination, which inseparably connects this outside something with my inner sense.

Bx1.1 ftnt a 33-38

Outer sense is already itself a relation of intuition to something actual outside me.

Bx1.1 ftnt a 38-42

If, with the intellectual consciousness of my existence in the representation 'I am", which accompanies all my judgments and acts of understanding, I could at the same time connect a determination of my existence through intellectual intuition, the consciousness of a relation to something outside me would not be required.

A107.12-17	This unity of consciousness which precedes all data— pure, original, unchangeable consciousness is *Transcendental Apperception.*
A107.17-21	All unity is possible only through the unity of consciousness.
A107.21-24	Numerical unity of apperception is the *a priori* ground of all concepts.
A108.1-4	This transcendental unity of apperception forms a connection of representations according to laws.
A108.4-7	Transcendental unity of apperception is possible because the mind is conscious of the identity of function in its synthesis.
A108.7-14	The original and necessary consciousness of the identity of the self is the consciousness of the necessary unity of synthesis.
A108.14-20	The mind could not think its identity *a priori* unless it saw the identity of the act by which it subordinates all apprehension to a transcendental unity according to *a priori* rules.
A109.15-18	The relation of knowledge to an object is the necessary unity of consciousness and also of synthesis thru a common function of mind.
A110.6-9	Appearances must stand under the necessary unity of apperception.
A111.23-A112.4	In original apperception everything must necessarily conform to the conditions of the thoroughgoing unity of self-consciousness, i.e., the universal functions of synthesis, i.e., of that synthesis in which alone apperception can demonstrate *a priori* its complete and necessary identity.
A112.6-10	Synthesis according to concepts as *a priori* rules makes it possible to meet a thoroughgoing, universal, necessary unity of consciousness in the manifold of perceptions.
A113.10-12	All possible appearances, as representations, belong to the totality of a possible self-consciousness.
A113.12-15	Self-consciousness is a transcendental representation— numerical identity is inseparable from it—nothing comes to knowledge except in terms of original apperception.
A114.4-13	Nature directs itself according to our subjective ground of apperception. Transcendental apperception is the radical faculty of all knowledge.
A115.3-6	There are three subjective sources of knowledge— sense, imagination, apperception.
A115.9-13	Apperception represents appearances in the *empirical consciousness* of the identity of the reproduced representations with the appearances—i.e., in recognition.

A115.14-A116.3   All empirical consciousness is grounded in pure apperception, i.e., int he thoroughgoing identity of the slef in all possible representatins.

A116.4-9   Pure apperception is the inner ground of the unity of representations in which they acquire the unity of knowledge necessary for experience.

A116.12-16   We are conscious *a priori* of the complete identity of the self

In respect of all representations which can belong to knowledge

As a necessary condition of the possibility of all representations.

A116.16-18   Representations can represent only if they belong to one consciousness.

A116.19-21   This is the *a priori* transcendental principle of all unity of manifold in representations.

A116.21-A117.2   Pure apperception supplies a principle of the synthetic unity of the manifold in all possible intuition.

A117.2 ftnt a 6-10   All empirical consciousness has a necessary relation to transcendental consciousness

Which precedes all special experience,

I.e., the consciousness of myself as original apperception.

It is absolutely necessary that all consciousness should belong to a single consciousness, that of myself.

A117.2 ftnt a 14-17   The synthetic proposition, that all variety of empirical consciousness must be combined in one single self-consciousness, is the absolutely first and synthetic principle of our thought in general.

A117.2 ftnt a 17-25   The bare representation 'I' in relation to all otehr representations (the collective unity of which it makes possible) is transcendental consciousness.

The possibility of the logical form of all knowledge is necessarily conditioned by relation to this apperception as a faculty.

A118.3-6   The transcendental unity of apperception relates to the pure synthesis of imagination as the *a priori* condition of its possibility.

A118.8-11   The principle of the necessary unity of pure (productive) synthesis of imagination is prior to apperception.

A118.12-14 + 14-17   The unity of the synthesis of the manifold in imagination which is directed exclusively to the *a priori* combination of the manifold is called transcendental if it is represented as *a priori* necessary in relation to the original unity of apperception.

A118.17-20   The unity of apperception underlies the possibility of all knowledge—therefore the transcendental unity of the synthesis of imagination is the pure form of all possible knowledge.

B132.4-15   All the manifold of intuition has a necessary relation
                   to the 'I think' in the subject in which the manifold is
                   found. This representation is an act of spontaneity.
                   It is pure original apperception because it is that self-
                   consciousness which is generating the representation
                   'I think'. It cannot itself be accompanied by any fur-
                   ther representation.

B132.17-B133.2   The manifold of representation given in intuition
                   would not be mine if they did not all belong to one
                   self-consciousness. To be my representations they must
                   conform to the unique condition under which they
                   can stand together in one universal self-consciousness.

B133.4-7   This thoroughgoing identity of the apperception of a
                   manifold which is given in an intuition contains a syn-
                   thesis of representations—And is possible only through
                   the consciousness of this synthesis.

B133.7-13   The empirical consciousness which accompanies dif-
                   ferent representations is in itself diverse and without
                   relation to the identity of the subject.
                   That relation comes about, not simply by my accom-
                   panying each representation with consciousness, but
                   only in so far as I conjoin one representation with
                   another—
                   And am conscious of their synthesis.

B133.13-18   Only in so far as I can unite a manifold of given repre-
                   sentations in one consciousness, is it possible for me
                   to represent to myself the identity of the conscious-
                   ness in these representations.

B133.18 ftnt a 12-15   The synthetic unity of apperception is that highest
                   point to which we must ascribe all employment of the
                   understanding.

B133.18 ftnt a 15-16   The understanding is the faculty of apperception.

B134.1-6   The thought that the representations given in intu-
                   ition all belong to me is equivalent to the thought that
                   I unite (or can unity them) in one self-consciousness—.
                   This thought is not itself the consciousness of the syn-
                   thesis of representation, but it does presuppose the
                   possibility of that synthesis.

B134.6-8   Only is so far as I can grasp the manifold of represen-
                   tations in one consciousness are they mine.

B134.10-13   Synthetic unity of the manifold of intuitions, as gener-
                   ated *a priori*, is the ground of the identity of appercep-
                   tion itself—
                   Which precedes all my determinate thought.

B134.16-B135.3   Combination belongs exclusively to the understand-
                   ing, which is the faculty of combining *a priori* and
                   bringing the manifold of given representations under
                   the unity of apperception.

B135.3-5   The principle of apperception is the highest principle
                   in the whole sphere of human knowledge.

B135.6-10	The principle of the necessary unity of apperception is identical and therefore analytic. Nevertheless, it reveals the necessity of a synthesis of the manifold given in intuition
	Without which the thoroughgoing identity of self-consciousness cannot be thought.
B135.10-14	Through the 'I', as simple representation nothing manifold is given.
	Only in intuition which is distinct from the 'I' can a manifold be given—.
	And only through combination in one consciousness can it be thought.
B135.17-21	I am consious of the self as identical in respect fo the manifold of representations that are given to me in an intuition
	Because I call them mine and so apprehend them as constituting one intuition.
B135.21-B136.1	I am consious to myself *a priori* of a necessary synthesis of representations, i.e., the original synthetic unity of apperception—
	Under which all representations that are given me must stand,
	But under which they must first be brought by synthesis.
B136.2-8	The supreme principle of the possibility of all intuition in its relation to understanding is that all the manifold of intuition should be subject to the conditions of the original synthetic unity of apperception.
B137.1-5	Without combination nothing can be thought of known since the given representations would not have in common the act of the apperception 'I think' and so could not be apprehended in one self-consciousness.
B137.11-15	The unity of consciousness alone constitutes the relation of representations to an object.
B137.17-21	The first pure knowledge of understanding upon which all the rest of its employment is based and which is also completely independent of all the conditions of sensible intuition is the principle of the original synthetic unity of apperception.
B138.2-4	The unity of the act of the synthesis of drawing a figure is the unity of consicousness as in the concept of a line.
B138.4-5	It is through the unity of this act that a determinate space as object is first known.
B138.6-7	The synthetic unity of consciousness is an objective condition of all knowledge.
B138.7-10	It is a condition under which every intuition must stand in order to become an object for me.

B144.1-4	By means of the category, the understanding through synthesis represents the manifold contained in an intuition which I call mine as belonging to the necessary unity of self-consciousness.
B144.4 ftnt a 1-5	This is proven by the fact that the represented unity of intuition through which an object is given always includes a synthesis of the manifold, and therefore already contains the relation of this manifold to the unity of apperception.
B144.4-8	The category shows that the empirical consciousness of a given manifold in a single intuition is subject to a pure self-consciousness *a priori*.
B145.22-B146.4	No further explanation is possible as to why: 1. our understanding can produce *a priori* unity of apperception solely by means of the categories; 2. we have these and no other functions of judgment; 3. space and time are the only forms of our possible intuition.
B148.15-149.2	The synthetic unity of apperception constitutes the whole content of the categories as forms.
B150.6-9	The synthesis of the manifold through categories relates only to the unity of apperception.
B150.10-20	The understanding, as spontaneity, is able to determine inner sense through the manifold of given representations in accordance with the synthetic unity of apperception And so to think synthetic unity of apperception of the manifold of *a priori* sensible intuition.
B151.13-18	Transcendental synthesis of imagination is figurative synthesis which is directed merely to the original synthetic unity of apperception, i.e., the transcendental unity which is thought in the categories.
B151.23-B152.4	Imagination is a faculty that determines sensibility *a priori* to the extent that it determines sense *a priori* in respect of its form in accordance with the unity of apperception.
B152.20-B153.2	Inner sense represents to consciousness our own selves only as we appear, to ourselves, not as we are in ourselves.
B153.2-5	We intuit ourselves only as we are inwardly affected. But this seems to be a contradiction since we would then have to be in a passive relation (of active affection) to ourselves.
B153.10-13	Inner sense is determined by the understanding and its original power of combining the manifold of intuition, i.e., of bringing it under apperception— Upon which the very possibility of understanding rests.
B153.17-21	The synthesis of understanding, if the synthesis be viewed by itself alone, is nothing but the unity of the act of which, as an act, it is conscious to itself,

Even without (the aid of) sensibility, but through
which it is yet able to determine sensibility.

B153.24-B154.2   The understanding, under the title of a transcendental
synthesis of imagination, performs this determinative
act upon the passive subject, whose faculty it is, and
therefore it affects inner sense.

B154.2-3   Apperception and its synthetic unity are not inner
sense.

B154.3-6   The former is the source of all combination and
applies to the manifold of intuition in general, and
through the categories to objects in general prior to
all sensible intuition.

B154.23-B155.4   Motion, as an act of the subject (not as a determination of an object) and therefore the synthesis of the
manifold in space, first produces the concept of succession—if we abstract from this manifold and attend
solely to the act through which we determine inner
sense according to its form.

B155.8-11   How the 'I' that thinks can be distinct from the 'I' that
intuits itself (for I can represent still other modes of
intuition as at least possible), and yet, as being the
same subject, can be identical with the latter,

B155.11-B156.1   How, therefore, I as intelligence and thinking subject
know myself as an object that is thought in so far as I
am given to myself, and yet know myself, like other
phenomena, only as I appear to myself, not as I am to
understanding—these are questions on a par with how
I can be an object to myself at all in inner perception.

B156.14-20   If we know objects only in so far as we are affected,
then we intuit ourselves only as we are inwardly
affected by ourselves—we know our own subject only
as appearance, not as it is in itself.

B157.1-5   In the transcendental synthesis of the manifold of representations in general, and therefore in the synthetic
original unity of apperception, I am conscious of
myself, not as I appear to myself, nor as I am in myself,
but only that I am.

B157.5-6   This representation is a thought, not an intuition.

B157.6-9   In order to know ourselves, there is required in addi-
tion to the act of thought, which brings the manifold
of every possible intuition into the unity of apperception, a determinate mode of intuition by which the
manifold is given.

B157.10-B158.3   Although my existence is not appearance, the determination of my existence can take place only in conformity with the form of inner sense.

B158.1 ftnt a 1   The 'I think' expresses the act of determining my existence.

B158.1 ftnt a 2-4	Existence is already given thereby, but the mode in which I am to determine this existence, i.e., the manifold belonging to it, is not so given.
B158.1 ftnt a 4-7	In order that it be given, self-intuition is required—and such intuition is conditioned by a given *a priori* from, i.e., time.
B158.1 ftnt a 7-11	Since I do not have another self-intuition which gives the determining in me (I am conscious only of the spontaneity of it) prior to the act of determination, I cannot determine my existence as that of a self-active being.
B158.1 ftnt a 11-12	I can only represent to myself the spontaneity of my thought, i.e., of the determination.
B158.1 ftnt a 13-14	My existence is only determinable sensibly, i.e., as the existence of an appearance.
B158.1 ftnt a 14-15	But it is owing to this spontaneity that I call myself an intellegence.
B158.5-9	Consciousness of the self is not knowledge of the self in spite of all the categories which are being used to constitute the thought of an object in general through combination of the manifold in one apperception.
B158.9-15	As for the knowledge of an object distinct from me I need, beside the thought of an object in general, an intuition by which I determine that general concept, so for knowledge of myself I require, besides the consciousness, i.e., the thought of myself, an intuition of the manifold in me by which I determine this thought.
B158.15-B159.1	I exist an intelligence which is conscious solely of its power of combination.
B159.6-9	Such an intelligence can know itself only as it appears to itself in respect of an intuition which is not intellectual and cannot be given by the understanding itself, not as it would know itself if its intuition were intellectual.
B161.6-10	Synthetic unity can be no other than the unity of combination of the manifold of a given intuition in general in an original consciousness in accordance with the categories.
B162.11 ftnt a 1-4	The synthesis of apprehension, which is empirical, must necessarily be in conformity with the synthesis ofI apperception which is intellectual and contained in the category *a priori*.
A142.11-16	The schema of a pure concept of the understanding (as distinguished from the schema of sensible concepts such as figures in space) is a transcendental product of imagination which concerns the determination of inner sense in general according to conditions of its form (time), in respect of all representations, in so far

as these representations are to be connected *a priori* in one concept in conformity with the unity of apperception.

A145.20-24   By means of the transcendental synethsis of imagination, the schematism of understanding effects the unity of all the manifold of intuition in inner sense, and so indirectly the unity of apperception which as a function corresponds to the receptivity of inner sense.

A379.4-8   In the connection of experience matter, as substance in the field of appearance, is really given to outer sense,

Just as the thinking 'I', also as substance in the fields of appearance, is given to inner sense.

A379.19-22   Though the 'I', as represented through inner sense in time, and objects in space outside me, are specifically quite distinct appearances, they are not for that reason thought to be different things.

A379.23-A380.5   Neither the transcendental object which underlies outer appearances nor that which underlies inner intuition, is in itself either matter or a thinking being

But a ground (to us unknown) of the appearance which supply to us the empirical concept of the former as well as the latter mode of existence.

A381.1-9   Nothing whatsoever that is *a priori* can be

known synthetically from the concept of a thinking being.

A381.13-17   Time is the sole form of our inner intuition. It has nothing abiding and therefore yields knowledge only of the change of determination, not of any object that can be determined.

A381.17-19   In the 'soul' everything is in continual flux and there is nothing abiding except the 'I'.

A381.19-20   It is simple only because its representation has no content, and therefore no manifold.

A381.20-A382.2   For this reason it seems to denote a simple object.

A382.2-6   In order for it to be possible by pure reason to obtain knowledge of the nature of a thinking being in general, the 'I' would have to be an intuition, which in being presupposed in all thought (prior to experience) might as intuition yield *a priori* synthetic propositions.

A382.6-8   The 'I' is neither an intuition nor the concept of an object.

A382.12-18   The limits of the possibility of knowing the soul.

A383.13-10   The limits of the possibility of knowing the thinking self.

A391.1-4   We cannot know anything in regard to the transcendental cause of our representations of outer senses.

A392.15-20   The alleged communion between two kinds of substances, the thinking and the extended, rests on a crude dualism, and treats extended substances, which are really nothing but mere representations of the thinking subject, as existing by themselves.

A392.23-A393.4   The question of the communion between thinking and the extended comes simply to this: how in a thinking subject outer intuition, i.e., that of space, with its shape and motion, is possible.

A393.4-6   This is a question which cannot be answered. This gap in our knowledge can never be filled.

A393.6-8   It can merely be indicated through the ascription of outer appearances to that transcendental object which is the cause of this species of representation.

A393.8-10   We have no knowledge of this object.

A394.3-10   The opinion that the soul after the cessation of all communion with corporeal world could still continue to think, would be formulated as the view that, if that species of sensibility, in virtue of which transcendental objects would not for that reason be removed.

A394.10-12   It would still be possible that the transcendental (unknown) object should continue to be known by the thinking subject, though no longer in the quality of bodies.

A397.13-18   Since, in thinking in general, we abstract from all relation of the thgought to any object, the synthesis of the conditions of a thought in general is not objective, but merely a synthesis of the thought with the subject.

A398.3-6   Since the one condition which accompanies all thought is the 'I' in the universal proposition 'I think' reason has to deal with this condition in so far as it is itself unconditioned.

A398.6-8   The 'I' is only the formal condition, i.e., the logical unity of every thought, in which I abstract from all objects.

A398.8-9   Nevertheless it is represented as an object which I think, i.e., I myself and its unconditioned unity.

A398.10-12   The is no *a priori* answer to the question, 'What is the constitution of a thing which thinks'.

A400.12-14   The bare apperception, 'I' is in concept substance, simple, etc.

A401.21-22   Apperception is itself the ground of the possibility of the categories.

A401.23-25   The categories represent only the synthesis of the manifold of intuition in so far as the manifold has unity in apperception.

A401.27-A402.6   The thinking 'I' (the soul) does not know itself through the categories, but knows the categories, and through them all objects, in the absolute unity of apperception, and so through itself.

A402.6-8   I cannot know as an object that which I must presuppose in order to know any object.

thought as a mere predicate, must be granted. it is an apodeictic and identical proposition.

B407.20-24   That the 'I' of apperception, and therfore the 'I' in every act of thought, is one, and connot be resolved into a plurality of subjects,a nd consequently signifies a logically simple subject, is already contained in the very concept of thought, and is therefore an analytic propositon.

B408.1-2   This does not mean that the thinking 'I' is a simple substance.

B408.13-15   The proposition, that in all the manifold of which I am conscious I am identical with myself, is implied in the concepts themselves and is therefore an analytic proposition.

B408.16-18   This identity of the subject, of which I can be conscious in all my representations, does not concern any intuition of the subject, wherby it is given as an object.

B408.18-22   It cannot signify the identity of the person, if by that is understood the consciousness of the identity of one's own substance, as a thinking being, in all change of states.

B409.3-5   That I distinguish my own existence as that of a thinking being, from other things outside me—among them my body—is also an analytic proposition.

B409.5-6   For other things are such as I think to be distinct from myself.

B409.6-11   I do not learn from this whether my consciousness of myself would be possible apart from things outside me throught which representations are given to me,
Whether therefore I could exist merely as a thinking being.

B409.12-14   The analysis of the ocnsciousness of myself in thought in general, yields nothing towards the knowledge of myself as object.

B409.17-23   It would be the one unanswerable objection to the whole critique if there were a possibility of proving *a priori* that all thinking beings are in themselves simple substances, and that consequently personality is inseparable from them, and that consequently personality is inseparable from them, and that they are conscious of their existence as separate and distinct from all matter.

B410.4-10   The proposition, 'Every thinking being is, as such, a simple substance,' is a synthetic *a priori* proposition, i.e., it *both* goes beyond the concept from which it starts and adds to the thougt in

A145.20-24   By means of the transcendental synthesis of imagination, the schematism aof understanding effects the unity of all the manifold of intuition in inner sense, and so indirectly the unity of apperception which as a function corresponds to the receptivity of inner sense.

A155.10-12   The synthesis of representations rests on imagination, and their synthetic unity, which is required for judgment, on the unity of apperception.

A177.15-16   The original apperception stands in relation to inner sense (the sum of all representations) and *a priori* to its form, that is, to the time-order of the manifold of empirical consciousness.

A177.18-19   All this manifold must, as regards its time-relations, thus be united in the original apperception.

A177.19-23   This is demanded by the *a priori* transcendental unity of apperception, to which everything that is to belong to my knowledge (that is, to my united knowledge), and so can be an object for me, has to conform.

B275.11-13   The mere, but empirically determined, consciousness of my own existence proves the existence of objects in space outside me.

B275.14-15   I am conscious of my own existence as determined in time.

B275.16-19   This permanent cannot be something in me, since it is only through this permanent that my existence in time can itself be determined.

B275.21-B276.1   The determination of my existence in time is possible only through the existence of actual things which I percieve outside me.

B276.2-4   Consciousness of my existence in time is necessarily bound up with consciousness of the condition of the possibility of this time-determination.

B276.17-B277.3   Outer experience is really immediate and only by means of it is inner experience—not the consciousness of my own existence but the determination of it—possible.

B277.3-5   The representation 'I am' expresses the consciousness that can accompany all thought.

B277.5-6   The representation 'I am' certainly includes in itself the existence of the subject.

B277.6-8   It does not include any knowledge of the subject, and therefore also no empirical knowledge, that is, no experience of it.

B278.7-10   The consciousness of myself in the representation 'I' is not an intuition, but merely an intellectual representation of the spontaneity of a thinking subject.

B278.10-14   The 'I' has not the least predicate of intuition which, as permanent, might serve as correlate for the determination of time in inner sense.

B278.15-20   The existence of outer things is required for the possibility of a determinate consciousness of the self.

A242.15-A243.2   If I leave out permanence (which is existence in all time), nothing remains in the concept of substance except the logical representation of a subject—a representation which I try to realize by representing to myself something which can exist only as a subject and never as a predicate.

A250.18-22   This something is only the transcendental objects, i.e., a something = x, of which we can know nothing whatsoever.

and

A250.22-24   This transcendental object, as the correlate of the unity of apperception, serves for the unity of the manifold in sensible intuition.

A278.11-13   We cannot observe our own mind with any other intuition than that of inner sense.

A278.14-22   We know ourselves only through inner sense and therefore as appearance.

A289.14-16   Apperception and thought precede all possible determinate ordering of representations.

A289.19-A334.3   The relations which are universally found in all our representations are (1) relation to the subject; (2) relation to objects, either as appearances or as objects of thought in general.

A334.3-7   All relation of representations is (1) relation to the subject; (2) relation to the manifold; (3) relation to all things in general.

A334.12-14   All transcendental ideas can therefore be arranged in three classes: the first containing the absolute unity of the thinking subject.

A335.16-21   Reason, by the synthetic employment of the function of which it makes use in categorical syllogisms, is necessarily brought to the concept of the absolute unity of the thinking subject.

A340.2-5   In the first kind of syllogism I conclude from the transcendental concept of the subject, which contains no manifold, the absolute unity of this subject, of which, however, even in so doing, I possess no concept whatever.

A341.8-12   The 'I think' is a concept, or judgment, which was not included in the general list of transcendental oconcepts, but which must be counted as belonging to that list without at least altering it or declaring it defective.

A341.12-15   This is the vehicle of all concepts, including the transcendental concepts, and so is always included in the conceiving of the latter, and is itself transcendental.

A341.15-17   It can have no special designation because it serves only to introduce all our thought, as belonging to consciousness.

A342.3-4   'I' as thinking, am an object of inner sense and am called 'soul'.

A343.2-5   This inner perception is nothing more than the mere apperception 'I think', by which even transcendental concepts are made possible—what we assert in them is I think substance, cause, etc.

	the simple), nor of yielding apodeictic knowledg regarding the nature of thinking beings in general.
A347.24-25	It would not be a rational psychology.
A348.1-3	The proposition 'I think' (taken problematically) contains the form of each and every judgment of the understanding and accompanies all categories as their vehicle.
A348.3-5	Inferences from the proposition 'I think' admit of only transcendental employment of understanding.
A349.6-8	In all our thought the 'I' is the subject in which thoughts inhere only as determinations.
A349.8-9	This 'I' cannot employed as the determination of another thing.
A350.5-6	The 'I' is in all thoughts, but there is not in this representation the least trace of intuition distinguishing the 'I' from other objects of intuition.
A350.7-10	We can perceive that this representation is invariable present in all thought, But not that it is an abiding intuition, wherein the thoughts as being transitory, give place to one another.
A350.15-16	The logical subject of thought cannot be an object of knowledge.
A350.16-18	Consciousness is, indeed, that which alone makes all representations to be thoughts.
A350.18-19	In it, as in the transcendental subject, all our perceptions must be found.
A350.19-21	Beyond the logical meaning of the 'I' we have no knowledge of the subject in itself.
A350.21-22	The subject in itself is the substratum which underlies the 'I' as it does all thoughts.
A350.22-A351.4	The proposition '*The Soul is Substance*' may be allowed to stand if we recognise that this concept signifies a substance in idea, not in reality.
A352.15-18	It cannot be proven that if a multiplicity of representations are to form a single representation they must be contained in the absolute unity of the thinking subject.
A352.18-19	This cannot be proven from concepts.
A353.1-3	The proposition, 'A thought can only be the effect of the absolute unity of the thinking being' is not analytic.
A353.3-8	The unity of the thought, which consists of many representations, is collective And as far as mere concepts can show, may relate just as well to the collective unity of different substances acting together as to the absolute unity of the subject.
A353.8-11	The necessity of presupposing, in the case of composite thought, a simple substance, cannot be demonstrated in accordance with the principle of identity.

A355.19-21	The simplicity of the representation of a subject is not *eo ipso* knowledge of the simplicity of the subject itself.
A355.21-24	We abstract altogether from its properties when we designate it solely by the entirely empty expression 'I', An expression on which I can apply to every thinking subject.
A356.1-3	Through the 'I' I always entertain the thought of an absolute, but logical, unity of subject (simplicity).
A356.3-4	It does not follow that I thereby know the actual simplicity of any subject.
A357.13-17	We are justified in saying that our thinking subject is not corporeal In as much as it is represented by us as an object of inner sense, it cannot, in so far as it things, be an object of outer sense, i.e., an appearance in space.
A357.17-20	Thinking beings, as such, can never be found among outer appearances, and their thoughts, consciousness, desires, etc., cannot be outwardly intuited.
A358.4-7	Extension, impenetrability, cohesion, and motion—in short, everything which outer sense can give us—neither are nor contain thoughts, feelings, desires, or resolution, since these are never objects of outer intuition.
A358.7-12	The something which underlies the outer appearances and which so affects sense that it obtain the reviewed as noumenon (or better, as transcendental object), be at the same time the subject of out thoughts.
A358.15-19	This something is not extended, nor is it impenetrable or composit, since all these predicates concern only sensibility and its intuition, in so far as we are affected by certain (to us unknown) objects.
A359.2-4	The predicates of inner sense, representations and thought, are not inconsistent with its nature.
A359.12-15	It is possible that it is in itself simple, although owing to the manner in which it affects our senses it produces in us the intuition of the extended and so of the composit.
A359.15-18	I may assume that the substance which in relation to outer sense possesses extension is in itself the possessor of thoughts And that these thoughts can by means of its own inner sense be consciously represented.
A359.18-21	In this way, what in one relation is entitled corporeal would in another relation is entitled corporeal would in another relation be at the same time a thinking being, Whose thoughts we cannot intuit.
A359.21-22	Though we can indeed intuit their signs in the field of appearance.

A359.22-A360.4   The thesis that only souls (as particular kinds of substances) think, would have to be given up; and we should have to fall back on the common expression that men think.

That is, that the very same being which, as outer appearance, is extended, is (in itself) internally a subject, and is not composit, but simple and thinks.

A360.13-17   If, on the other hand, we compare the thinking 'I' not with matter but the the intelligible that lies at the basis of outer appearance which we call matter, we have no knowledge whatsoever of the intelligible, and therefore are in no position to say that the soul is in any inward respect different from it.

A360.18-20   The simple sonsciousness is not, therefore, knowledge of the simple nature of the self as subject, such as might enable us to distinguish it from matter, as from a composite being.

A360.24-A361.4   Though we may still profess to know that the thinking 'I' the soul (a name for the transcendental object of inner sense), is simple, such a way of speaking has no application to real objects, and cannot extend our knowledge.

A362.3-5   I am an object of inner sense, and all time is merely the form of inner sense.

A362.6-8   I refer all of my successive determinations to the numerically indentical self, and do so through time, i.e., in the form of the inner intuition of myself.

A362.8-11   The personality of the soul is not inferred but is a completely identical proposition of self-consciousness in time and is valid *a priori*.

A362.12-14   It says only that in the whole time in which I am conscious of myself, I am conscious of this time as belonging to the unity of myself.

A362.14-16   To say that this whole time is in me, as individual unity, is the same as to say that I am to be found as numerically identical in all this time.

A362.17-18   In my own consciousness, identity of person is unfailingly met with.

A362.18-20   If I view myself from the standpoint of another person (as object of his outer intuition), it is this outer observer who first represents *me in time*.

A362.20-21   In the apperception, *time* is represented, strictly speaking, only *in me*.

A362.21-A363.3   Although he admits, therefore, the 'I' which accompanies with complete identity all representations at all times in my consciousness, he will draw no inference from this to the objective permanence of myself.

A363.3-8   Just as the time in which the observer sets me is not the time of my own but of his sensibility, so the identity which is necessarily bound up with my consciousness is not therefore bound up with his, that is, with the consciousness which contains the outer intuition of my subject.

A363.9-12   The identity of the consciousness of myself at different times is therefore only a formal condition of my thoughts and their coherence, and so in no way proves the numerical identity of my subject.

A363.12-14   In spite of the logical identity of the 'I' such a change may have occurred in it as does not allow of the retention of its identity.

A363.14-18   And yet we may ascribe to it the same sounding 'I' which in every different state, even in one involving change of the (thinking) subject, might still retain the thought of the preceding subject and so hand it over to the subsequent subject.

A363.18 ftnt a 4-15   The conceivability of the transferability of states of consciousness from one substance to another which shows that unity of consciousness does not necessarily entail unity of subject.

A364.5-6   We are unable from our own consciousness to determine whether, as souls, we are permanent or not.

A364.6-8   We reckon as belonging to our identical self only that of which we are conscious.

A364.8-9   We must necessarily judge that we are one and the same throughout the whole time of which we are conscious.

A364.10-11   We cannot claim that this judgment would be valid from the standpoint of an outside observer.

A364.11-16   Since the only permanent appearance in the soul is the representation 'I' we are unable to prove that this 'I' a mere thought, may not be in the same state of flux as the other thoughts, which through it, are connected with one another.

A365.8-9   Personality does not cease because its activity is interrupted.

A365.9-12   This permanence, however, is not given prior to that numerical identity of our self which we infer from identical apperception, but on the contrary, is inferred first from the numerical identity.

A365.15-20   The identity of person does not follow from the identity of the 'I' in the consciousness of all the time in which I know myself.

A365.21-26   The concept of personality may still be retained as merely transcendental, i.e., as concerns the unity of the subject, which is unknown to us, in the determination of which there is a thoroughgoing connection through apperception.

A365.26-A366.1   This concept is necessary for practical employment and is sufficient for such use.

A366.1-4   This concept is not an extension of self-knowledge.

A381.19-20	It is simple only because its representation has no content, and therefore no manifold.
A381.20-A382.2	For this reason it seems to denote a simple object.
A382.2-6	In order for it to be possible by pure reason to obtain knowledge of the nature of a thinking being in general, the 'I' would have to be an intuition, which in being presupposed in all thought (prior to experience) might as intuition yield *a priori* synthetic propositions.
A382.6-8	The 'I' is neither an intuition nor the concept of an object.
A382.12-18	The limits of the possibility of knowing the soul.
A383.13-20	The limits of the possibility of knowing the thinking self.
A391.1-4	We cannot know anything in regard to the transcendental cause of our representations of outer senses.
A392.15-20	The alleged communion between two kinds of substances, the thinking and the extended, rests on a crude dualism, and treats extended substances, which are really nothing but mere representations of the thinking subject, as existing by themselves.
A392.23-A393.4	The question of the communion between thinking and the extended comes simply to this: how in a thinking subject outer intuition, i.e., that of space, with its shape and motion, is possible.
A393.4-6	This is a question which cannot be answered. This gap in our knowledge can never be filled.
A393.6-8	It can merely be indicated through the ascription of outer appearances to that transcendental object which is the cause of this species of representation.
A393.8-10	We have no knowledge of this object.
A394.3-10	The opinion that the soul after the cessation of all communion with corporeal world could still continue to think, would be formulated as the view that, if that species of sensibility, in virtue of which transcendental objects appear to us in a material world, should cease, all intuition of the transcendental objects would not for that reason be removed.
A394.10-12	It would still be possible that the transcendental (unknown) object should continue to be known by the thinking subject, though no longer in the quality of bodies.
A397.13-18	Since, in thinking in general, we abstract from all relation of the thought to any object, the synthesis of the conditions of a thought in general is not objective, but merely a synthesis of the thought with the subject.
A398.3-6	Since the one condition which accompanies all thought is the 'I' in the universal proposition 'I think' reason has to deal with this condition in so far as it is itself unconditioned.

evident that inferences from it admit only of transcendental employment.

B406.26-32   I do not know myself through being conscious of myself as thinking, but only in so far as I determine a given intuition with respect to the unity of consciousness in which all thought consists,

I.e., only when I am conscious of the intuition of myself as determined with respect to the function of thought.

B406.32-B407.1   Modes of self-consciousness in thought are not by themselves concepts of objects (categories).

B407.2-4   They are mere functions which do not give thought an object to be known.

They do not give even myself as object.

B407.4-8   The object is not the consciousness of the determining self, but only that of the determinable self, i.e., of my inner intuition (in so far as its manifold can be combined in accordance with the universal condition of the unity of apperception in thought).

B407.9-10   In all judgments I am the determining subject of that relation which constitutes the judgment.

B407.10-13   That the 'I' the 'I' that thinks, can be regarded as subject, and as something which does not belong to thought as a mere predicate, must be granted.

It is an apodeictic and identical proposition.

B407.20-24   That the 'I' of apperception, and therefore the 'I' in every act of thought, is one, and cannot be resolved into a plurality of subjects, and consequently signifies a logically simple subject, is already contained in the very concept of thought, and is therefore an analytic proposition.

B408.1-2   This does not mean that the thinking 'I' is a simple substance.

B408.13-15   The proposition, that in all the manifold of which I am conscious I am identical with myself, is implied in the concepts themselves and is therefore an analytic proposition.

B408.16-18   This identity of the subject, of which I can be conscious in all my representations, does not concern any intuition of the subject, whereby it is given as an object.

B408.18-22   It cannot signify the identity of the person, if by that is understood the consciousness of the identity of one's own substance, as a thinking being, in all change of states.

B409.3-5   That I distinguish my own existence as that of a thinking being, from other things outside me—among them my body—is also an analytic proposition.

B409.5-6   For other things are such as I think to be distinct from myself.

the manner in which I exist, whether it be as substance or accident.

B420.19-22   We know the unity of consciousness only because, as indispensable for the possibility of experience, we must make use of it.

B421.21-B422.1   The unity of consciousness, which underlies the categories is here mistaken for an intuition of the subject as object.

B422.1-2   This unity is only unity in thought by which no object is given.

B422.2-4   The category of substance cannot be applied to this unity.

B422.4-5   This subject cannot be known.

B422.5-7   The subject of the categories cannot by thinking the categories acquire a concept of itself as an object of the categories.

B422.7-9   In order to think them, its pure self-consciousness, which is what was to be explained, must itself be presupposed.

B422.9-11   Similarly, the subject, in which the representation of time has its original ground, cannot thereby determine its own existence in time.

B422.11-14   If this is impossible, then the determination of the self as thinking being in general by means of the categories is equally so.

B422.14 ftnt a 1   The 'I think' is an empirical proposition.

B422.14 ftnt a 2   It contains the proposition 'I exist'.

B422.14 ftnt a 2-3   I cannot say 'Everything which thinks, exists'. (cf B420.3-8)

B422.14 ftnt a 3-4   For in that case the property of thought would render all beings which possess it necessary beings.

B422.14 ftnt a 5-6   My existence cannot, therefore, be regarded as an inference from the proposition 'I think' as Descartes sought to contend.

B422.14 ftnt a 6-8   For it would then have to be preceded by the major premise 'Everything which thinks exists'. Rather it is identical with it.

B422.14 ftnt a 8-9   The 'I think' expresses an indeterminate empirical intuition,

B422.14 ftnt a 9-11   I.e., perception, which shows that sensation, which as such belongs to sensibility, lies at the basis of this existential proposition.

B422.14 ftnt a 11-13   But the 'I think' precedes the experience which is required to determine the object of perception through the category in respect of time.

B422.14 ftnt a 13-14   The existence referred to here is not a category.

B422.14 ftnt a 14-15   The category as such does not apply to an indeterminately given object.

B422.14 ftnt a 15-17   It applies only to an object of which we have a concept

B429.1-3	Thought takes no account of the mode of intuition, whether it be sensible or intellectual.
B429.3-5	Through thought, I represent myslef neither as I am nor as I appear to myself.
B429.5-6	I think myself only as I do any object in general from whose mode of intuition I abstract.
B429.6-9	If I here represent myself as subject of thoughts or a ground of thoughts, these modes of representation do not signify the categories of substance or of cause.
B429.9-11	Categories are those functions of thought (of judgment) as already applied to our sensible intuition which is required if I am to know myself.
B429.12-16	If I would be conscious of myself simply as thinking, then since I am not considering how my own self may be given in intuition, the self may be mere appearance to me (the 'I' that thinks), but is no mere appearance in so far as I think.
B429.16-18	In the consciousness ofmyself in mere thought I am the being itself, Although nothing in myself is thereby given for thought.
B429.19-20	The proposition 'I think' in so far as it amounts to the assertion 'I exist thinking', is no mere logical function.
B429.20-22	It determines the subject (which is then at the same time object) in respect of its existence.
B429.22-23	This cannot take place without inner sense.
B429.23-B430.1	The intuition in inner sense presents the object not as a thing in itself but merely as appearance.
B430.1-3	There is here, therefore, not simply spontaneity of thought, but also receptivity of intuition.
B430.3-4	That is, there is the thought of myself applied to the empirical intuition of myself. (cf A347.5-6, A353.23-A354.1)
B430.4-8	It is to this intuition that the thinking self would have to look for the conditions of the employment of its logical functions as categories of substance, casue, etc., It is not merely to distinguish itself as objct in itself through the 'I'.
B430.8-9	But it is also to determine the mdoe of its existence, i.e., to know itself as noumenon.
B430.9-13	To know the self as noumenon is impossible since the empirical intuition is sensible and yields only data of appearance Which furnish nothing to the object of pure consciousness for the knowledge of its spearate existence, But can serve only for the obtaining of experience.
B430.14-22	If we discover not in experience but in certain laws of the pure employment of reason, Laws which are not merely logical rules,

A537.8-10	While the effects are to be found in the series of empirical conditions, The intelligible cause, together with its causality, is outside the series.
A537.10-13	The effect may be regarded as free in respect of its intelligible cause And at the same time in respect of appearances as resulting from them according to the necessity of nature.
A538.1-2	Whatever in an object of the senses is not itself appearance, I entitle intelligible.
A538.2-6	If that which in the sensible world must be regarded as appearance has in itself a faculty which is not an object of sensible intuition, but through which it canb be the cause of appearances, the causality of this being can be regarded from two points of view..
A538.6-7	Regarded as the causality of a thing in itself, it is intelligible in its action.
A538.7-9	Regarded as the causality of an appearance in the world of sense, it is sensible in its effects.
A538.9-12	We should therefore have to form both an empirical and intellectual concept of the causality of the faculty of such a subject And to regard both as referring to one and the same effect.
A539.10-17	We must allow the subject an intelligible character by which it is the cause of those same actions as appearances But which itself does not stand under any conditions of sensibility, and is not itself appearance.
A539.20-22	This acting subject does not, in its intelligible character, stand under any conditions of time. Time is only a condition of appearances, not of things in themselves.
A540.3-6	Its causality, so far as it is intelligible, does not have a place in the series of those empirical conditions through which the event is rendered necessary in the world of sense.
A540.7-9	This intelligible character can never be known immediately.
A540.9-10	It would have to be thought in accordance with the empirical character.
A540.10-12	Just as we are constrained to think a transcendental object as underlying appearances Though we know nothing of it in itself.
A540.13-15	In its empirical character, the subject, as appearance, must conform to all the laws of causal determination.
A541.1-4	In its intelligible character (thought we can only have a general concept of that character) this same subject must be considered to be free from all influence of

the action of which cannot be ascribed to the receptivity of sensibility, a purely intelligible object.

A552.18-20	Man is himself an appearance.
A553.4-9	Reason is not itself an appearance.
A553.10-11	Reason is the abiding condition of all those actions of the will under which man appears.
A555.16-17	The action is ascribed to the agent's intelligible character.
A561.8-10	The thing itself is a cause (*substantia phanonenon*) conceived to belong to the series of conditions.
A561.10-11	Only its causality is thought as intelligible.
A672.1-7	In conformity with these ideas as principles we shall, first, in psychology, under the guidance of inner experience, connect all appearances, all the actions and receptivity of our mind, *as if* the mind were a simple substance
	Which persists with personal identity (in this life at least).
A682.6-8	In order to investigate the properties of a thinking being, one must interrogate experience.
A682.8-10	None of the categories can be applied to this object except to the extent that a schema of the category is given in sensible intuition.
A682.10-11	In this way, however, one never attains a systematic unity of all appearances in inner sense.
A682.12-19	Instead of the empirical concept of that which the soul actually is, which cannot take us far, reason takes the concept of the empirical unity of all thought
	And by thinking this unity as unconditioned and original
	It forms from it a concept of reason, i.e., the idea of a simple substance
	Which, unchangeable in itself (personally identical), stands in association with other real things outside it,
	In a word, the idea of a simple self-subsisting intelligence.
A682.19-A683.2	In so doing it has only in view the principles of systematic unity in the explanation of all appearances of the soul.
A683.2-7	It is trying to represent all determinations as existing in a single subject, all powers, so far as possible, as derived from a single fundamental power, all change as belonging to the states of one and the same permanent being, and all appearances in space as completely different from the actions of thought.
A683.7-11	The simplicity and other properties of substance are intended to be only the schema of this regulatory principle
	And are not presupposed as being the actual ground of the properties of the soul.

A771.24-A772.3	To assume the soul is a simple substance (a transcendent concept) would be to offer a proposition which is indemonstrable.
A772.7-12	Reason does not afford any sufficient ground for assuming, even as a matter of opinion, merely intelligible beings, or merely intelligible properties of things belonging to the sensible world.
A785.6-10	Though the 'I' taken in abstraction, can contain in itself no manifold, in its other meaning, as signifying the soul itself, it can be a highly complex concept, as containing under itself, and as denoting, what is very composite.

35. Subject: Topics

Contents

1. Consciousness
2. Subject-Existence Awareness
3. A. Limit of Subject Knowledge
   B. Transcendental Knowledge of Subject
   C. Mind Acts on and the Affects Itself
   D. Real Object as Involved in Subject Awareness and in Subject Determination
   E. Thought of "Object" as Involved in Subject Awareness and in Subject Determination
4. Ontological Unity of Subject:
   A. Appearance, Thing in itself Paradigms
   B. Intelligible, Transcendental, Subject in itself, Noumenon Paradigms
   C. Aspect Paradigm
   D. "I" and "I think" as Representations and Their Relations to the "I" that Thinks Them
   E. Apperception
   F. Continuity of Identity (Personality)
   G. Mind-Body
5. A. Other Minds
   B. Communication
6. Equivalences and Identities
7. Priorities

1. Consciousness
A346.10-14
A350.16-18
A350.18-19
B414.17-B415.2

2. Subject-Existence Awareness
 (see Topic 14.4)

Bx1.1 ftnt a 24-33
Bx1.1 ftnt a 38-42

4. C. *Ontological Unity of Subject:*
    Aspect Paradigm
  (see Topic 21.)

A358.7-12
A359.18-21
A359.22-A360.4
A538.2-6
A538.6-7
A538.7-9
A538.9-12
A539.10-17
A540.9-10
A540.13-15
A541.1-4
A541.4-5
A541.5-7
A541.18-22
A544.14-17
A545.11-18
A546.23-A547.2
A561.8-10
A561.10-11

4. D. *Ontological Unity of Subject:*
    "I" and "I think" as Repre-
    sentations and Their Relation
    to the "I" that Thinks Them
  (See Topic 22.)

A117.2 ftnt a 17-25
A123.20-22
B131.15-B132.4
B132.4-15
B135.10-14
B137.1-4
B138.13-20
B138.21-24
B140.3-9
B155.8-11
B155.11-B156.1
B157.1-5
B157.5-6
B158.1 ftnt a 1
B158.1 ftnt a 7-11
B158.1 ftnt a 11-12
B158.9-15
B158.15-B159.1
B277.3-5
B277.5-6

B277.6-8
B278.7-10
B278.10-14
A242.15-A243.2
A341.12-15
A341.15-17
A342.3-4
A343.2-5
A345.15-A346.1
A346.1-2
A346.2-3
A346.3-5
A346.5-8
A346.8-10
A346.16-18
A346.18-19
A347.8-13
A348.1-3
A348.3-5
A349.6-8
A349.8-9
A350.4-6
A350.7-10
A350.15-16
A350.16-18
A350.18-19
A350.19-21
A350.21-22
A354.2-4
A354.4-7
A354.7-8
A354.12-13
A354.14-17
A354.23-25
A354.25-A355.1
A355.1-4
A355.4-7
A355.8-10
A355.10-14
A355.14-15
A355.15-17
A355.19-21
A355.21-29
A357.1-3
A357.3-4
A357.13-17
A357.17-20
A358.4-7
A360.13-17
A362.21-A363.3

Section IX

Agency

36. Causality

Abbreviations

1

C   Category of "Cause"

2

C1.   Causality as time-succession
C2   Causality as simultaneous
C3   Causality as not temporal
F   Cause as free
2C   Multiple Causality (in regard to the same effect)

3

Gc   God as cause
Oc   Object as cause
Rc   Reason as cause
Uc   Understanding and/or Imagination as cause
W   Will

4

CS   Cause and substance

Axvii.7-10	Uc	B3.5-8	C
Bxxvii.2-12	2C	B3.10-12	C
Bxxvii.14-Bxxviii.4	C	B4.23-B5.2	C
Bxxviii.7-9	F	B5.2-10	C
Bxxviii.9-12	F	A9.6-9	C, C1
Bxxviii.12-16	F	A9.9-12	C
Bxxviii.16-18	C	A9.12-15	C
Bxxxii.23-Bxxxiii.3	F	A9.16-20	C
		A9.21-25	C
A1.1-3	Uc	A19.1-10	Oc
		A19.15-16	Oc
B1.1-8	Oc, Uc	A20.8-10	Uc

B136.10-B137.1	Uc	A144.1-3	C, Cl
B138.1-2	Uc	A144.3-5	C, Cl
B138.24-B139.4	Uc	A144.6-9	C2, Cs
B141.8-14	Uc	A144.10-12	
B143.7-10	Uc	A145.7-8	Uc
B143.10-12	Uc	A145.20-24	Uc
B144.1-4	Uc	B202.12-B203.2	Uc
B144.10-16	Uc	B203.2-10	Uc
B150.10-20	Oc, Uc	A162.21-A163.3	Uc
B151.23-B152.4	Uc, Oc	A163.3-6	Uc
B152.6-7	Uc	A163.6-10	Uc
B153.2-5	Uc	A163.15-17	Uc
B153.10-13	Uc	B208.5-8	Uc
B153.17-21	Uc	B208.11-14	Uc
B153.21-24	Uc	B208.14-18	Oc
B153.24-B154.2	Uc	A168.21-24	Oc
B154.3-6	Uc	A171.4-20	C
B154.6-13	Uc	B219.5-8	Uc
B154.13-22	Uc	A177.18-19	Uc
B154.23-B155.4	Uc	A179.8-12	Uc
B155.4-7	UC	A179.10-15	Uc
B155.1		B232.11-12	C
ftnt a 4-7	Uc	B233.12-13	Uc
B156.2-8	Uc	B233.16-18	Uc
B156.8-14	Oc, Uc	B233.20-22	Uc
B156.14-20	Oc, Uc	B234.3-7	Uc
B156.20		B234.7-14	C
ftnt a 1-8	Uc	B234.14-19	Uc, Cl
B158.1		A189.9-10	Cl
ftnt a 1-4	Uc	A190.7-9	Oc
B158.1		A193.20-21	Uc, Cl
ftnt a 7-11	Uc	A193.22-24	Cl
B160.19		A193.24-A194.2	Cl
ftnt a 10-12	Uc	A194.5-7	Cl
B162.4-6	Uc	A194.7-10	Cl
B162.11		A194.11-12	Cl
ftnt a 4-7	Uc	A195.12-17	Uc, Cl
B163.4-11	Uc, C	A196.9-14	Uc
B163.11-15	Uc	A197.16-20	Uc, C
B163.18-24	Uc	A198.8-11	Cl
B164.1-5	Uc	A198.16-19	Cl
B164.15-16	Uc	A198.19-24	Cl
B168.3-11	C	A199.2-5	Cl
A139.21-23	Oc	A199.2-5	Cl
A140.10	Uc	A199.6-9	Cl
A141.21-23	Uc	A199.9-15	Cl
A141.23-A142.4	Uc	A199.17-20	Uc
A142.11-16	Uc	A199.20-21	Uc
A143.1-4	Uc	A199.22-24	Uc
A143.22-27	Uc	A199.24-A200.2	Cl

A317.19-23	Rc		A450.51-54	F, C3
A317.23-A318.1	Rc		A450.54-58	F, C3
A318.6-9	Rc		A445.5-27	F, C3
A328.19-20	Rc		A445.30-38	F, C3
A351.18-A352.4	2C		A445.38-40	F, C3
A368.8-10	2C		A445.40-A447.4	F, C, C
A372.8-15	Oc		A449.36-42	F, C3
A372.15-22	Oc		A451.1-10	F, C3
A386.9-A387.24	Oc		A451.11-13	F, C3
A391.1-4	Oc		A451.23-36	F, C3, C
A391.4-11	Oc		A452.5-12	Cl
A393.3-10	Oc		A452.13-16	Cl
A394.17-19	Oc		A452.22-27	C3
A401.21-22	Uc		A452.27-A454.3	C3, Cl
A402.8-11	Uc		A454.3-14	Cl
B431.21-B432.5	Rc, C, Cs		A454.15-19	Cl
A409.14-17	(C, Cl These		A454.21-25	C3, Cl
A409.17-21	(explain how		A460.45-51	Cl
A40921-24	(Reason con-		A460.52-54	C
A409.24-A410.1	(verts Cate-		A560.54-59	Cl
A410.13-16	(gories into		A455.5	C
A411.21-22	(Ideas.		ftnt a 1-5	
A411.24-A412.5	(How one *must*		A459.23-30	Cl
A412.7-11	(think time.)		A495.31-A461.3	Cl
A414.21-25	C, Cl		A470.1-3	Oc
A415.1-7	C, Cl		A494.4-6	Oc
A419.1	C		A494.10-12	Oc
ftnt b 1-3			A494.15-17	Oc
A419.1	C		A494.19-20	Oc
ftnt b 3-6			A496.4-8	Oc
A419.1-5	C		A496.8-11	Oc, C
A419.5-6	F		A511.15-17	Uc
A419.6-8	Oc		A521.13-A522.1	Cl
A427.13-23	C3		A530.14-17	C, Cl
A444.1-5	C, Cs, F		A532.8-9	C
A444.5-9	F		A532.9-10	F
A446.5-9	C, F		A532.10-12	Cl
A446.9-17	C, F		A532.12-19	Cl
A446.18-19	C3, F		A533.1-3	F
A446.30-35	F, C		A533.3-5	F, C3
A448.1-6	F, C		A533.5-8	F
A448.6-10	F		A533.8-10	C, Cl
A448.17-22	F		A533.10-12	C, Cl
A448.22-27	F		A533.14-15	Cl
A448.44-50	F		A533.15-18	F
A450.3-15	F		A533.19-20	F
A450.15-27	F		A533.20-22	F
A450.27-31	F, C3		A534.1-2	F
A450.43-48	F, C3		A534.2-3	W
A450.48-51	F, C3		A534.4-5	W

A553.15-17	Rc, 2C	A636.1-6	C, Gc
A553. 17-20	Rc, C3	A636.6-10	C
A553.20-A554.1	Rc	A636.21-A637.1	C, Gc
A554.1-2	Rc	A637.1-7	C, Gc
A554.2-4	Rc, C3	A643.19-22	Rc
A554.4-6	Rc, C3	A648.22-A649.9	Cs, Rc
A555.9-13	Rc, 2C	A680.20-23	Gc
A555.13-17	Rc, 2C	A670.23-A571.2	Gc
A555.17-20	Rc, 2C	A672.16-23	Gc
A555.23-A556.1	Rc, C3	A672.23-A673.4	Gc
A556.1-5	Rc, C3	A673.7-12	Gc
A556.5-8	Rc, C3	A675.10-13	Gc, Cs
A556.8-9	Rc, C3	A678.6-9	Gc
A556.9-12	Rc, C3	A679.16-17	Gc
A556.14-18	Rc, C3	A685.11-15	Rc
A556.21-22	Rc, C3	A685.17-19	Rc
A557.1-3	Rc, C3	A685.25-27	Gc
A557.3-5	Rc, C3	A688.18-24	Gc
A557.13-15	2C, F	A694.2-9	Gc
A557.15-20	2C	A694.17-23	Gc
A557.21-A558.2	2C	A696.4-7	Gc
A558.10-13	Rc	A697.11-14	Gc
A558.16-19	2C, F	A697.14-16	Gc
A559.1-4	C1	A700.4-9	Gc
A559.4-7	Gc	A700.10-18	Gc
A561.10-11	Rc	A715.11-13	C
A561.26-A562.3	Rc, 2C, Gc	A722.12	C
A564.17-20	Rc, Gc	ftnt a 1-5	
A564.21-23	Gc, Oc	A724.4-7	Cs
A569.1-5	Rc	A723.2-8	C
A569.8-11	Rc	A736.25-A737.4	C
A609.19-21	C	A737.4-7	C
A609.16-19	C	A737.8-10	C
A609.21-23	C	A737.10-13	C
A610.1-6	Gc	A737.13-17	C
A613.21-A614.1	Oc	A760.8-15	C
A621.23-A622.2	C	A760.15-18	C
A622.12-14	C	A765.20-22	C
A622.14-A623.3		A766.1-4	C
A625.12-A626.4	F, Gc	A766.10-17	C, C1
A626.5-18	Gc	A766.17-19	C
A626.19-26	Gc	A766.19-23	C
A628.14-22	Gc	A766.23-A767.3	C
A632.20-A633.8	Gc, F	A767.8-11	C, Cs
A634.4-6	C	A770.10-16	C
A635.4-7	C	A773.9-14	C3
A635.7-13	C3, Gc	A783.4-7	C
A635.13-16	C3, Gc	A783.7-10	C
A635.17-19	C, Gc	A786.11-17	C
A635.19-22	C	A788.3-10	C

A788.10-13	C	A807.20-24	F
A798.15-16	Rc	A808.5-7	Rc, C
A800.3-4	Rc	A808.11-15	Rc
A802.2-4	W	A808.15-20	Rc
A802.5-7	Rc	A809.15-23	F, Rc
A802.8-9	Rc	A810.14-16	Gc, Rc
A802.9-10	Rc	A812.21-A813.2	Rc
A802.12-15	Rc	A814.14-17	Gc
A802.17-22	Rc	A815.3-9	Gc, C
A803.10-15	2C, Rc	A815.26-A816.5	Gc, Rc
A803.15-18	2C, Rc	A816.14-17	Gc
A805.25-A806.5	Rc, Gc	A817.8-11	Rc
A806.18-24	F	A818.19-22	Gc
A807.1-11	F	A820.1-4	Uc
A807.12-16	Rc	A826.10-13	Gc
A807.16-18	Rc, C	A826.13-16	Gc

37. Morals

Abbreviations

a	*A priori*
BL	Beyond limits
D	Duty, moral law, moral consciousness
E	Ends, interests, purposes
F	Freedom
Fa	Faith, postulate
G	God
Go	Good
H	Happiness
I	Immortality
K	Knowledge
L	Limits
M	Motives
P	Principles, ideas, ideals, concepts, rules, maxims
Po	Politics
R	Reason
S	System

(See Topics 7, R; 10, F1; 14.9; 14.28; 19; 21; 36, R, Gc)

Bxxi.1-9	K, R, L, BL, a
Bxxiv.20-21 +	
Bxxiv.21 - Bxxv.2	
= Bxxv.2-3	K, R, L, P
Bxxv.3-7	K, R, L

Bxxv.7-10	K, R, BL
Bxxv.10-14	K, R, L
Bxxix.11-15	F
Bxxiv.16-21	L, BL, K
Bxxix.26-Bxx.9	R, L, BL, G, I, F, K, P
Bxxx.9-11	Fa, K, L
Bxxxii.6-20	K, L, F, I, G
Bxxxii.20-23	I, Hope
Bxxxii.23-Bxxxiii.3	F, K
Bxxxiii.3-5	G, Fa
Bxxxiii.5-14	L, K, E
B7.6-7	R, G, F, I
A14.23-A15.9	a, K, P, L, S, D, M
A15.11-13	M, L
A314.9-12	E
A314.12-17	R, L, K
A314.18-A315.2	F, K, R, P
A315.2-8	P, L, K, Go
A315.8-12	Go, R, L
A315.12-15	Go, L, P, D
A315.15-18	Go, L, P
A315.18-20	Go, K, L, P
A315.20-21	Go, P
A315.21-24	Go, L
A316.10-15	Po, F, P, L, S, H
A316.22-A317.4	Po, P
A317.8-13	Po, R, S
A317.17-19	F, L
A317.19-23	R, P
A318.4-6	P
A318.16-21	P, Go, Po
A318.24-A319.1	P, L
A328.8-12	P, R, BL, L
A328.12-13	P, R
A328.13-16	P, L, BL
A328.16-18	P
A328.19-22	R, P, BL
A328.22-25	P, E, S, L
A329.10-15	S, P
A365.26-A366	P, L
B423.1-B424.2	E, BL
B424.14-23	I, P, R, BL
B424.23-B425.3	BL
B425.3-9	R, E, F, BL
B425.9-18	E
B425.19-B426.6	P, D
B430.14-22	P, R, a, F, D
B430.22-B431.3	a, BL, R
B431.5-8	R, D, P
B431.17-21	F, P (analogical meaning of concepts)

A776.17-20	R, Fa, BL
A776.20-A777.14	L, E, R, K
A795.17-A796.4	K, R, E, BL
A796.4-5	R, E
A797.1-4	R, K, L
A797.13-15	R, E
A798.5-8	R, E, F, I, Go
A798.15-16	F, L, K
A799.23-A800.2	K, L, R
A800.3-4	F
A800.7-11	P, E, H
A800.11-14	L, P, F, E
A800.14-15	L, P, a
A800.15-19	D, P, R, E, a, BL
A800.19-21	D, R
A800.22-A801.1	R, E, F, Go, I, D
A801.1-5	E, R
A801.7 ftnt a 1-5	P, H, K, L
A801.15-A802.2	R, R, L
A802.5-7	F
A802.8-9	F
A802.9-10	F, K
A802.10-12	F, BL
A802.12-15	F, BL
A802.15-17	R, Go, P
A802.17-22	R, P, D, F, BL
A803.1-9	R, F, D, K, L
A803.10-15	F, K, R, BL
A803.15-18	F, K, L
A803.18-A804.4	R, K, L, E, Go, I, F
A804.5-9	R, P, E, BL
A804.19-A805.3	R, E, K, D, Hope
A805.16-19	R, K, L, D
A805.20-25	Hope, K
A806.6-8	A
A806.9-12	P, H, D
A806.12-15	P, H, D
A806.15-18	P, H, L
A806.18-24	D, BL, F, H, S, P, R, a, K
A807.1-11	D, a, H, BL, F, R, K
A807.12-16	R, P, D
A807.16-18	R, D
A807.18-19	S, D
A807.20-26	F, R, L, D
A808.1-3	P, R
A808.4-5	D, S
A808.5-7	F, R, D
A808.7-10	D, L
A808.10-11	BL, S, D
A808.11-15	P, L, S, E

A817.20-24	P, D, R, E
A817.24-27	BL
A818.1-5	P, D, G, R, S
A818.5-9	R, D, E, K, L
A818.9-12	K, L, Fa, R, E
A818.13-19	R, G, Go, K, L, D
A818.19-22	P, D, Fa, G
A818.22-A819.2	G, D
A819.2-6	R, G, D
A819.6-8	F, E, P, R
A819.8-11	D, G, R
A819.11-13	Go, D, G
A819.13-14	K, L
A819.14-16	E, S
A819.16-20	R, D, G, L
A819.20-23	K, L, E, R
A823.5-10	D, K, L
A823.21-23	Fa
A823.23-26	D, D
A823.27-A824.8	E, K, Fa
A824.8-13	Fa, L
A824.13-15	Fa, L
A824.16-A825.8	Fa, L
A825.9-23	Fa
A826.1-7	F, Fa, K, L
A826.21-22	Fa, G, L
A826.22-A827.3	Fa, L
A827.3-7	Fa, I
A827.8-16	Fa, L
A827.16-19	Fa, L
A828.3-5	Fa, D
A828.5-6	D, E
A828.6-9	E, S, G, I
A828.10-12	E, S, D, K, L
A828.12-15	D, P, R, Fa, G, I
A828.15-17	Fa, D
A828.17-18	D, E
A828.19-A829.6	R, K, L, G, I
A829.6-7	Fa
A829.7-10	Fa, G
A829.10-13	Fa, G, I, D
A829.14-15	Fa, G
A829.16-A830.1	D, L, R, L
A830.1 ftnt a 1-3	R, E, D, L
A830.1 ftnt a 4-8	E, D, R, Go, Fa
A830.1-14	E, G, I, K, L, Fa
A830.15-A831.2	Fa, G, I, BL
A831.12-15	R, E, K, L
A831.15-19	E, K, L
A840.5-7	E

Section X

Language

38. Language

Contents

(For 1, 2, and 3 below, see Topics 1, U pm; 8, P Predicates)

1. Theory of Predication

4. Communicability as Truth-criterion

5. Perspective